PROTECTING YELLOWSTONE

Protecting Yellowstone

Science and the Politics of National Park Management

MICHAEL J. YOCHIM

University of New Mexico Press   Albuquerque

First paperbound printing, 2015
Paperbound ISBN: 978-0-8263-0785-9

20 19 18 17 16 15   1 2 3 4 5 6

Although the author is an employee of the National Park Service, he wrote this book entirely on his own time and at his own expense. Consequently, the views expressed in this book are entirely those of the author, not the National Park Service.

LIBRARY OF CONGRESS CATALOGING-IN-PUBLICATION DATA

Yochim, Michael J.
Protecting Yellowstone : science and the politics of
national park management / Michael J. Yochim.
p. cm.
Includes bibliographical references and index.
SUMMARY: "In Protecting Yellowstone, Michael Yochim considers
how park managers may best work within the contemporary policy-
making context to preserve national parks"—Provided by publisher.
ISBN 978-0-8263-5303-0 (cloth : alk. paper) — ISBN 978-0-8263-5304-7 (electronic)
1. Yellowstone National Park—Management. 2. Wildlife management—Yellowstone
National Park. 3. Environmental protection—Yellowstone National Park.
4. Environmental policy—Yellowstone National Park. 5. Yellowstone National Park
(Agency : U.S.) I. Title.
F722.Y63 2013
978.7'52—dc23
2012042471

BOOK DESIGN AND TYPESETTING BY LILA SANCHEZ
Composed in Minion Pro 10.25/13.5
Display type is Minion Pro and Adobe Garamond Pro

To Mom and Dad, who, more than anyone,

have helped make me the person that I am.

Contents

Acknowledgments

SHORTLY AFTER PUBLISHING MY FIRST BOOK, *YELLOWSTONE AND the Snowmobile*, I left Yellowstone National Park to go to the other "Big-Y" park, Yosemite, where I have continued to work. The change in location has brought me new career possibilities, new wild places to explore, and new friendships. Like any change, though, this one came with upheavals, from leaving the house and landscape I loved to ending my relationship with the woman I thought I would marry.

Writing this book became the creative endeavor I needed to fill the holes in my life, to refocus my attention on the possibilities of the present, to enhance my budding career at Yosemite, and to help me look again to the future. It was with the support of many friends and colleagues that this new endeavor became a successful one.

First, I'd like to thank Bill Lowry, my colleague in St. Louis. Bill is one of just a few academics publishing book-length examinations of *current* National Park Service policy making and the influences—especially the political ones—on such efforts. He is the one who recognized the strength of my methodological approach and encouraged me to publish the results in this book. Bill was also gracious enough to encourage me to expand on the findings of his own books about the parks.

Paul Schullery, Lee Whittlesey, Don Bachman, Jeff Pappas, Denice Swanke, Wade Vagias, Kathleen Morse, Jim Donovan, Jim Bacon, Jim Roche, Sabrina Stadler, Brenna Lissoway, Don Neubacher, Laura Kirn, and my many other "Big-Y" park friends and colleagues have also provided ongoing support, encouragement, and interest in this work. Most of these people work for the very agency whose policy-making successes and struggles I critique in this book; the others regularly interact with those who do. They are the men and women who struggle day in and day out to preserve the national parks for now and the future, for you and me.

Without the support of my family, I could never have made the transition to my new life and workplace in Yosemite. All of them helped make this new place and job enjoyable and productive, and all of them supported me in my new after-work writing endeavor. Whether it is our regular chats on the phone, our hikes together, or the expressions of love and support that they have provided, I have nothing but thanks to offer them.

Librarians and archivists are the often unsung heroes of scholarship; they are the ones who patiently dig out dusty archives to examine, who suggest related and important collections to peruse, and who critically think about a patron's project, all with the goal of making the work as complete as possible. This book could not have been possible without the help and always cheerful assistance of the librarians and archivists in Yellowstone, Yosemite, the National Park Service Denver Service Center, the University of Wisconsin-Madison, and the Denver Public Library.

On the same note, a special thanks to the Greater Yellowstone Coalition staff, who also opened up their files to me. While we may disagree on some issues, we have the same ultimate goal: preserving the Greater Yellowstone Area for future generations. They were gracious enough to trust me with their files, without which this book would have been incomplete.

Finally, Thomas R. Vale, William Cronon, Nancy Langston, Bob Ostergren, and Matt Turner, as well as the two anonymous reviewers who reviewed the manuscript and my editor at the University of New Mexico Press, all consistently pushed me to examine all perspectives, to faithfully record events as objectively and clearly as possible, and in general make this work as excellent as possible. Any mistakes or oversights in this book are my own.

Introduction

WHILE TRAVELING TO OLD FAITHFUL GEYSER IN YELLOWSTONE National Park, the visitor today passes by many of the great sights of the American West. Snow-covered mountains and sparkling waterfalls abound in all directions. The serene beauty of Yellowstone Lake and Hayden Valley invite a peaceful calm not ordinarily enjoyed by most Americans. Making the place their home and bringing the landscape alive are the park's wildlife, ranging from stolidly grazing bison and reclusive grizzly bears to graceful trumpeter swans and majestic bald eagles. For many, there are few American landscapes as compelling as Yellowstone.

Yet, if one looks closer or views the landscape over time, there are things that do not seem to belong. Along the north and west boundaries of the park, for example, are large corrals with bison droppings inside, suggesting that the bison do not always range freely. In the winter, snowmobile noise intrudes upon the park's profound winter silence, even in places like Shoshone Geyser Basin, more than five miles from the nearest snowmobile route. In an awkward juxtaposition, some tourist villages are situated amid prime grizzly bear habitat, such as Fishing Bridge Village. Similarly, some things that do seem to belong make one wonder how the National Park Service (NPS), Yellowstone's managing agency, is able to retain them in the modern world. Gray wolves are the single best example; eliminated from much of the country by the early 1900s, wolves now thrive in Yellowstone. Lightning-caused fires often burn in the park as well, fulfilling an ecological role despite the country's long history of putting them out elsewhere. Finally, the New World Mine—a gold mine that was proposed just outside Yellowstone's boundary—is absent; mines such as this are typically present in many western landscapes.

The landscape itself, then, prompts the following question: why do these anomalies occur? More specifically, and in the order presented above, why are bison corralled and prevented from leaving the park when all other large animals are allowed this freedom? Why are noisy snowmobiles allowed in the park at all? Why does the NPS build tourist villages in the middle of important grizzly bear habitat when other less sensitive locations are plentiful? If these problems were the result of agency weakness or a lack of foresight (two possibilities among many potential explanations), then how did the same agency manage to restore the gray wolf to Yellowstone, allow naturally ignited fires to burn, and keep that gold mine from intruding?

As this study will demonstrate, the answers to these questions are complex. Each of these issues—bison, snowmobiles, Fishing Bridge and grizzly bears, gray wolves, fires, and the New World Mine—was the center of a policy-making controversy. All of these controversies erupted after 1980 and involved federal politicians, vigorous debates with interested members of the public, and animated discussion about the relevant science. As is clear from the landscape itself, however, the outcome of these policy contests varied according to the issue. What factors, then, determined the outcome? Why did the NPS create these policies?

The answers to these questions have been little examined, gathering dust in Yellowstone's files and archives, aging in the memories and minds of former park managers, and receiving little attention from national park critics and observers. Whatever the reason, only a handful of accounts exist detailing the influences upon contemporary NPS policy making, and these tend to be incomplete.[1] Unfortunately, no one has painted a complete picture of the primary influences upon contemporary National Park Service policy making.

This book strives to provide the important missing details. In brief, and as explained more fully below, by examining *every* recent, major policy-making controversy from this one park—a "controlled comparison," which will be explained in more detail below—this book hopes to answer the following questions: what are the primary influences upon contemporary national park policy making, how do they function in the public policy process, and how may park managers best work within their contemporary policy-making context to preserve the national parks? The controversies to be examined are the six major issues Yellowstone managers have faced since 1980, as presented briefly above. The park is, of course, Yellowstone, the country's first—and to many, a bellwether for policy making in other national parks. The debates, all elevated to the national level, showcase the full suite of policy-making influences: 1) park managers and how well they built a supportive coalition with external interests all working toward a common goal; 2) how well park managers framed the issue for public debate; 3) the existing scientific data and its thoroughness; 4) the policy implications for public access to the park; 5) the policy implications for local and regional economies; and 6) elected or appointed federal politicians.

Before explaining this book's direction in more detail, it is important to take note of what answers other authors have already provided to these questions. Virtually all students of NPS policy making discuss the roles played by the men and women working for the agency. These authors agree that from the earliest days, national parks have reflected the managers' dispositions, ideas, and ideals. Some were (are) visionary, while others were (are) bureaucratic tyrants, but all had (or have) profound and ultimately human influences upon their parks.[2] Often, the influences of such managers are manifested through their personal interpretations of the agency's mandates. As can be recited by heart by many NPS employees, the agency's stated purpose is to "conserve the scenery and the natural and historic objects and the wild life therein and to provide for the enjoyment of the same in such manner and by such means as will leave them unimpaired for the enjoyment of future generations."[3] Some managers err toward resource preservation, others toward visitor accommodation, and still others somewhere in between—and all can defend their actions as implementing the Organic Act. Whatever their interpretation, park superintendents and other key officials have strong influence over policy-making outcomes.[4]

Over time, national parks have expanded their purpose from the preservation of scenic landscapes ("scenic monuments," in the words of one historian) to include the preservation of natural processes such as predation, wildfire, flooding, and the damaging effects of wind. Embracing such natural process management has come with calls for science-based management; the agency has experienced fits and starts in encouraging research and in using science as a basis for management. With the exception of an ill-fated thrust toward encouraging research and science-based management in the 1930s, the agency has only recently embraced scientific research more broadly, with consequent effects on NPS policies. While there are some who disagree, the consensus among park observers is that science has been playing an increasingly important role in park management in the last few decades, with both scholars and park managers expressing support for science-based decision making.[5]

Managers and observers of the parks also express support for allowing local residents to influence park policies, although there is disagreement over to what extent.[6] Often, local and stakeholder perspectives are manifestations of their core values. Because such values are also held by most Americans, the values and conflicts between them are also critical management influences. Indeed, values could be considered the ultimate policy influence, since most other influences derive their strength from various American values. (A full analysis of these values is beyond the scope of this book, which seeks to present the primary policy influences in ways that park managers and students of NPS policies can best apply in their day-to-day policy workings).[7]

Motivated in part by their values, stakeholders frequently bring their elected or appointed officials into the policy-making debates. A number of different authors, including several former NPS directors, argue that such politicians exert considerable influence over the NPS in its policy-making efforts.[8] Only one author, however, has methodically examined this topic: political scientist William R. Lowry. In two different works, Lowry demonstrates that political influence on the NPS has increased over time and that the agency is more politicized than the park management agencies of some other countries, though less so than others.[9]

In a third book, Lowry examines the primary influences on contemporary national park management. Examining four different NPS controversies from as many national parks, Lowry found that park managers were more likely to succeed in a policy-making endeavor when they framed the fundamental issue compellingly; formed strong coalitions with affected stakeholders (such as environmentalists, gateway or local communities, and other government agencies); convincingly demonstrated that their proposal would protect local and regional economies; demonstrated consistent commitment toward their policy-making ends; and tapped into a robust and convincing scientific research base.[10]

Collectively, these authors demonstrate that parks are subject to a variety of influences, including park managers, gateway communities, scientists and proponents of science-based management, conservationists, politicians, and the values held by such stakeholders. However, many questions are still left unanswered, such as whether some of these influences are more important than others in determining policy outcomes. Similarly, the conditions under which scientific research is useful in park policy making remain unexplored. Also, the means by which politicians affect park policy creation and the ways that park managers can successfully work with them to ensure such influence is positive need further explication.

As touched upon briefly, this book will provide insight into these questions by examining every major policy-making controversy regarding Yellowstone in the last thirty-two years. Each controversy will be examined critically, looking for those forces most influential in the controversy's outcome. By examining every major controversy from one national park in the modern policy-making era, this book thus conducts a *controlled comparison*. Controlled comparisons seek to control as many variables as possible in all the case studies pertinent to the inquiry, in an effort to discern common trends or influences among them, as well as substantive differences between them.[11] The variables that will be controlled are: 1) the *place* and *agency*—Yellowstone National Park and its managing agency, the NPS; 2) the *scale* of the controversy—all must have been major policy-making controversies occurring on a national stage, so that as many policy influences are experienced as possible; and 3) the *era*—all controversies must have occurred in the contemporary policy-making era, beginning in early 1981, so that all are subject to influences (which can change over time) within one era. Each of these variables will now be discussed in more detail.

First, all policy-making controversies must be from the same *place* and involve the same *agency*—Yellowstone National Park and the NPS. This exclusive focus is appropriate for three reasons. First, restricting the inquiry to one national park minimizes the variability inherent in examining controversies from different national parks; therefore, all controversies occurred on the same playing field, subject to similar influences. Second, the focus on all Yellowstone issues can discern associated policy influences, as well as demonstrate that each park has some unique influences, something that a park-by-park approach may not uncover. By comparing this study to others—see William Lowry's books, for example—such unique influences can become obvious. In Yellowstone's case, there is more political involvement than in other smaller or lesser-known parks. Finally, what happens in America's first national park often transfers to, or is evident at, other parks in the country.

The focus on Yellowstone and NPS policy making is important and sometimes nuanced, as illustrated by one controversy that occurred in the region in the years 1989–1992. The controversy involved the "Vision" document, which would have developed a framework for coordinated land management among the six national forests, two national parks, and two national wildlife refuges in the Greater Yellowstone Area (GYA), whose managers collectively form a group known as the Greater Yellowstone Coordinating Committee (GYCC). When released to the public in 1990, the seventy-four-page draft document was perceived by some members of the public as an attempt to extend preservationist NPS policies to the area's national forests. Under political pressure, the GYCC revised the draft to a slim eleven-page booklet that made little change in the area's federal lands management. While the controversy was certainly major (the next criterion) and contemporary (the final criterion), it did not directly involve Yellowstone National Park policy making; policies *inside* the park were never under debate. Consequently, this controversy, and others like it that did not involve policy making for the national park itself, were excluded from this book because they did not meet the first criterion.[12]

Next, the *scale* of the policy-making controversies must have been major in order to be included in this book. All the policy-making influences are evident in such larger controversies, which produced more visible public debate, thereby capturing more public interest and opinion and introducing a full suite of stakeholders, perspectives on park purposes, and influences. There have also been a number of minor controversies in the modern era—the last thirty-two years—but these are excluded because they do not always involve the full complement of policy-making influences. While some of the forces evident in the major issues are also at play in the minor ones, other influences are absent. For example, in the mid-1990s, lake trout (or *Salvelinus namaycush*) were discovered in Yellowstone Lake. Native to the Great Lakes, lake trout have wiped out local trout populations when introduced to other western waters. Alarmed that Yellowstone Lake's native cutthroat trout (or *Oncorhynchus clarki bouvieri*) would suffer the same fate, park managers sought scientific input and, based on that opinion, began a program of selectively netting exotic trout to keep the species suppressed. The program continues today with uncertain results: plenty of lake trout have been caught, but cutthroat trout populations have plummeted, perhaps also due to drought and whirling disease, which makes them more vulnerable to predation. While scientific research was clearly pivotal in the managers' response to this crisis, the issue did not rise to the level of a controversy and has not seen much interest-group or political involvement. No major public debate resulted—a debate that would have introduced varying perspectives about the purpose of the park and what response was appropriate to preserve the park and the park experience. Consequently, this policy-making issue and other minor ones like it were unnecessary to include in

FIGURE 1: Old Faithful Geyser, 2008. Loved by many, Yellowstone National Park has been the focus of many controversies since 1981—most of which have included some of the region's politicians. An examination of those controversies may suggest to some that Yellowstone, therefore, is synonymous with political intrigue. Author photo.

the controlled comparison. The focus on the six highly visible controversies produces a sufficiently comprehensive picture of the forces influencing NPS policy-making successes.

FIGURE 2: Wolf in acclimation pen, mid-1990s. Working with the U.S. Fish and Wildlife Service, the National Park Service returned the wolf to Yellowstone in the 1990s. The wolves were held for two months in acclimation pens before being released into the wild. Wolf reintroduction was a hotly and nationally debated issue during which the full suite of policy-making determinants came into play. Consequently, it is one of the primary case studies of the controlled comparison discussed in this book. NPS photo.

Finally, all policy-making controversies must be from the contemporary *era*, defined as 1981 to the present. During this roughly thirty-two-year period, the policy-making framework for federal land managers has not changed substantially. That framework rests primarily upon the National Environmental Policy Act, signed into law by President Nixon on January 1, 1970, and the other environmental laws of the 1960s and 1970s. They include the Clean Air Act (1970), the Clean Water Act (CWA) (passed in 1948 as the Federal Water Pollution Control Act but amended and renamed in 1972), the National Historic Preservation Act (1966), the Endangered Species Act (1973), the Wilderness Act (1964), and the Wild and Scenic Rivers Act (1968). By the early 1980s, the NPS had prescribed procedures for complying with these laws, and agency staff throughout the country had become familiar with those procedures. These laws and procedures mandated public involvement and maximum use of the scientific data pertaining to the issue at hand, a mandate that brought new (today, familiar) influences upon NPS policy making. Standard NPS policy-making procedures have changed little since then.

President Reagan, who took office in 1981, marked a turning point in federal policy making. He essentially turned the Republican Party into the "state's rights" party, generally opposing federal government intrusion into state-level policies. Because the environmental and historic preservation laws mentioned above were all federal, the Republican Party largely turned against environmental preservation (less so against historic preservation). For park managers, this has meant that the Democratic Party has more often been their friend, the Republican Party, their foe. Little has changed in

FIGURE 3: Snowmobiles parked at Old Faithful, early 2000s. Although snowmobiles have been present in Yellowstone National Park since the late 1960s, national public debate about their appropriateness in the park did not occur until the late 1990s and 2000s (the contemporary era, as defined in this book). During that time, park managers completed several examinations of the environmental impacts snowmobiles have on the park. Winter use of Yellowstone, therefore, is a good example of a contemporary issue that fits the requirements for this book's controlled comparison. Author photo.

this regard since Reagan's presidency. Both for this reason and because the environmental laws and associated processes have remained the same since 1981, the six controversies in this book have all occurred on a similar policy-making stage.[13]

By applying these criteria to Yellowstone's recent policymaking, we find six controversies comprising the controlled comparison. As mentioned earlier, these controversies are the 1980s Fishing Bridge Village and grizzly bear issue; the review of wildfire policy (which took place after the 1988 fires); the 1990s New World Mine controversy; gray wolf reintroduction (which spanned the 1980s and 1990s); the ongoing snowmobile and winter use controversy (which began in the 1990s); and the bison management issue (which also began in the 1990s). Because there are no comprehensive, scholarly accounts of the first three issues, the first three chapters in this book chronicle them and illuminate the role of the policy influences as the stories unfold. The other three case studies (wolf reintroduction, the snowmobile issue, and bison management) have all been discussed in at least one book; thus, chapter 4 will present them in an abbreviated form, drawing upon these published works.[14] Reviews of the latter three issues will focus, like the more detailed narrations, upon those factors most important in NPS's policy-making success or failure.

The six influences mentioned previously will be evident throughout the studies comprising this controlled comparison. Because these influences are pivotal in determining the outcome of the policy-making controversies, I will refer to them as "determinants." These determinants consist of the following. First, park managers are usually more successful in policy-making efforts when they form a strong coalition with members of the environmental community, gateway (or nearby) towns, and/or other federal agencies. Such coalitions help to build support for the NPS's proposals among local residents, the interested public, and elected and appointed representatives. Second, framing the issue in a way that compels the public to support the park managers' cause also contributes to policy-making success. When an issue is framed succinctly and compellingly, members of the public (as well as federal politicians) are more likely to support the agency's proposal. Third, park managers are more successful when they can demonstrate that their proposed policies will not harm local and regional economies. Proposals that are seen as threatening such economies usually fail (in part due to the expected political opposition). Fourth, the public is more likely to support policy proposals if they perceive that their ability to tour Yellowstone on motorized vehicles will not be diminished. Park managers, then, are more likely to succeed if their proposals preserve public access. Fifth, it is best when park managers have a strong and easily understood scientific research base informing the policy question. A robust science base, with unanimity among the relevant scientists, greatly aids the NPS in a policy-making controversy; lacking such, the park managers' proposals often fail. Finally, park managers must take care to build political support at either the congressional or executive branch level. Having the other determinants already aligned in their favor substantially assists in building the necessary political capital.[15]

The controlled comparison will also illustrate that park managers must have all, or almost all, of the six policy-making determinants working in their favor to be successful in a policy-making endeavor. While there is no guarantee of success, in every example of policy success explored in this book, park managers had at least five of the six determinants aiding their cause. When they are not able to align the determinants in such a manner, the policy-making controversies are more often settled via compromise, or they fester for many years. While such compromises and lingering debates may be the best available solution in those circumstances, they do not always assure adequate natural resource protection. For example, meadows in bear habitats may see their ecological function compromised (as in the Fishing Bridge Village and grizzly bear issue), park soundscapes may be harmed by snowmobile noise, and bison leaving the park in winter may be sent to slaughter because they could transmit a harmful disease to domestic cattle. Additionally, visitors may find their experiences in the park compromised, such as through hearing snowmobile noise or being unable to afford winter visits (because fractious debate obscures solutions that would provide for less expensive transportation options). Such compromises, though, are not always permanent; park managers are often able to revisit them and adjust them to better protect park resources and experiences. Contemporary policy making in Yellowstone, then, means that park managers must achieve near complete alignment of the policy-making determinants in their favor, with a long-term focus being necessary much of the time.

Therefore, by examining all recent major policy-making controversies from Yellowstone National Park, this book discerns the dominant influences upon NPS policy making today. Those influences are public perceptions as to whether motorized *access* will be affected; public perceptions as to whether gateway (or local) *economies* will be harmed; the NPS's success or failure in building a supportive *coalition* with external interests; the NPS's ability (often with the assistance of its coalition members) to *frame* the issue in a succinct, compelling manner; the robustness and unanimity of the relevant *scientific research base* and its ability to be easily understood; and the support or opposition of the appropriate elected or appointed federal *politicians*. Of these, the controlled comparison will indicate that the last two determinants—science and politics—appear to be most influential and that park managers usually need all, or almost all, of the determinants aligned in their favor to be successful. Aligning the determinants can take time—sometimes a decade or more, with natural resource or park experiential degradations sometimes an associated short-term consequence—but the result is improved resource and experience protection. By carefully attending to the influences revealed in this book, managers can further improve their use of the existing policy-making context to preserve Yellowstone and our country's other national parks.

CHAPTER ONE

Fishing Bridge and the Son of Cody

It's about power. F***ing power.
—Alan Simpson

The Fishing Bridge area and nearby Pelican Valley
constitute an extraordinarily diverse setting . . . a crossroads of
energy flows and life forms that is unique in Yellowstone Park.
—Paul Schullery

IN SUMMER 1986, YELLOWSTONE NATIONAL PARK MANAGERS WERE
confronted with something more commonly found in the country's large
cities: a protest. Organized by the radical environmental group Earth First!,
the protest was held on Fishing Bridge, a historic bridge at the mouth of
Yellowstone Lake, to bring attention to the declining population of grizzly
bears in the park and the high number of grizzly deaths occurring in a tourist village just east of the bridge. Park managers were considering closing the
village to protect the bears, but seemed to be flagging in their determination to proceed. So, the Earth First! protestors, some dressed in animal costumes, did many of the things that so captivate the media: chanting, holding
placards, and eventually trying to block traffic across the historic bridge
(figure 4). At that point, National Park Service (NPS) law enforcement officers moved in, breaking up the blockade and arresting several protestors.

FIGURE 4: Earth First! protestors demonstrating against the National Park Service's decision to allow portions of Fishing Bridge Village to remain open, 1988. The activist environmental group held several protests in Yellowstone National Park in the late 1980s. Concerned about the drop in grizzly bear numbers, the group attempted to call attention to actions (or inaction) by park managers that they felt threatened the bears' survival in the park. NPS photo.

Despite its visibility, the Earth First! protest on Fishing Bridge, along with others the group held that same year, did little to affect the outcome of the debate over whether to close the village.[1] Additionally, lawsuits filed later against the NPS by the National Wildlife Federation (NWF) were unsuccessful; parts of Fishing Bridge Village remain open to this day. Both extremes of the environmental political spectrum—the radical Earth First! and the staid NWF—had little influence on the outcome of the Fishing Bridge Village controversy. More influential were science (or the lack of it) and certain elected politicians (mainly Senator Alan Simpson, a Republican from Wyoming, whose thoughts on the controversy are evident in the quote above).[2] Caught up in a controversy without a coalition of allies, helpful scientific data, or political friends, park managers had few to turn to for support and thus found their efforts largely thwarted.[3]

This issue—the first of Yellowstone's major policy-making controversies in the contemporary era—will introduce many of the determining influences upon NPS policy making. The agency's ability to form coalitions with external interests, the presence or absence of supportive scientific data, public perceptions about policy impacts on local economies or visitor access to the park, the manner in which the issue was framed, and whether the agency had political friends all would come to play important roles in park managers' ability to achieve success. In a pattern that would come to repeat itself, the presence or absence of supportive scientific information and friendly politicians essentially determined the issue's outcome; the other influences largely served as avenues to gain political attention—whether positive or negative.

The Fishing Bridge Story: Grizzly Bears, Science, and Power

Fishing Bridge spans the Yellowstone River just below the outlet of Yellowstone Lake (figures 5, 6). In the early 1980s, just east of the bridge was a tourist village consisting of a recreational vehicle (RV) park with 353 sites, an NPS campground with 308 sites, a collection of several hundred tourist cabins, a general store, a gas and service station, and a visitor center, all of which were built between about 1920 and the mid-1960s. Located on the lakeshore and with good fishing both there and from the nearby bridge, the village was consistently popular. Three miles farther east, the lake's second-largest tributary, Pelican Creek, flows into the lake in a meadow-studded area. The area offers grizzlies a rich mixture of wet meadows, sheltering forest, riparian bottoms, spawning cutthroat trout, elk, and bison. It is near-perfect bear habitat, with a variety of edible plants and suitable prey.[4]

Having a major park development right in the middle of such excellent habitat compromised it. As early as the 1940s, conservationists recognized the potential to improve bear habitat in Yellowstone by removing Fishing Bridge Village. Conservationist Olaus Murie, who helped found The Wilderness Society and gain passage of the Wilderness Act, was the first to make such a suggestion. Later, in 1963, the Leopold report (entitled "Wildlife Management in the National Parks"), an influential management review commissioned by the NPS, promoted more natural conditions for park wildlife. The lead author on the report was A. Starker Leopold, son of noted 1940s conservationist Aldo Leopold. Starker and his coauthors pushed park managers to consider whether they were preserving zoos and amusement parks rather than wild places. They suggested the NPS manage the country's national parks to be "vignettes of primitive America," or reminders of how the country once appeared and functioned.[5] The report revolutionized national park management in the late 1960s and early 1970s.[6]

The idea of closing Fishing Bridge Village was mostly idle speculation until the 1960s, when park staff working on a new master plan for Yellowstone echoed Murie's idea. Finalized in 1974, the plan did indeed propose closing the village and replacing it with a new one about 25 miles away. Dubbed Grant Village (for President U.S. Grant, who signed the Yellowstone National Park Act into law in 1872), the new village site was thought to be low-quality grizzly bear habitat. On the southwest shore of Yellowstone Lake, Grant Village would also have a campground, general store, visitor center, and about seven hundred hotel rooms. Those rooms would replace the cabins at Fishing Bridge, which were aging or obsolete.[7]

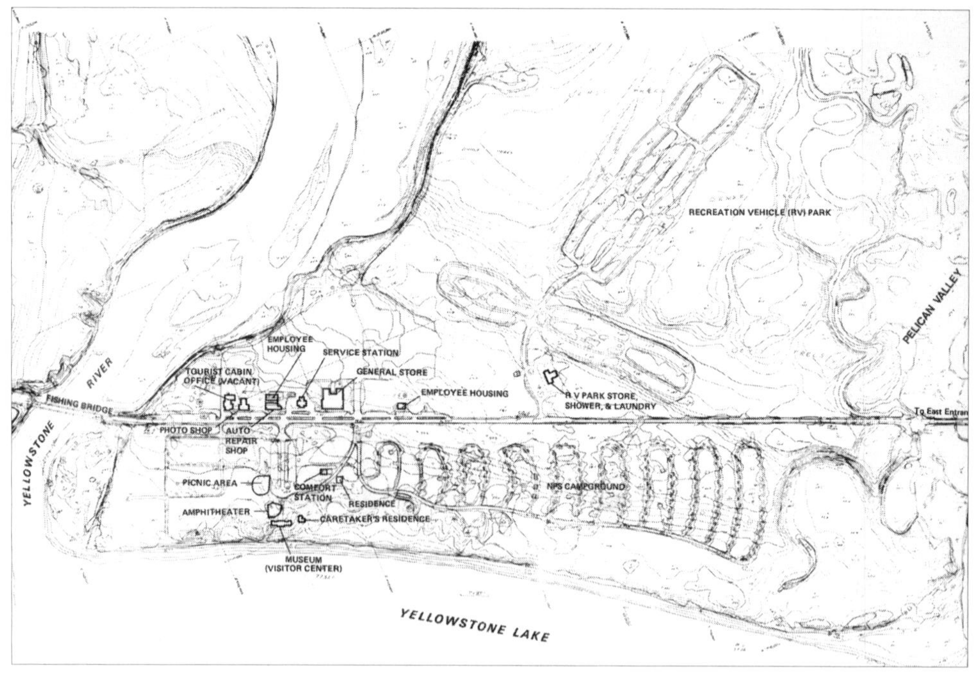

FIGURE 5: The Fishing Bridge area, and nearby Yellowstone River, Yellowstone Lake, and Pelican Creek. Source: USDI/NPS, *Draft Environmental Impact Statement, Development Concept Plan* (Denver: NPS, 1987), 27.

FIGURE 6: Fishing Bridge, 2011. The bridge spans the outlet of Yellowstone Lake, just visible through the trees at the top left of the photo. At the east end (left) of the bridge is Fishing Bridge Village, which in the mid-1980s had a campground, general store, gas and service station, visitor center, and RV Park. Author photo.

Five years after the master plan was completed, park managers began planning for Grant Village's construction by completing an environmental assessment (EA), as required by the 1970 National Environmental Policy Act (NEPA). This law requires federal agencies to consider the impact of any proposed action on natural and human environments. The agencies prepare an EA if they think their project or proposal will not have significant impacts. If they do expect significant impacts or public controversy, they must prepare a more comprehensive environmental impact statement (EIS). As part of such planning processes, the agencies must also gather public opinion, in at least two different phases during the process. The law, however, does not obligate managers to minimize the environmental impacts of a proposal; rather, it only requires them to assess and disclose those impacts. Similarly, the law does not obligate managers to adhere to majority public opinion, just to consider substantive comments—though going against a prevailing point of view, particularly if it is preservationist in nature, is certainly awkward for the NPS and requires creative justification.[8]

In addition, as part of the NEPA planning process, federal agencies must obtain the opinion of the U.S. Fish and Wildlife Service (FWS) on a project's potential impacts on endangered or threatened species. As one would assume, the agencies are also required to avoid jeopardizing the existence of any such species. In the language of the bureaucracy, this process is called "Section 7 consultation" and the FWS's opinion is referred to as a "biological opinion." In these ways, federal land managers ensure that they are protecting rare species and complying with the Endangered Species Act.[9]

At about the same time that Yellowstone managers were beginning their homework for building Grant Village, the park's grizzly bear population was hitting an all-time low, possibly less than two hundred in the entire Yellowstone region (including the bear's range outside the park).[10] Alarmed at the drop in numbers, the FWS had designated the bear a threatened species in 1975. The designation was perhaps the culmination of one of the first disputes park managers had had regarding scientific research and its use in park management. The research involved the grizzly bear and its use of the NPS's last open dump in Yellowstone's interior, the Trout Creek dump, located just 5 miles north of Fishing Bridge in Hayden Valley. The researchers, Frank and John Craighead (twin brothers), had pioneered the use of radio collars to track grizzly movements, finding that a high percentage of park grizzlies fed at the dump at some point in the year. Human food— even garbage—is more attractive to most grizzly bears than many naturally occurring foods, especially when it is readily available at an open dump. When park managers proposed closing the dump to implement some of the Leopold report recommendations, the Craighead brothers reacted in alarm, fearing that doing so would imperil the bears. They cautioned park managers against full or rapid closure, but park managers closed the dump anyway, in 1970, with the threatened-species listing soon following. Not only did the listing and dispute sensitize all those concerned with the bear's survival to the animal's current situation, but they also highlighted the need to foster and utilize scientific research in park management more consistently, something many scholars had criticized the agency for not doing. Unfortunately, in this situation, the somewhat desperate need to stop the grizzly bear population decline placed more demands on research tools—particularly a nascent computer model—than they were capable of addressing, given the need to take action immediately.[11]

The threatened-species listing brought strong federal protection for the grizzly bear, requiring both the FWS and NPS to develop a recovery plan. Since almost all the surviving bears were in Yellowstone, the NPS began developing a recovery plan for the species, consulting with the FWS in 1980. Examining where grizzly bears were dying, the NPS realized that the Fishing Bridge area accounted for more fatalities than any other area in the park. With the nearby dump now closed, many bears escalated their search for food at other campgrounds in the vicinity, like those at Fishing Bridge, where they had also long obtained human food. Coming into more contact with people in the Fishing Bridge campgrounds than at the former dump, bears were causing more and more human injuries and property damage. The end result was that park managers were removing an increasing number of bears from the population (either by sending them to zoos or by killing them) to prevent human injuries. That park managers were more aggressive in their efforts to separate bears from human foods at this time merely added to the number of bear removals, again especially in the campgrounds.[12]

Hoping to save the bears and to implement its master plan, the NPS promised the FWS in 1981 that it would close the Fishing Bridge campgrounds within five years. At the same time, the NPS could move forward on building Grant Village, thereby implementing a portion of the master plan and the now-complete EA for the project. A year later, Yellowstone superintendent John Townsley and his staff also completed an EIS on grizzly bear management, again consulting with the FWS. The latter concurred with that plan and carefully monitored NPS's progress in implementing both the EIS and the earlier Grant Village and Fishing Bridge agreement. As the months passed, though, the campground closure stalled and the issue soon became controversial.[13]

One reason the closure stalled was that Superintendent Townsley had other things on his mind: a struggle against cancer. Townsley lost that battle in 1982, at which point the NPS appointed Robert "Bob" Barbee to Yellowstone's superintendency. Barbee was a friendly, approachable person who possessed the political savvy to cope with controversy while achieving park goals. Shortly after taking office, for example, he approved the new bear management plan for Yellowstone and never wavered from its more difficult stipulations, such as the closure of some backcountry areas to the public so bears could forage there without human interruption. Barbee would find the Fishing Bridge Village situation to be a true test of his managerial and political skills.[14]

Picking up where Townsley left off, Barbee quickly initiated the government procedure necessary to close Fishing Bridge, including the campgrounds, general store, cabins, and gas station. He directed his staff to begin writing a Development Concept Plan (DCP) and associated EA for Fishing Bridge and two nearby tourist villages on the northwest shore of Yellowstone Lake, called Lake Village and Bridge Bay (figure 7). The DCP, adhering to the FWS agreement, presented several different proposals, all of which involved closing Fishing Bridge Village. In August 1983, Barbee's staff held seven public meetings in the area to present the proposals and found that the proposed Fishing Bridge closures had struck a nerve with local residents, especially those living in Cody. They were upset that favorite camping areas would be closed and that the NPS evidently did not plan to replace them, at least not nearby (for Cody residents, Grant Village was not a satisfactory replacement). The controversy did not extend to the Lake or Bridge Bay villages, but rather focused on Fishing Bridge specifically.[15]

Those who were upset with the proposed closure questioned it on both scientific and economic grounds, two areas of concern that would play pivotal roles in the developing controversy. The scientific concerns revolved around the agency's ability to prove that the closure would help the grizzly bear. For example, Cody Country Chamber of Commerce president William D. Weiss demanded that the agency prove "specifically and conclusively" that closing the campgrounds would benefit the bear.[16] In addition, Terry Povah, president of Hamilton Stores (the line of general stores in Yellowstone at the time) (figure 8) asked Yellowstone's bear expert, Gary Brown, how many grizzly bears would be saved by the closure of the tourist complex. Brown, perhaps not yet ready to answer this question with a specific number, replied six, a number that would probably have been too low to justify the closure, at least for Povah and like-minded critics. Later, evolving scientific study would change that number, but would not change the request to prove that closure would protect a specific number of bears. Unfortunately for the NPS, the numbers-game debate would consistently obscure the agency's larger concern about preserving a charismatic animal species in Yellowstone. The obfuscation was due partly to consistently weak research and, as time would tell, to increasingly powerful political interest in the issue.[17]

Questions about the economic impacts of the proposed closure were similarly pointed, revolving around the effects of closure upon visitor travel through Fishing Bridge and out Yellowstone's East Entrance to Cody, fifty-two miles away. Led by the Cody Country Chamber of Commerce, those raising this concern feared that closing Fishing Bridge would dampen the flow of tourists through Cody, a town that prides itself on its tourist services. This concern would continue to fester and grow. Meanwhile, the park's two primary tourist service providers raised another issue: they did not want to lose large capital investments, such as the park's only RV park, its largest general store, and associated profits—$20 million dollars in property, plus almost as much in annual sales. Terry Povah of Hamilton Stores stated the issue most succinctly: to him it was a matter of "economics and common sense."[18] He later exerted considerable pressure on the secretary of the interior to compel the NPS to rethink its plan and produce better supporting science.[19]

Quickly, the NPS began receiving inquiries from members of Congress, wondering what the agency was doing to get their constituents so upset. In the fall of 1983, Superintendent Barbee traveled to Washington, D.C. to confer with NPS director Russell Dickenson, who had received the brunt of many of the inquiries. Barbee pitched his case for closure, stating that he felt the scientific consensus supported it but that his biologists could not make an air-tight case that it would preserve the grizzly bear. He also told Dickenson that he was worried that a retreat or delay in closing the campgrounds would violate the FWS agreement, which would in turn make the NPS vulnerable to lawsuits from environmentalists upset with the delay. In response, Dickenson told Barbee to gather the data necessary to make his case before proceeding any further.[20]

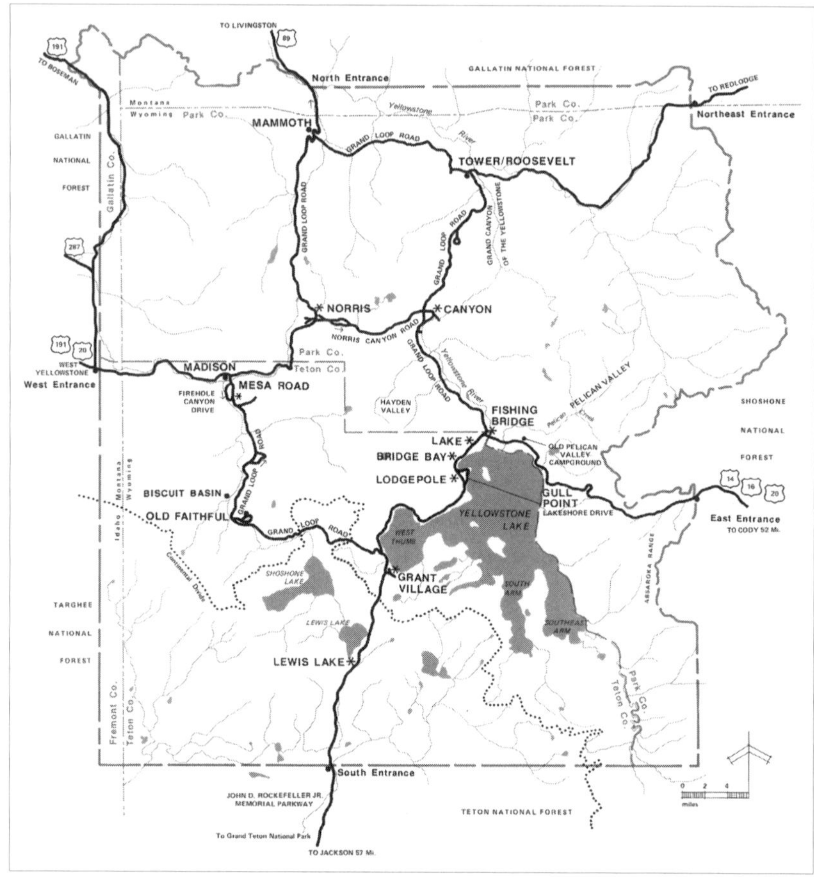

FIGURE 7: Yellowstone National Park, showing developments on the shores of Yellowstone Lake, as well as the Fishing Bridge campground replacement sites proposed in 1987. The primary replacement site is shown on the map as "Lodgepole." Earlier in the controversy it was called "Weasel Creek." Source: USDI/NPS, *Draft Environmental Impact Statement, Development Concept Plan* (Denver: NPS, 1987), 25.

Meanwhile, RV advocacy groups, such as the Good Sam Club and Trailer Life, began urging their members to write Barbee opposing the closure. The Fishing Bridge RV Park was one of the few campgrounds in the national park system that offered full hookups (electricity, water, and sewer connections) (figure 9), and this constituency did not want to lose access to a place with such nice conveniences. Throughout the first half of 1984,

FIGURE 8: Fishing Bridge Village, with the General Store visible across the road, 2011. The store is part of the Hamilton Stores franchise in Yellowstone. This store's owner, Terry Povah, defended the economic importance of his business by questioning the scientific basis for the National Park Service's proposal to close Fishing Bridge Village. Author photo.

Barbee received a firestorm of letters against the closure. Representatives of the RV groups also met with U.S. senators Alan Simpson and Malcolm Wallop (another Republican from Wyoming) to insist that NPS replace any RV sites that would be closed with others situated elsewhere in Yellowstone. This meeting clarified for Barbee the senators' attention to the issue.[21]

In June 1984, Barbee's staff produced a draft report responding to Dickenson's directive and summarizing the ecological importance and human impact of the Fishing Bridge area. NPS writer Paul Schullery was the primary organizer and editor of the report, which was more than 150 pages long and entitled *Fishing Bridge and the Yellowstone Ecosystem: Report to the Director.* He and his coauthors found that Pelican Creek and the Yellowstone Lake area produced abundant trout (not preyed upon by grizzlies at that time, though they were certainly available to them), while the meadows, wetlands, and forests of the area produced an exceptional diversity of

FIGURE 9: The Fishing Bridge RV Park, 2011. Located across the road from the NPS-managed campground, the RV Park featured full hook-ups for RV owners, including electricity, water, and sewer connections. RV advocacy groups, such as the Good Sam Club and RV Life, opposed the proposed closure of Fishing Village RV Park. Author photo.

wildlife habitat. Grizzlies were strongly attracted to the area because of its abundance of natural foods (figure 10), but the human development and activity in the area were widespread and dangerous for the bears. Anglers, hikers, and campers all frightened them away from their natural food sources. Moreover, by allowing bears to obtain human foods, visitors perpetuated the cycle of human food addiction, habituation, and eventual bear removal to protect humans. The situation was critical at Fishing Bridge Village: the area had had more bear deaths through such NPS removals between 1968 and 1983 than at all other Yellowstone developments combined. Calling the Fishing Bridge development an "ecological mistake," Schullery and his co-authors concluded: "The results are predictable and grave. . . . Fishing Bridge operating in concert with Grant Village has a potential cumulative effect that is disastrous [for grizzly bears]."[22]

FIGURE 10: Bear in meadows near Fishing Bridge. Due to the abundance of natural foods in the area, the suite of meadows, forest, and lake habitats available near Fishing Bridge and Lake attracts numerous grizzlies. A 1984 National Park Service assessment of the importance of these habitats to the park's grizzly bear population concluded that business as usual in the Fishing Bridge area could have grave consequences for the bruins. NPS photo by Jim Roche.

While the report convincingly portrayed the Fishing Bridge area as important to the grizzly bear, it failed in other ways. First, it was rushed into production; six months was simply not enough time to assess long-term trends in grizzly bear survival and the NPS's management of the bruins. The report's authors did explain that when bears obtained human foods, park managers would either move the bears away from developed areas or send them to zoos where they could not harm people. Such actions were growing increasingly rare, however, because since the mid-1970s Yellowstone Park's managers had made human foods difficult for bears to get. They had closed the last open garbage dump, installed bear-proof trash cans for visitors to use, and had begun educating visitors about, and enforcing the laws against, people feeding bears.[23]

Fishing Bridge, however, seemed immune from the declining bear removal trend. While bear removals were indeed beginning to decline there, the report's authors feared that this trend was only illusory, because the area's prime habitat would continue to put bears into proximity to people and their tempting foods. As time would tell, however, the concern was unfounded, for bear removals at Fishing Bridge eventually fell in line with those taking place throughout the park. The luxury of hindsight tells us that that the impact of the 1970s bear management changes merely took longer to affect Fishing Bridge's bear numbers.

Without that hindsight, however, park managers and the report's authors overemphasized the continuing impact that Fishing Bridge would have on bear populations.[24] To make the point that Fishing Bridge was indeed good habitat, managers compared the area to other nearby habitats. Specifically, they considered those around Lake and Bridge Bay separately from habitat at Fishing Bridge. Such a division of habitats in immediate proximity to each other (they were at most only 2 miles apart) was artificial and a division that the grizzly bears did not observe. The three areas were merely parts of a greater whole, one park region that was especially rich in resources. Also, such a division belied the casual observations of those familiar with the areas. All three tourist developments were characterized by extensive meadows on the lakeshore, with forests nearby. The public was unable to understand why Fishing Bridge Village had to be removed when developments in similar areas within walking distance could remain. Such findings did not square with common perceptions.[25]

Finally, the report did not definitively state that continued operation of the Fishing Bridge campgrounds would cause the grizzly bear to become extinct. The authors could predict that more bears would die, but making a stronger statement was considered scientifically imprudent. Nonetheless, the report's reluctance to do so was its greatest single shortcoming, because park managers would pin their entire justification for closure on the connection between grizzly deaths and the Fishing Bridge developments (especially the campgrounds). Before long, the public defined the core question as: "Will grizzly bears become extinct if we leave Fishing Bridge open?" The scientific community, even today, struggles to answer such a question, but park managers had left themselves little choice but to attempt to answer it. They would soon make that attempt using a brand new computer program, one that was as fallible as its developers. Ultimately, park managers would find that they had framed the issue in a way that was unanswerable.[26]

Hints of that conclusion came within a month of the report's release, in June 1984. With the report providing some justification for the proposed closure, Superintendent Barbee and his staff resumed the planning for Fishing Bridge closure. After digesting the report and seeing renewed signs of planning, interested Cody residents clarified their central question. Karen Gibbons, new president of the Cody Country Chamber of Commerce, wrote NPS director Dickenson in July to request that Yellowstone prepare a full EIS, not the less rigorous EA. She not only wanted the EIS to evaluate the socioeconomic impacts of the closure, but wanted it to show "specifically, if at all, how the one square mile of improvements [at Fishing Bridge] when removed . . . will increase bear numbers in that one square mile area."[27] Gibbons's request for hard scientific evidence indicates the extent to which the debate was centering on grizzly bear research. She knew that a conclusive scientific finding proving that continued operation of the "one square mile" of development would seriously hurt the grizzly bear was unlikely. However, by framing the debate around unachievable results, she knew the analysis would support what she wanted: continued operation of the village.[28]

Scientific study was not the only focal point of debate; continued motorized access to Yellowstone was becoming a concern as well. Cody residents were beginning to speculate that closing Fishing Bridge Village was just the tip of the iceberg—that Barbee was going to ban all automobiles from Yellowstone. The 1974 master plan for Yellowstone had called for a drastic reduction in automobile use in the park, but had not yet been implemented (and remains unimplemented and mostly obsolete today). Cody residents feared that park administrators were finally beginning to restrict automobile use, effectively closing down the park to them. The long distances between Cody and Yellowstone's primary attractions (52 miles from Cody to the East Entrance, another 27 miles to Fishing Bridge, and another 38 miles to Old Faithful), and the tendency for most Cody visitors to tour the park via automobile, had precluded the development of public transportation, making automobile travel an absolute must for Yellowstone access. Anything park administrators did that threatened the use of automobiles in Yellowstone, therefore, was perceived as a threat to Cody's economy as well as the freedom of its residents to tour their own backyard park.[29]

Concerned Cody residents turned to the "Son of Cody," Alan Simpson, Wyoming's junior senator on Capitol Hill.[30] Because Simpson was from Cody,

Gibbons found it easy to get his attention concerning the issues they faced. Simpson and the other two members of the Wyoming congressional delegation—Senator Malcolm Wallop and Representative Dick Cheney, both Republicans—quickly seconded Gibbons's request for a comprehensive EIS and demanded that the document's socioeconomic analysis focus on the potential loss of sales tax revenue that Park County (of which Cody is the seat) collected at Fishing Bridge Village. Simpson may have been partly motivated by the economic decline his state was experiencing at the time, but his desire to attend to his neighbor's needs, as well as those of his voting constituents in Cody probably motivated him even more. A few months after the politicians made their request, Dickenson and Barbee responded by agreeing to write the EIS.[31]

By this time Barbee and his staff were feeling "the water getting hot." Their neighbors to the east in Cody were not happy at their proposal and were mounting an increasingly adversarial campaign. A controversy was clearly brewing and park managers needed allies. The FWS could be a solid ally if park managers indeed closed the Fishing Bridge campgrounds. Environmentalists, their other likely ally, had not yet been heard from. Although some environmental groups were following the controversy, they were not yet partnering with the NPS or lobbying their members to get involved; they were likely waiting to see what position the agency actually ended up adopting in the EIS. As time would tell, neither the environmental community nor the FWS would support the NPS, because both ultimately disliked the agency's final proposal. For park managers, both groups would prove to be adversaries, not allies, over the issue of Fishing Bridge Village.[32]

In 1985, Barbee's staff began working on the EIS, developing a range of options to consider regarding the Fishing Bridge area. These included preserving the status quo (in NEPA language, the "no action" alternative); closing the area, but replacing its facilities elsewhere; and completely closing the area without replacing the village. When gauging initial public opinion that May, park managers found that most respondents favored closure without replacement. Ultimately, however, the park managers knew that one of their options had to meet the congressional delegation's approval—a hint at both the controversy's outcome and the strength of political influence on NPS policy making.[33]

As the snow melted that spring, Barbee and his staff started doing the research for the EIS. They found the results from some visitor surveys done the year before encouraging: when asked if they would alter their route if

Fishing Bridge Village were closed, only 3 percent of those surveyed said yes. For the other 97 percent, Fishing Bridge was incidental to their journey, and they would go through Cody regardless of any change at Fishing Bridge. To park managers, this information seemed as though it would allay the concerns of those in Cody; it also seemed to indicate that a full blown EIS was not really necessary. Additionally, Barbee knew that the more comprehensive EIS would take two to three years to complete. If the campgrounds remained open that entire time, he would be in violation of the FWS agreement, which stipulated closing both campgrounds by the end of 1986. Such a delay meant that the NPS would either have to amend the agreement or risk a lawsuit from the environmental community. In the end, Barbee decided to revert to the original EA, which could still be completed in time to close the campground and live up to the FWS agreement.[34]

However, because Senator Simpson had asked—demanded—the EIS, any change in course needed to pass muster with him. The son of Milward Simpson, a former senator and governor of Wyoming, Alan Simpson knew how to get his way. Though he had a good sense of humor, he was not afraid to use four-letter words (especially in the absence of women), or to castigate people publicly in fairly personal terms. Such actions gave him the reputation of a bully, a word commonly used to describe him by those NPS staff who worked with him.[35] So, in September, Barbee, new NPS director William Penn Mott, and Assistant Secretary of the Interior William Horn convened a summit with Simpson, Senator Wallop, and Congressman Cheney. Barbee told the congressional delegation about the results of the visitor surveys, allaying their concerns over the socioeconomic effects of closing Fishing Bridge Village as best he could. He also assured them that he would seek to replace the campground in an area that was low-quality grizzly habitat, but as close to Fishing Bridge as possible, to preserve existing traffic patterns. Simpson and his two allies, however, would have none of this. Telling a constituent that he was going to "stay with this one," Simpson and the other delegation members insisted again on the full EIS.[36] Knowing they needed to preserve good speaking terms with the three (especially Simpson), Barbee and Mott backed down and agreed to continue the EIS preparation.[37]

This meant that the agreement with the FWS was in jeopardy, because the campgrounds would remain open beyond the agreed upon closure date, posing a continued threat to the grizzly bears. Barbee turned to the FWS, an NPS sister agency, for help. Understanding his predicament, his colleagues at FWS agreed to the postponement of the campground closure on the condition that Barbee use a new computer model to assess the likely impacts of NPS actions on grizzly bear habitat and the likelihood of consequent grizzly mortalities in the Yellowstone area. Known as the Cumulative Effects Model (CEM), the model had been under development by the NPS and the U.S. Forest Service (USFS) (the agency that managed extensive grizzly habitat surrounding Yellowstone) for several years. The FWS believed the model was close to completion and would provide an accurate assessment of effects on the bear—two assumptions that would prove fateful in the next three years. With the model's readiness unquestioned, Barbee agreed to use it.[38]

Barbee also agreed to close the portion of the Fishing Bridge campground closest to Pelican Creek, because a more detailed analysis demonstrated that this area saw a disproportionately high level of grizzly mortality. Barbee and his staff took several other steps designed to protect the bear: they implemented backcountry hiking restrictions in the best grizzly habitats like Pelican Valley; they established more frequent monitoring and ranger patrolling of the Fishing Bridge Village and Grant Village campgrounds and nearby trout streams; and they removed some unimportant facilities at Fishing Bridge. He and his staff also reemphasized the park's education program designed to teach park employees and visitors how to prevent bears from attaining human foods, and they recommitted themselves to prompt and effective garbage removal from the campgrounds.[39]

However meritorious these efforts were, they seemed like Band-Aids to conservationist groups such as the NWF, one of the country's most respected wildlife advocacy groups.[40] Leaders of the NWF had been growing increasingly frustrated by the NPS's delays and inability to carry through on its promise to close Fishing Bridge Village. The organization had threatened to sue the NPS for violating the Endangered Species Act if the agency did not close the campground as agreed upon with the FWS, but held off when NPS director Mott personally appealed to NWF leaders for patience. That patience ended when the September summit with Senator Simpson failed; six months later, the NWF sued the NPS, alleging that continued operation of Fishing Bridge Village imperiled the grizzly bear's survival. The group argued that scientific studies indicated that grizzlies would be lost; they based much of their claims on the agency's own 1984 *Report to the Director*. With the lawsuit, it was increasingly clear that park managers did not have an ally in either the environmental community or the FWS.[41]

As part of its suit, the NWF requested a temporary restraining order preventing the NPS from opening the Fishing Bridge campgrounds for the 1986 season. District Judge Ewing Kerr denied the order in May, asserting that the organization had failed to prove that opening the campground would harm the bears.[42] Kerr's decision highlighted the difficulty of using scientific research and study to prove harm would come to the grizzlies at Yellowstone; such research could not be done successfully, especially in so short a time. Moreover, his decision hinted at the likely outcome of the court case—and the controversy.

Meanwhile, Barbee's staff researched and wrote the EIS. Following up on their own visitor surveys, they contracted with Scott Atkinson of the University of Wyoming to determine what impact, if any, closure of Fishing Bridge Village would have on the economy of Cody and Park County. Surveying more than four hundred Yellowstone campers, Atkinson concluded there would be negligible, if any, socioeconomic effects. Nearly all campers still would have visited Yellowstone despite the closure of Fishing Village campgrounds and virtually none would have altered their travel patterns. Essentially, Atkinson showed that people come to Yellowstone to see bears and geysers, not to camp in a specific campground. Finding that visitors typically spent fifty dollars or less in surrounding communities, he concluded that "[t]he economic impact in the public sectors of Cody and Park County will be insignificant."[43]

Barbee and his staff specifically chose the state's only university to conduct the research in order to gain credibility among Cody residents. And yet, the report was not what Cody, Senator Simpson, and the rest of the Wyoming delegation wanted to hear. Almost as soon as it was issued, Simpson discarded its findings, stating: "I don't agree with it in any way."[44] The Senator reflected the general public opinion in Cody, which would not be changed by new research such as this (no matter the research source). Even though Cody residents soon stopped using economic decline as their reason to oppose the NPS proposal, gradually shifting their rhetoric to claim the closure would impede their access to the park, they still remained opposed to the proposed closure.[45] This situation illustrates that to be useful to park managers, scientific studies must be published well before a controversy erupts, so that the research findings become accepted among the general public. If a controversy is already flaring, new studies will only be used if they support the preconceived agendas of the involved stakeholders (even if the studies force participants to alter their logic).[46] Further, fear of loss of public access could be just as motivating to public officials like Senator Simpson as is the fear of a harmed economy. Finally, the situation indicates that *perceptions* of economic harm or loss of access are more important than the relevant research in determining the final policy outcome.

Further work on the EIS progressed slowly. The CEM, being used for the first time, needed refinement and therefore delayed the EIS development. Park managers had little choice but to take the delays in stride, since the FWS agreement mandated use of the model. While they waited, they canvassed the park for campground replacement sites and settled upon Weasel Creek, an area about 5 miles south of Fishing Bridge. A new campground there would be close enough to Fishing Bridge to preserve existing travel patterns but would not harm grizzly bear habitat, as it was in a dense lodgepole pine (or *Pinus contorta*) forest that provided little food to grizzly bears. Pleased that they had found such a site, park managers sent out a public newsletter in April of 1986 presenting five potential options, all of which would close the Fishing Bridge campgrounds and replace them with new campgrounds at Weasel Creek, or elsewhere in the park.[47]

In their newsletter, park managers also solicited public input—and got it, in more ways than one. Entering the fray for the first time was the Wyoming Heritage Society, directed by a former Cody Country Chamber of Commerce director, Bill Schilling. Coming from the tightly connected Cody political community, Schilling joined his friends in the Wyoming congressional delegation in opposing the closure. In his comments, Schilling poked holes in the weak scientific research results and reverted to the public access defense trope. Specifically, he noted that more bear deaths had occurred since 1970 at nearby Bridge Bay and Canyon campgrounds than at Fishing Bridge. He then concluded, "[T]he dual objectives of 'enjoyment of people' and 'preservation' now seems to have become a secondary concept."[48] Like Senator Simpson, Schilling and his group stuck with the issue, consistently advocating their cause.[49]

Comments like these from the public, which were fairly evenly split between those defending the campgrounds and those defending the NPS, were expected reactions to the 1986 newsletter; public protests, however, were not.[50] Having followed the issue for a while, Earth First! found the newsletter to be the final straw. This group, like the NWF, was annoyed that NPS seemed to be vacillating on its promise to close Fishing Bridge. However, the group used very different methods to voice its concern. Not only did Earth First! orchestrate its protest on the bridge, but members also engaged in other publicity stunts typical of interest groups lacking litigation resources. In March 1986, they embarrassed Superintendent Bob Barbee in front of NBC News by presenting him with their "Conservationist of the Year Award"—a buffalo chip—to which Barbee replied that they could "shove it."[51] Calling park rangers "bioprostitutes," Earth First! held other protests as well, including chaining themselves across the entrance to the Grant Village Visitor Center. Because Grant Village was being constructed in good (but not great) grizzly bear habitat, ostensibly to replace Fishing Bridge, the group opposed it as well. Elevating the need for grizzly bear protection over human concerns, Earth First! opposed all of NPS's initial options listed in the newsletter; instead, they favored complete closure of Fishing Bridge without replacement elsewhere, either at Grant Village or Weasel Creek.[52]

Thus, the summer of 1986 was the summer of discontent among radical environmentalists watching the Fishing Bridge events unfold. At least four other splinter groups joined the fray, each garnering small numbers of members and agitating for complete closure through newsletters to their members and others. For example, the Grizzly Bear Task Force formed in Bozeman, Montana, and disseminated literature in the park that summer. Even a group of Yellowstone National Park employees was so dissatisfied with the EIS and Barbee's perceived capitulation to Senator Simpson that they formed the Yellowstone Park Preservation Council to lobby for improved protection of the grizzly bear and its habitat.[53]

As suggested earlier, these groups and their antics caught public attention, but did little to influence the final outcome. Because the protestors were dressed in grizzly bear costumes and engaged in antics most people enjoyed watching more than participating in, observers focused more on the messengers than on the message. In this case, however, the performers ended up persuading the NPS to include a fifth alternative in its draft EIS, one that proposed removing all Fishing Bridge facilities (except the historic visitor center) without replacing them elsewhere in Yellowstone. This idea may have found its way into the EIS, but given the political climate of the day Superintendent Barbee and the environmental movement's radical left were not able to form an effective coalition in favor of village closure. Ultimately, as Barbee himself said, the Earth First! contingent was little more than a "gnat in my ear."[54]

The political climate also made an effective coalition with the more mainstream elements of the environmental movement difficult. The NWF may have lost its initial lawsuit against the NPS, but it continued to watch the NPS's actions—with increasing dismay. Caught under the critical gaze of the powerful Wyoming congressional delegation, Barbee and his staff soon announced a compromise between protecting the bear and retaining the village. Identified as the "preferred alternative" in the draft EIS, the compromise would retain the RV Park but close the Fishing Bridge campground across the road and replace it at Weasel Creek, where it would be called the Lodgepole Campground. A more detailed analysis of bear-human conflicts at Fishing Bridge had shown that 80 percent of them occurred in the campground and not the RV park, where campers usually cooked, ate, and stored their food inside their vehicles. By closing the NPS campground, park managers felt they were addressing both the bear problem and Cody's concerns. Ultimately, that may have been true, but at this point the compromise only further alienated the environmental community. Complete closure of the Fishing Bridge area, as originally sought by the NPS itself, was rapidly becoming impossible.[55]

The CEM was not helping the situation either. Still in its infancy, the model was plagued with errors and data gaps. Additionally, Yellowstone staff did not have a computer powerful enough to run the program, so they were borrowing a USFS computer. Not only were there technical issues, but early model runs produced results that went against park managers' current thinking—namely, that the campground redevelopment sites they were initially considering were shown by the model to be almost equal in quality to the habitat at Fishing Bridge. So, Barbee and his staff took yet another delay in stride, while they searched for a more suitable redevelopment site, eventually settling upon Weasel Creek. All told, such delays added up to almost another year of waiting. By the end of 1986 it was clear that the draft EIS would not be ready before late spring of 1987. The delays and disharmonious model runs also threw open the question of what park management should do with research results that went against their thinking: should park management bend to accommodate those results, question the modeling, or disregard the unexpected research results?[56]

The answer would depend on the contemporary political context. Further model runs continued to draw into question the idea of replacing Fishing Bridge elsewhere in the park—even at Weasel Creek. The model attempted to quantify acres of high-quality bear habitat—called Prime Equivalent Acres (PEAs)—that each of the EIS alternatives would restore or destroy, as well as identify the number of grizzly mortalities under each alternative. Replacing Fishing Bridge with Weasel Creek would restore some PEAs and result in fewer grizzly bear deaths, but not enough; early 1987 model runs indicated that grizzlies would still risk extinction. Presented with this dilemma, the park's planning team held a conference call in April of 1987 to decide what to do. In his notes on the call, team captain Howie Thompson recorded the following:

> The grizzly bear analysis data of the prime equivalent acres (PEAs) and mortality figures do not appear to provide enough justification to implement most of the Fishing Bridge action alternatives. . . . The data support the No Action Alternative and Alternative E (removal without replacement). As a result, Joel Kussman and Dan Huff [NPS Rocky Mountain region chief scientist, who with Kussman were the model's programmers] requested that Alternative E be considered as a replacement for the preferred alternative. [NPS Assistant Regional Director] Jack Neckels admitted that Alternative E had merit as a preferred alternative but commitments by Superintendent Barbee, Regional Director Mintzmyer and Deputy Director Galvin to the Wyoming Congressional Delegation precluded major modifications to the preferred alternative at this time. Howie Thompson recommended that if the preferred alternative remained as the NPS plan for Fishing Bridge, that additional rationale, such as opening up the grizzly bear corridor along the lakefront, reducing human/bear conflicts and visitor injuries, continuing to provide most of the visitor facilities in the park, and the total ecosysterm [*sic*]–wide approach to helping the grizzly bear, should be discussed in the report [or EIS].[57]

In other words, because the model would not support the preferred alternative demanded by Senator Simpson, park staff needed to find additional justification for it. The alternative had to stay, so they needed to find other reasons to support it. The scientific research, however late in the game, actually supported a position that complete closure would benefit the bear, but the park planners clearly feared the consequences of going against the congressional delegation. Barbee, in fact, openly acknowledged that he had "underestimated the political bottom line" and that "the parks are very much the children of politics."[58] Had such research results been produced earlier, with enough time to become accepted by the affected groups of stakeholders, they might have been more influential. Unfortunately, for Barbee the model runs came too late to help the efforts to close Fishing Bridge; Senator Simpson and his colleagues had made up their minds.

As Thompson's notes made clear, it was obvious that Simpson and his colleagues were calling the shots. They were not motivated by grizzly bear protection or wilderness preservation, but rather a desire to protect Cody's economy and access to Yellowstone. Simpson said as much at a press conference around this time: "I've worked as hard as anyone else in preserving endangered species, but for heaven's sake to try and save 243 in an area [Yellowstone] where there are two million people a year in a road system of hundreds of miles, is bizarre when there are 40,000 to 50,000 in Alaska and 30,000 to 40,000 in Canada."[59] While his comment suggests less sympathy than he actually had toward grizzly bear preservation in Yellowstone, Simpson did sustain the pressure to keep facilities open at Fishing Bridge.[60]

Also preoccupying park managers at the time was public discussion about a recently published book that was highly critical of Yellowstone management and associated NPS policies. In his provocatively titled *Playing God in Yellowstone*, author and journalist Alston Chase argues that environmentalists adversely drive park policies. He asserts that environmentalists think nature is sacred, making it intrinsically good and right. Research to them is unnecessary, therefore, because nature knows best. Humans are not a part of nature, so their effects should be minimized. Criticizing this idea of nature, Chase argues that humans have long played integral roles in creating the natural scene. Native Americans have been particularly influential, so nature being preserved in Yellowstone should include the role of humans, and national parks should reflect an inhabited and human-managed system. Chase suggests that park management should be based on objective scientific study that would provide a clearer concept of the human role in nature management.[61]

While a full review and critique of Chase's book is beyond the scope of this book, it is the timing of his publication that is most important.[62] Published at the height of the Fishing Bridge controversy, *Playing God* cast further doubt on a park administration that was already looking weak and indecisive, and as if they were capitulating to powerful Wyoming politicians. Right when park managers needed support the most, Chase's book closed the door on any such support, especially from Wyoming officials or the popular press. With the environmental community also reluctant to support the NPS, park managers were caught in the middle between the various stakeholders, very much alone.

Anxious to move forward, Barbee and his staff released the draft EIS to the public in October of 1987. To no one's surprise, the preferred alternative called only for the closure of the NPS campground at Fishing Bridge, with its replacement at nearby Weasel Creek. All other Fishing Bridge Village facilities, including the RV park, general store, visitor center, and picnic area would remain open. Five other alternatives presented variations on the closure theme, with the last, "Alternative E," calling for the complete closure of the area, except for the historic visitor center, and no replacement campground elsewhere in the park.[63]

Justifying the agency's proposal, the EIS presented CEM results, which indicated that the preferred alternative would add forty-seven PEAs and 1.1 bears (between one and two, but more likely just one bear) to the ecosystem over ten years, compared to 961 PEAs and 2.4 bears over the same time period if park managers totally closed the area. Even the FWS agreed that such a small difference would not save the grizzly bear at Yellowstone National Park. Scientific research did not carry the day; its results were tardy and ultimately could not prove that complete closure was necessary. The conclusion to the controversy was becoming obvious.[64]

The EIS also noted that closing the Fishing Bridge campground was only one of many actions already being taken throughout Yellowstone to restore the grizzly's numbers and that "[s]uch an incremental approach is the only means available for improving the grizzly's prospects for recovery."[65] Park managers cited the popularity of Fishing Bridge RV Park with visitors as an additional reason to keep it around.[66] As team captain Howie Thompson suggested, if political reality mandates a compromise, one might as well make it as justified as possible. Justified or not, politics was about to prevail, particularly with the scientific study being so inconclusive.

Pleased with NPS's proposal, Senator Simpson stated: "I think it's a pretty good compromise." Acknowledging reality (and implicitly acknowledging the agency's need to preserve the grizzly bear), he added that the issue was a "very tough, emotional" one.[67] He could afford to be sanguine, as he knew by now that he had won the battle. Getting the NPS to alter its preferred alternative was the major effort; now all he had to do was hold the agency's feet to the fire and preserve the compromise. His constituents would end up mounting that effort without his help, although they needed a wake-up call first.

That call came not from Senator Simpson but from the environmental community, which finally got involved in the issue. Most major environmental groups filed comments on the EIS, universally opposing the preferred alternative and largely favoring Alternative E that called for complete closure without replacement elsewhere. Concerns over the grizzly bear's recovery dominated their remarks, and several groups criticized the previously untested CEM and its assumptions. Many noted that if the NPS implemented the preferred alternative, Yellowstone would end up with three separate developed areas—Fishing Bridge, Lake and Bridge Bay, and Lodgepole and Weasel Creek—rather than just one in this part of the park, as called for in the original FWS and NPS agreement to build Grant Village. Deploring this "fight over the politics of land use," most environmentalists called for complete closure.[68]

For the environmental community, more was at stake than merely the bear's survival. Requiring huge areas of wild land, grizzlies were then (and still are today) found only in those areas of the West dominated by large blocks of wilderness—essentially, only the large areas of mostly federal land surrounding and including Glacier and Yellowstone national parks. In their comments on the draft EIS, two environmental groups enunciated the connection between bears and wilderness. One said: "Yellowstone's most powerful symbol of American wilderness may forever be lost," while another group stated: "The grizzly is wilderness incarnate."[69] In other words, if the grizzly perished, so did the wilderness.

Why this connection did not motivate more people within the environmental community to respond earlier is not clear. Perhaps the Reagan Administration's assault on nature preservation on many other fronts had them spread thin. Regardless, it soon did provide motivation for many. By December 16, 1987, the NPS reported that public comments (in about seven hundred letters) on the draft EIS were running 95 percent in favor of Alternative E and complete closure, with only 2 percent supporting the agency's preferred alternative of partial closure with replacement nearby.[70]

NEPA public comment periods are not considered "votes," although the public often perceives them as such. Still, when public comment is disproportionately opposed to an agency's preferred alternative, the agency is wise to reconsider its thinking. Certainly, it seemed as though the NPS might need to do so in this case, but soon the Cody Country Chamber of Commerce, Wyoming Heritage Society, and Good Sam Club organized their troops to defend continued campground access at Fishing Bridge. By the end of the comment period, in January of 1988, supporters of the preferred alternative had narrowed the gap to 33 percent in favor of it, 49 percent in favor of Alternative E, and much smaller numbers favoring the other alternatives (in about 2,905 letters in total). The Good Sam Club, being the only national group of the three, generated the most comment letters. Both Wyoming governor Mike Sullivan and Hamilton Stores president Terry Povah also supported the preferred alternative, again illustrating the political support.[71]

The most common theme articulated by the Wyoming and RV groups was perceived loss of access. The Cody Country Chamber of Commerce, for example, stated: "[T]he entire Fishing Bridge Areas may be closed . . . forever. This important issue provides a great opportunity for those that support the idea of 'the people's right to enjoy our National Parks' to have a positive influence on the National Park Service's decision-making process."[72] Few mentioned the economic impact to Cody that had been so feared just a few months earlier. If the focal point for conservationists was wilderness preservation under the guise of grizzly bear protection, it was now access to the park for the Wyoming constituents.[73]

These two themes—wilderness and public access—illustrate the differing lenses through which stakeholders framed the debate. Park managers, like the conservationists, attempted to structure the debate in terms of grizzly bear preservation, but found their efforts thwarted by incomplete scientific studies and strong opposition by Wyoming stakeholders. The latter, taking advantage of the weak scientific framing, were considerably more successful at framing the issue as one of public access. In a pattern that would recur in Yellowstone's snowmobile issue (see chapter 4) and public access issues in other national parks, the NPS generally loses its policy battles when the public perceives that a form of access is at stake. And, as with Fishing Bridge, it is usually *motorized* public access.

In the Fishing Bridge debate, the plurality of public comment in favor of complete closure led park managers to impose several conditions upon campground replacement. Superintendent Barbee and his staff revised the proposed action in several ways, all of which were intended to defer the replacement campground construction until absolutely necessary. They would develop a reservation system for the nearby Bridge Bay campground—the largest in the park—to provide more efficient use of it; defer replacement of Fishing Bridge campground until the remaining park campgrounds were filled to 95 percent capacity in the peak summer visitation period for any three out of five summers; and reanalyze any replacement sites in light of evolving grizzly bear research, to determine which locations would minimize impacts on the bear the most. By adopting these strategies, Barbee and his staff would see if campground replacement was really necessary and, in so doing, address the environmental groups' concerns as best as they could. Finally, in addition, they proposed building a visitor center in Cody where tourists could effectively plan their trips to Yellowstone (such as by reserving a campground space). A visitor center would help heal the wounds in the Cody-NPS relationship.[74]

In early 1988, events rapidly reached a foreordained conclusion. After consulting once again with the Wyoming delegation, Barbee published the Final EIS and the Record of Decision (the formal record of the agency's decision) in late May. The NPS campground would go, the other structures at Fishing Bridge would remain, and NPS would adopt the mitigating measures listed above. The environmental community cried foul, but left it at that. By late 1988 it was becoming clear that the NPS's decision would stand.[75]

In 1989, the NPS campground at Fishing Bridge saw its last season. Throughout 1990, it sat vacant with picnic tables and fire pits still ready for use. Ecological restoration of the area, as called for in the Final EIS, languished, the result of a lack of funding. By late 1990 the inaction began to bother Yellowstone National Park personnel. Despite the lack of a specific restoration appropriation, they began holding annual work parties at Fishing Bridge the next year. In this manner, they removed all campground structures; and by 1997 they had revegetated the campground.[76]

Some of the other projects called for in the EIS were also realized, while still others have yet to happen. Park managers closed Turbid Lake Road, a side road through Pelican Valley, to restore the roadbed to grizzly bear habitat. Managers also strengthened their commitment to keeping human foods unavailable to bears. At Fishing Bridge Village, managers removed the photo shop and cabin office building, but the service station remains because suitable replacement sites do not exist nearby. The agency removed 256 obsolete tourist cabins even before the controversy erupted, but the area on which the cabins stood has not been restored to natural conditions. Unfortunately, it is today used as a staging area, temporary storage area (or dump), and occasional camp for hundreds of firefighters who camp there for two or more weeks at a time when forest fires are being fought in the area (about two or three times per decade) (figure 11). Firefighters' boots trampling the grounds and piles of debris left behind do little toward helping restore the area for grizzly bear use. Finally, the Cody visitor center virtually disappeared from consideration and still does not exist, despite the town's request that it be built.[77]

FIGURE 11: The former Fishing Bridge cabin area, 2011. Yellowstone National Park staff completed restoration of the former NPS campground at Fishing Bridge in the 1990s, but the former cabin area has not received the same attention. Throughout the 1990s and into the first decade of the twenty-first century, the cabin area has been used for various purposes, including a fire camp, baseball field, storage area, and construction staging area. In 2012, Yellowstone managers proposed restoring it to natural conditions, but that has not yet been accomplished. Author photo.

Park managers did quickly institute a reservation system for camping at Bridge Bay and found it to be successful. Within only three summers of the reservation system coming online, campgrounds in the park met the 95 percent occupancy rate that was to trigger replacement of the Fishing Bridge campground. Beginning that process, park managers obtained updated information on grizzly bear populations and other park resources, finding that the cutthroat trout population in Yellowstone Lake and the grizzly bear population in the park had both significantly increased. Grizzlies had begun using Weasel Creek, in spring and early summer, making the site unsuitable for development into the proposed Lodgepole Campground.

Managers inaugurated another EIS to find a place (or places) for replacement campsites. In the resulting draft EIS, released in late 1994, the agency proposed adding 175 campsites to the existing campground at Norris, 100 campsites to the Canyon campground, and 35 campsites to Grant Village. Using updated methodologies, the agency affirmed that new development in these areas would not compromise essential grizzly bear habitat or bear population.[78]

After releasing the new EIS to the public for review, planning for the campsite replacement stopped. Superintendent Barbee was about to leave for a position as regional director of the national parks in Alaska, and refused to sign the final document. His replacement, Mike Finley, also refused to make a final decision, so no final EIS was ever issued. With President Clinton in the White House and Bruce Babbitt in the secretary of the interior's chair, Finley enjoyed a climate more amenable to park-resource preservation than Barbee. More importantly, he also found the Wyoming political situation had changed. Senator Alan Simpson retired in early 1997, having served Wyoming for more than thirty years. Without the Son of Cody goading the park into campground replacement, Finley felt no need to pursue the project. To this date, none of the Fishing Bridge campsites have been replaced.[79]

Reflections

The Fishing Bridge controversy introduced most of the major determinants of contemporary policy-making outcomes for the NPS. Among the most influential were the science base (and the problems associated with it, if it is weak) and politicians (who pressured Yellowstone managers to preserve Fishing Bridge). Also influencing the outcome were the fears of Cody residents that their economy would decline or access to Yellowstone be limited; the park managers' inability to form a successful coalition with interest groups or other members of the public; and the park managers' inability to frame the issue in a manner that compelled others to become involved. By examining each of these in more detail, it becomes clear that the NPS had the deck stacked against it; it was practically doomed to failure, at least on the policy front line.

Without a strong proposal to protect grizzly bears, park managers were unable to build a supportive coalition with environmentalists of any type.

Neither the activists of Earth First! nor the more staid members of the NWF believed the NPS was doing enough to protect the grizzly bear. Outside of the conservation community, the NPS also found few friends; such a lonely road to travel, as the agency came to find, was also an uphill one.

In addition to its failure to advance a strong vision for grizzly bear survival, the NPS also found itself unable to build successful coalitions because neither the agency nor its would-be supporters succeeded in framing the issue in a manner that resonated with the public. Sure, grizzlies had died at Fishing Bridge, but they seemed to be faring better in the rest of the park. In part for this reason, the image of "wilderness threatened" did not have much effect. Earth First!'s failure to stick with the issue after their arrests and the NWF's failure in court further challenged the "wilderness threatened" framing. More resonant, at least for those exerting the power in this issue, was the vision of public access at stake. For park management, few things carry more visibility than threatened public access (especially motorized access). With a threatened economy also catching the public's attention, it was not long before regional politicians got involved and basically determined the issue's outcome.

Scientific research, and its problems, tremendously influenced the Fishing Bridge outcome. When the issue first erupted, relations between park managers and the premier grizzly bear researchers were strained at best. Learning from the unhappy dispute and hoping to protect bears better, park managers were anxious to chart a new course for the NPS by basing their decision upon the best available scientific studies. Unfortunately, the research techniques upon which they pinned their hopes were too new for the task. Scientific research could show that grizzlies were dying at Fishing Bridge, but it could not prove that any form of closure there would save the bear. Instead of responding to a science-based decision, participants in the debate interpreted the new research results in light of their already conceived notions of how the issue should be resolved. Ultimately, the park proposal was only as strong as the scientific research—which is to say, weak.[80]

Scientific research is, nevertheless, crucial in park policy making; for example, it produced some grizzly habitat gains at Fishing Bridge. Even if the scientific studies failed at proving grizzly bears would go extinct if Fishing Bridge remained open, they did clearly demonstrate that the area was important to the bruins and that most Fishing Bridge grizzly encounters were actually in the NPS campground. In so doing, the research provided a solid basis for closing at least some of the area. Happily—and thanks to other managerial changes happening at the time (those that made human foods unavailable to grizzlies)—grizzly bear populations soon began to recover; by 2007 the bear could be removed from the endangered species list. Overall, scientific research contributed to a compromise that was better for preservation than continued campground operation would have produced—a victory for the use of science, one that has often been overlooked by those reflecting on the controversy's political aspects.[81] Since the Fishing Bridge controversy, scientific research has become ever more important and the park staff has become ever more professional (by increasingly publishing their research and monitoring results in peer-reviewed media, for example).[82]

Senator Simpson was *the* political presence; he essentially bullied park managers into retaining most of the Fishing Bridge development and associated public access. Park managers watered down their proposal to the point where it was not clear they were gaining any ground for the bear at Fishing Bridge. Without any other policy determinants aiding their cause, though, park managers found little assistance in convincing Simpson and his cohorts otherwise. The final outcome was one park managers disliked, for it offered no clear assurance that grizzly bears would survive. Only by taking action internally to restore the old campground, and by refusing to build new campsites, did park managers realize any substantial gains at Fishing Bridge. Their other actions aimed at distancing bears from human foods were considerably more pivotal to the grizzly population's eventual upswing. All in all, Simpson's presence in this controversy appears to be the single strongest influence on the policy-making outcome.

As spring turned into summer in 1988, managers found their attention rapidly shifting to a fire situation unparalleled in park history. By that autumn Fishing Bridge would be mostly forgotten, as park managers conducted a thorough review of the policy that had allowed some of those fires to burn. In a marked departure from Fishing Bridge—and perhaps much of NPS's past management policies that have not strongly embraced scientific research—park managers would find that when reviewing Yellowstone's fire policy, their strong scientific research base would be their greatest defense.

CHAPTER TWO

Scientists and a "Barbeeque"

The fire is destroying Yellowstone—destroying it—
and the Park Service is just sitting around, letting it happen!
It's so bad, the park's rivers are running *black*!
—Ralph Regula, 1988

Yellowstone may well have been destroyed by the
very people who were assigned to protect it. . . .
Let me tell you, colleagues, the ground is sterilized.
It is blackened to the very depths of any root system within it.
—Alan Simpson

IN 1988, THE NATION WATCHED AS YELLOWSTONE WENT UP IN smoke—at least that's the image many Americans had, based on statements like those above from politicians, often repeated in the press.[1] Starting in June, ignited by lightning strikes and some by the actions of people, these fires ended up burning about 800,000 of Yellowstone's 2.2 million acres (or 36 percent of the park). With the advent of cooler and wetter weather in the fall, by which time the fires had been contained, public and NPS attention turned to the agency policy that had allowed such fires to burn unimpeded. The heat went "indoors," but like the fires themselves, quickly cooled as more tempered and scientific discourse began to prevail. While the NPS, like all federal agencies, did suspend its policy of allowing naturally-caused fires to burn, it reinstated this policy after four years of review, in 1992. The final policy closely resembled that which had allowed the fires to burn in the first place, with more attention paid to the conditions that favor fire and the national firefighting situation.

The 1988 fire policy review provides a contrast in almost all ways to the Fishing Bridge Village controversy (which it helped snuff out). Initially present during the review were familiar public fears about diminished park access and damaged economies; once the smoke cleared, however, it became clear that fires burning in Yellowstone would harm neither of these, and political interest (or opposition to continued natural-fire burning) largely disappeared. With a broad base of preexisting scientific research into the role of fire in wildland ecosystems like Yellowstone, and knowing that research scientists were nearly unanimous in asserting that allowing wildfires in places like Yellowstone was a good thing, Yellowstone's managers were able to again allow naturally-occurring fires to burn in the park. Managers enjoyed the support of some environmentalists as well, but carrying the day were the lack of political opposition and the strong scientific support.

Literature on the 1988 wildfires at Yellowstone, on fire ecology, and on NPS's specific fire policy is abundant; therefore, this chapter will only provide a brief overview of these subjects.[2] The major focus is an overview of the fire policy review that took place once the fires at Yellowstone National Park finally died out.[3] This chapter begins with a short overview of that summer, continues with the policy review, and concludes with a discussion of the major factors affecting NPS's policy making as regards wildland fire.

Wildfires and Fire Science in Yellowstone

Yellowstone's fire policy, and that of many national parks, evolved out of the Leopold report (formally known as *Wildlife Management in the National Parks*, and authored by A. Starker Leopold), the prominent management review that NPS had commissioned in 1963. In addition to closing inappropriate developments such as Fishing Bridge Village (or portions thereof), NPS managers in Yellowstone and many other national parks eventually changed their earlier management policies to allow natural forces such as wildfires, predation, and natural succession to prevail as much as possible. Eventually dubbed "natural regulation," or more accurately "natural process management," such management became dominant in most of the country's larger and wilder national parks.[4]

Regarding landscapes, A. Starker Leopold and his coauthors specifically suggested the NPS use "prescribed fires" to replicate natural scenes and processes. Park managers in California's Sequoia National Park were the first in a western national park to respond to the suggestion, in 1968, initially allowing naturally caused fires to burn. Yellowstone's managers followed suit in 1972, allowing lightning-caused fires to burn in two large backcountry areas totaling 340,000 acres. Four years later, nature put the Yellowstone policy to its first significant test, when twenty-nine lightning-caused fires started throughout the summer. Park managers allowed at least one fire to burn naturally (it grew to 1,500 acres); allowed others to initially burn and then suppressed them when they threatened human-made structures; and immediately suppressed other fires, again because they threatened structures. This variety of successful actions, done pursuant to the plan, seemed to verify its feasibility and gave managers the confidence to open much of the rest of Yellowstone National Park to prescribed natural fires, later in 1976.[5]

Throughout the late 1970s and early 1980s, the fire plan seemed to work adequately. In 1986, Yellowstone's managers began to refine the earlier plan; it was in the final stages of approval in the spring of 1988. By that time, after sixteen years of allowing fires to burn, it was clear that 80 percent of lightning-caused fires went out by themselves, that the average fire size was about 250 acres (with the largest at 7,400 acres), and that thousands of lightning strikes occurred annually, with only a small percentage leading to fires.[6]

In allowing fires to resume their ecological function, park managers were drawing upon an increasingly large and supportive research base. By 1988 scientists had published numerous papers on fire ecology in Yellowstone. They had found evidence of fire everywhere they looked, particularly in the park's higher-elevation forests. There, extensive patchworks of lodgepole pines blanketed the landscape, with each patch composed of trees all the same age. Such patches had their origin in fire and the lodgepole pine's serotinous cones, borne by a portion of the lodgepole population and opened only by fire. As the scientists discovered, once a fire burns through an area, lodgepole pines take root from the seeds released from the opened cones; the pines grow slowly, taking two hundred to three hundred years to reach the age of senescence, when they become significantly more flammable. By dating representative trees in each patch of forest, scientists further discovered that large fires swept the Yellowstone plateau in the 1850s, as well as around 1700. Biology professor William Romme, one of the leading Yellowstone fire experts, concluded that Yellowstone's high-elevation forests burned roughly every three hundred to four hundred years. Although it was impossible to predict the 1988 conflagration, Romme was clear in stating that large, high-intensity fires occurred regularly in Yellowstone. However, the full implications of his research were lost on park managers and the public alike—few realized the potentially large size of Yellowstone conflagrations; park managers' experience in allowing fires to burn between 1972 and 1987 provided no hint that fires in the area could be several hundred thousand acres in size.[7]

This all changed in 1988 and 1989, when the famous Yellowstone fires transformed the park's landscape and policy makers had to deal with the aftermath. Beginning in June and early July of 1988, lightning ignited a series of fires in the park's backcountry. Park managers initially allowed most of these to burn as prescribed fires, in part because extensive rains in April and May had supplemented the below-normal winter moisture levels (a dry winter/wet spring pattern had characterized most of the 1980s). With ample overall moisture, managers felt comfortable allowing these spring fires to burn under careful supervision. The fires exhibited little extreme behavior initially, thus confirming that park managers were operating within the prescriptions of their fire plan.[8]

In mid-July, weather patterns and associated fire behavior began to change. A high pressure ridge settled in over the Northern Rockies, ending the wet spring weather, and some fires began to burn entire trees, instead of just smoldering on the forest floor. Pushed by warm afternoon winds, fires began to move through the forest faster. One fire in Yellowstone even overtook some firefighters, who had to deploy their fire shelters (small, aluminum-clad, emergency pup tents in which firefighters can take cover). No one was injured, but this event and the changing fire behavior prompted park officials to declare all fires burning in the park as wildfires, on July 21, 1988; from that point forward, park managers attempted to suppress all fires. The size of the fires by that time—17,000 acres—meant that full suppression would require help from nature in the form of rain or snow; such moisture would not arrive until September.[9]

Instead, in August and early September, virtually no rain fell, making 1988 the driest summer in Yellowstone's 112 years of record keeping. Making matters worse was a series of dry cold fronts, each packing wind but no moisture. Relative humidity dropped as low as 6 percent; moisture in dead

FIGURE 12: Forest aflame in Yellowstone, 1988. By August 1988, the National Park Service was dealing with a summer of historic fire activity in Yellowstone. Many fires, such as the one pictured here, burned everything from the ground up (except for the thicker tree trunks and branches). NPS photo.

and downed wood was as low as 2 percent. Fire behavior became extreme, peaking on August 20, when one of the cold fronts pushed the fires across 160,000 acres in that single day. Adding to the difficult situation were several fires—all started by people and fought when first sighted—that burned into the park from nearby national forests around the same time. By month's end much of the Yellowstone area was aflame (figures 12, 13).[10]

The firefighting effort mushroomed along with the fires, with personnel from all four U.S. armed forces joining the effort in late August and September. At the peak in early September, over one hundred fire engines and dozens of helicopters were being used by almost ten thousand firefighters. Increasingly, however, their efforts seemed futile; the fire retardant dropped from helicopters and the hand-lines dug to deprive fires of fuel barely caused the fires to hesitate.[11] Driven by powerful winds that pushed the flames up to three-hundred-feet high, and casting burning embers a mile

FIGURE 13: Helicopter and bucket of water, 1988. Fire managers at Yellowstone use helicopters to douse hot spots and fire edges with water hauled from nearby rivers and lakes. At the peak of the fire activity in 1988, dozens of helicopters and planes (which drop a chemical fire retardant) along with almost 10,000 firefighters were at work fighting the Yellowstone conflagrations. The effort succeeded in protecting all significant park structures, but did little to stop the fires from burning across much of the Yellowstone landscape. NPS photo.

ahead of the main fire fronts, no technology in existence could stop these fires. Firefighters concentrated their efforts on saving human developments; they just let some fires in backcountry areas burn, perhaps in recognition of nature having the upper hand there. By summer's end the federal government had staged its largest firefighting effort to date in Yellowstone, but the park's wildfires remained beyond anyone's control (figure 14).[12]

Despite such efforts, public debate and criticism over the fires grew with the flames. Critics were especially dismayed by the early decisions to allow the fires to burn; many felt the NPS had not read the early signs of drought adequately. Had the agency fought those early fires, the critics reasoned, the fires in late summer would not have existed or would have been much smaller. Others felt the agency's reluctance to use bulldozers in carving out fire lines led to larger-size fires. While park managers had good reasons not to use bulldozers (for instance, dozer lines scar the landscape for decades, while fire scars disappear relatively quickly), such decisions perpetuated what seemed to be a cavalier attitude toward fire by the managers.[13] Worst of all, perhaps, was some of the rhetoric used by agency staff. For example, NPS biologist Don Despain, excited to see one of the plots he had set up to study the effects of fires actually burn, was overheard saying "Burn, baby burn."[14] His innocent, if poorly timed remark, was picked up by the press and used to illustrate the seemingly casual attitude of NPS managers toward the fires. Even into late summer, some NPS personnel were still promoting the ecological benefits of fire, putting a happy face on what most perceived as a tragedy. Such actions smacked of indifference at best and carelessness at worst.[15]

Inconsistent and confusing reports added to the summer's frustrations. Maps of the fires' extent distributed by the NPS, in which the fires were illustrated with black ink, gave the impression that most of the park had burned by the end of summer (figure 14). Although it was routinely noted on these maps that "only about half of the vegetation has burned within many fire perimeters," most reporters ignored the fine print, assuming instead that black on the map meant entirely black on the ground as well.[16] Certainly, these reporters added to the overall confusion and public frustration. Most of the reporters (as well as their audiences) were urbanites and brought with them the assumption that wildfires could be suppressed as easily as urban fires. They did not understand that wildfire suppression depends on weather-related events that, in Yellowstone's case, did not arrive until September. Moreover, the reporters characterized the fires as a traditional disaster story: an evil force marauding across a beloved and benign national icon, with a villain—

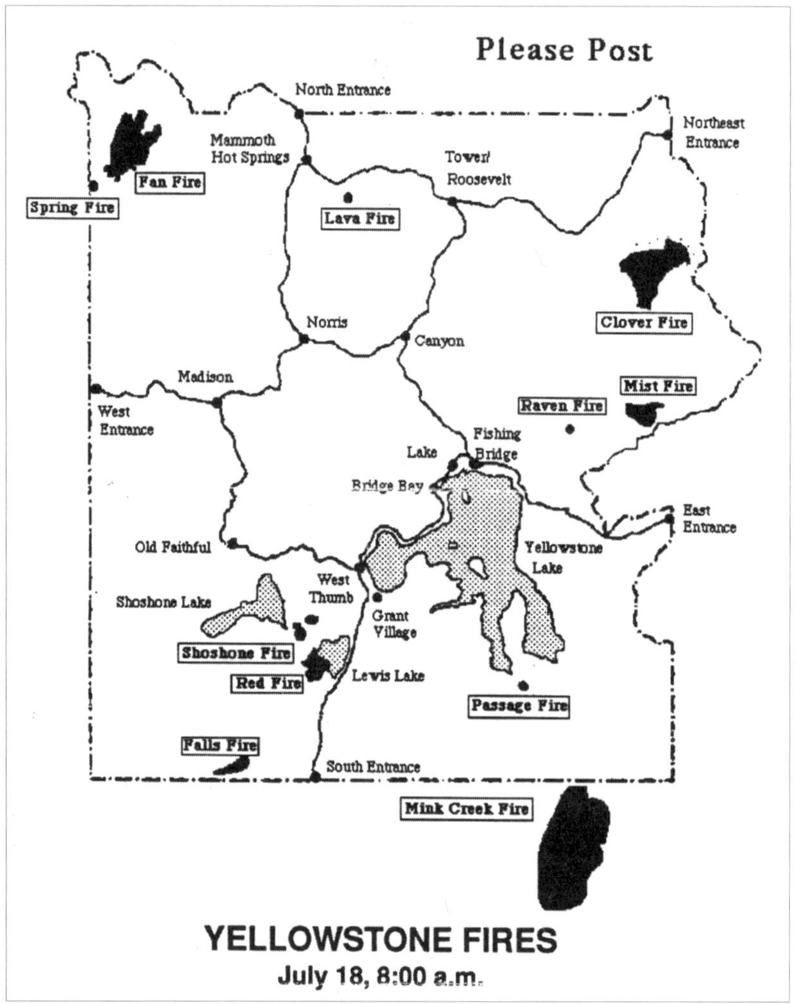

FIGURE 14a

FIGURE 14a, b, c, d: Maps depicting the progression of the 1988 fires across Yellowstone National Park. The Huck Fire and North Fork Fires were human-caused and park staff began fighting them immediately after they were discovered. These two fires, along with the Mink Creek, Storm Creek, and Hellroaring Fires all originated outside Yellowstone and burned into the park. Only the Clover-Mist Fire, Fan Fire, and Snake River Complex were lightning-caused; all three were allowed to burn initially. Note the change from dark-black coloration in the earliest map to shades of gray in the

FIGURE 14b

later ones, an attempt by park information officers to convey that not all acreage within each fire perimeter had burned. Variations in the extent of individual fires reflect the difficult mapping conditions that summer (mapping was usually done by sight—which was often obscured by smoke—and hand-drawn lines on a park map). Source: National Park Service fire maps, issued in the summer of 1988. (Note: these four images are unaltered scans of the maps, so they replicate the inconsistencies within them.) Author's collection.

North Entrance
Hellroaring Fire
Northeast Entrance
Mammoth Hot Springs
Tower–Roosevelt
Fan Fire
Lava Fire
Clover–Mist Fire
Norris
North Fork Fire
Canyon
West Entrance
Madison
Fishing Bridge
Lake
East Entrance
Bridge Bay
Old Faithful
West Thumb
Cub Fire
Yellowstone Lake
Shoshone Lake
Grant Village
Lewis Lake
Heart Lake
Falls Fire
Red-Shoshone Fire
Mink Creek Fire
South Entrance
Huck Fire
Emerald Fire
YELLOWSTONE FIRES
August 22, 1988, 8:00 a.m.

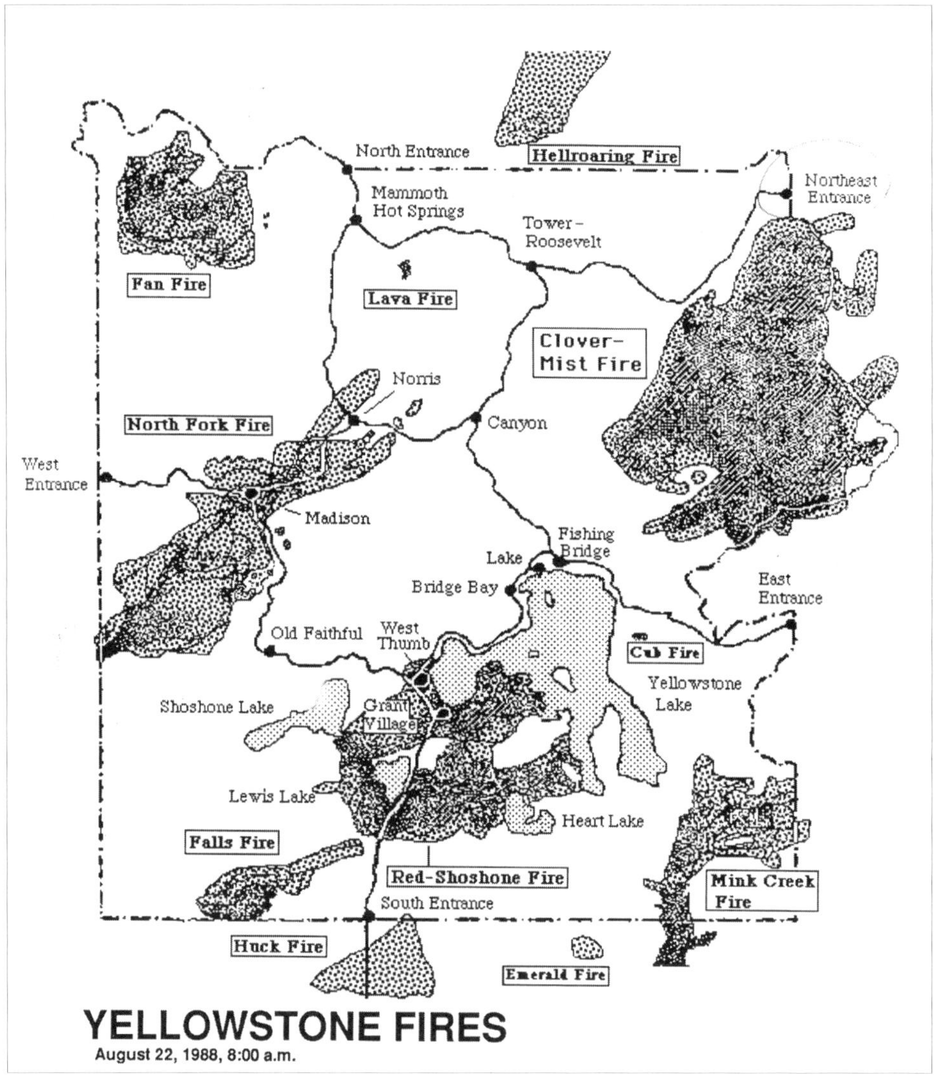

FIGURE 14C

Storm Creek Fire
Hellroaring Fire
Gardiner
North Entrance
Cooke City
Fan Fire
Mammoth
NE Entrance
Tower
?
?
Clover-Mist Fire
Wolf Lake Fire
Canyon
Norris
West Entrance
West Yellowstone
Madison
?
Fishing Bridge
Lake
North Fork Fire
Old Faithful
West Thumb
Bridge Bay
East Entrance
Yellowstone Lake
Grant Village
Shoshone Lake
Lewis Lake
Snake River Complex
Heart Lake
Mink Creek Fire
South Entrance
Huck Fire
?
YELLOWSTONE FIRES
September 26, 1988, 1:00 p.m.

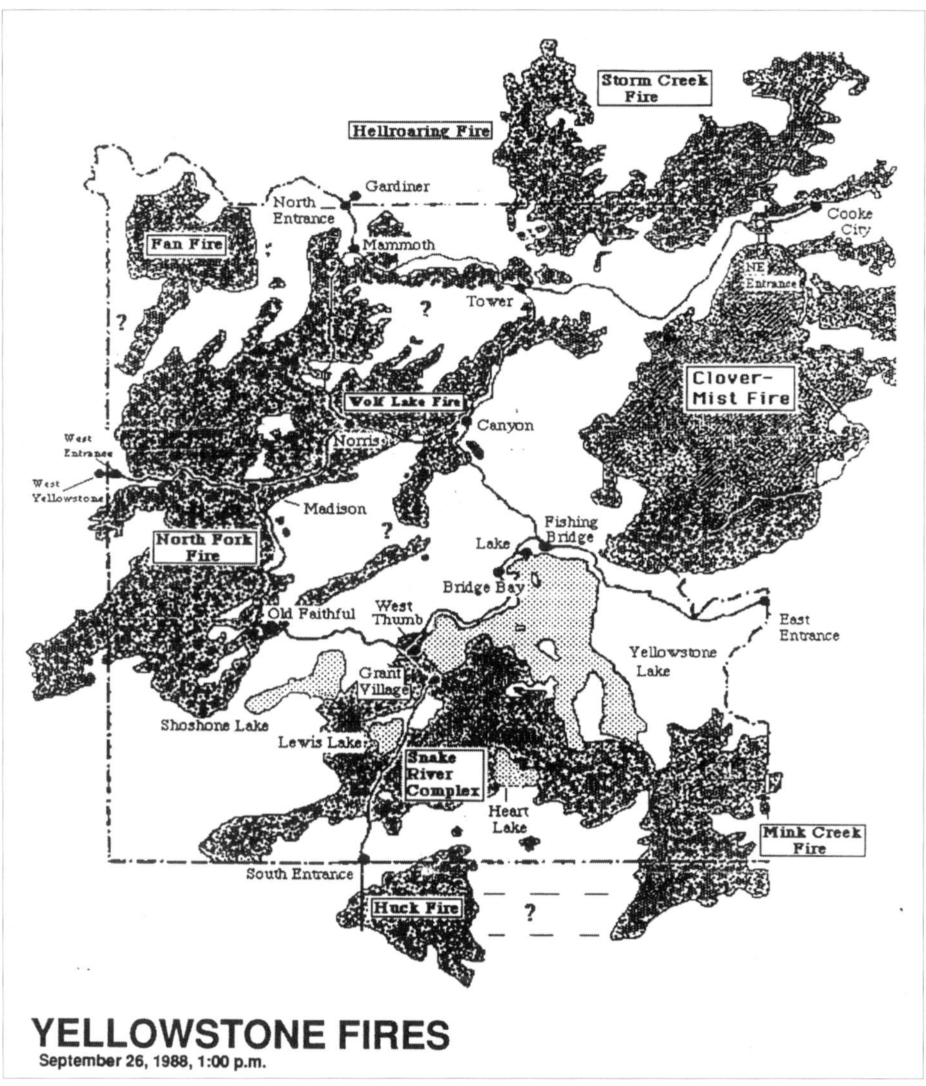

FIGURE 14d

the National Park Service—failing to put the fires out and even intentionally making them bigger. Overall, such reporting gave the impression that the entire park was "scorched" and "destroyed," heightening the emotion and frustration levels surrounding the fires.[17]

Given Yellowstone's prominence and the country's inexperience with large fires at that time (as compared to later, in the 1990s and 2000s, when many western states experienced similarly large fires), it was probably inevitable that controversy would erupt. Local residents certainly stimulated some political interest, by filing many complaints about reduced tourist numbers that summer (in August the park received 40 to 45 percent fewer visitors than on average). Through mid-September, public emotions ran high and congressional interest was inevitably stirred.[18] By September, Wyoming and Montana congressmen were demanding a policy review and planning to hold a hearing on the matter. With the Fishing Bridge controversy having heightened his sensitivities already, it was no real surprise that Senator Alan Simpson was the most vocal of the congressmen. In September, he gave a fiery speech on the Senate Floor, escalating the rhetoric and indicating that the fire policy review would soon occur.[19]

The fire policy review began with a congressional hearing in late September, chaired by Senator John Melcher, a Republican from Montana. Almost immediately it became clear that the policy review would focus more on revisions to the policy rather than its wholesale abandonment. At that hearing, for example, Senator James McClure, a Republican from Idaho, stated, "The smoke from these fires may obscure our vision, but let us keep our memories unclouded. The policy that resulted in what we see today has been supported and used by both Republican and Democratic Administrations for the past sixteen years. For fifteen of those years it worked."[20] Even Senator Malcom Wallop, Simpson's Wyoming colleague, largely agreed. The reason for the more tempered debate was scientific research: some at the hearing specifically referred to the conclusions of biologist William Romme and others. Room for debate about whether fire belonged in the Yellowstone ecosystem did not exist; the scientific research had been done and unequivocally proved that wildland fires did indeed belong in the Yellowstone ecosystem. Instead, debate would revolve around how to live with and manage such fires. From the start of this policy-making review, then, the solid and preexisting base of scientific research guided the discussions toward retaining the fire policy.[21]

Defending NPS actions at this preliminary hearing was Interior Secretary Donald Hodel, who had visited Yellowstone National Park twice that summer, getting a first-hand view of the fires and suppression efforts. Hodel's first visit was in late July, when he affirmed Superintendent Bob Barbee's decision to suppress all the fires. By the time of his second visit, on September 10, the fires had ballooned in size; the controversy surrounding them had grown to eclipse the Fishing Bridge controversy as the largest Yellowstone issue of the decade. Amazed at what he saw in September, Hodel promised to review the NPS's fire policy. However, at the hearing and throughout that fall, he vigorously defended the NPS, fending off accusations that the agency had ignored early warnings of drought and disregarding the calls for NPS director William Penn Mott's and Superintendent Bob Barbee's resignations.[22] Hodel, exhibiting a clear understanding of Yellowstone's distinctive fire ecology and the firefighting history of that summer, claimed "it was not within anybody's ability to stop that fire."[23]

Hodel concluded his remarks at the hearing by confirming that a high-level review of federal fire policy would be embarked upon by the departments of agriculture and interior, which included all federal land management agencies that had seen extensive fires burn that summer. (Yellowstone's prominence eclipsed most press coverage of fires on the other agencies' lands.) The two departments created an advisory team to review the events at Yellowstone, to consult with members of academia, and then report back by December 15.[24] Led by one high-ranking member from each department, the team was rounded out by two NPS officials, two USFS officials, and one representative each from the Bureau of Land Management, the FWS, and the Bureau of Indian Affairs. So that the team could complete its review in time for the 1989 fire season, Hodel and Secretary of Agriculture Richard Lyng restricted the team to government representatives; the team's draft report would be open to public comment that winter.[25]

The fire policy review was only the most visible of the reviews then occurring at Yellowstone. By the time Hodel made his announcement, Yellowstone's managers were already forming several other review committees, as well as plans of action, for the upcoming winter season. One team would compile information for NPS managers to use in response to further congressional oversight hearings. Another team, led by Norm Christensen, Duke University professor of forestry, botany, and environmental studies, would assess the resources affected by the fires, such as acreage burned, wildlife killed, and soils damaged. Similarly, a task force would guide rehabilitation efforts such as clearing trails, rebuilding damaged structures, and removing trees from along roadsides. With scientists expressing great interest in researching the various aspects of the fires, the NPS and USFS formed a research coordination team. Recognizing the need to educate the public about all aspects of the events at Yellowstone National Park, the park's Division of Interpretation (NPS's educational branch) planned to develop educational media, including new exhibits for the Grant Village Visitor Center. Finally, the NPS would expand cooperative efforts with the Montana and Wyoming tourism commissions, to market tourism and facilitate press interest in post-fire Yellowstone.[26]

The actions of these different teams were crucial in the fire policy review over the next few years. Therefore, most of this story revolves around these groups, especially the national fire policy-review team and their research results. The latter would play as crucial a role as the former; in fact, scientists' interest in the newfound research opportunities and their support for federal agencies' prescribed fire policies would end up carrying the day for the NPS and its fire policy.[27]

Support from conservationists was also important in helping retain a policy that allowed naturally caused fires to burn, though it was probably not as important as the support of the scientists. When the fires peaked in late August and early September, some conservationists and newspapers published articles supporting the role of fire in wildland ecosystems like Yellowstone. Such articles lent credence to the NPS's policies, although press coverage of the extreme fire behavior and firefighting activities probably dampened the benefits of such positive and educational coverage.[28] However, conservationist magazines and the general press turned up the volume on their ecology coverage that fall; not only did these articles directly support the fire policy, but they also reinforced its scientific basis by discussing fire ecology for both Yellowstone specifically and western forests in general. Even the *Wall Street Journal*, the nation's most respected conservative newspaper, jumped on the press bandwagon in late September and published an article affirming the policy allowing prescribed natural fires in places like Yellowstone.[29] Overall, park managers found widespread support for their fire policy among scientists, conservationists, and the press; the die was cast for a successful coalition.

Casting strong tools, though, requires good steel; for park managers, this meant gathering solid information on what had occurred at Yellowstone (both in the natural and human worlds) quickly, before the snow began to fly. Consequently, the resource assessment and rehabilitation teams rapidly got out into the field to gather data on acreage and structures burned, to clear trails, and to repair other visitor facilities damaged in the fires. They were wise to move quickly, as the winter of 1988–1989 would turn out to be the first normal winter, with cold temperatures and abundant snowfall, that Yellowstone had experienced so far that decade.

Recognizing that in America few coalitions can succeed without support from affected businesspeople and their political representatives, Interior Secretary Hodel and park managers quickly took action to salve the wounds of the businesses and try to sway popular opinion toward restoration of the fire policy. As a first step, Hodel convinced the White House to make federal aid available to businesses and communities affected by the fires. With the low-interest loans becoming available that fall, concerned citizens and Yellowstone's managers turned their attention toward addressing the fear that the destructive fires might curtail the volume of tourists in the region. Yellowstone managers soon met with state tourism officials to devise new marketing schemes that would bring tourism back to its normal flow in 1989. The tourism officials decided to market a new Yellowstone, one that would rise like a phoenix from its own ashes to become a vivid, exciting place embarking upon a natural rebirth. Yellowstone officials assisted by doing their own marketing, and also by contributing and disseminating the most accurate information on the fires possible.[30]

Economic aid and partnering with their neighbors to frame a new, positive message were two parts of the park managers' successful strategy; a third part was to simply roll out the perpetual tourist welcome mat. As a result of these actions, once the smoke cleared, visitors flocked to Yellowstone in numbers never before seen in autumn. They found a park that had changed and reflected the summer's events, but also found that Yellowstone still possessed its natural beauty, abundant wildlife, and vast spaces. One Wyoming state official, Gene Bryan, director of the state's travel commission, was among those visitors. He found that Yellowstone was indeed "alive, dynamic, changed, but definitely still there."[31] He wrote a long memo to his supervisor describing abundant wildlife, including the first bears he had seen in Yellowstone in more than twelve years. He liked the new vistas (burned forests opened up views previously hidden by the foliage of green forests) and found the park's major attractions unaltered. He left the park not frustrated, angry, or depressed (as he had been for the previous two months), but rather awed by Yellowstone. Bryan was influential in changing his state's attitude toward the park and its fires, a change that would soon be expressed by other state personnel in Wyoming, as well as in nearby Montana and Idaho.

All three states came to promote the park's future—an exciting response to the potentially devastating disaster. Unlike the Fishing Bridge controversy, then, park managers in this situation could turn to the majesty of nature itself to aid their cause, convincing most local residents and businesspeople that the fires, while dampening short-term tourist dollars, probably offered a long-term boost to local economies (figure 15).[32]

FIGURE 15: Park visitors waiting for Old Faithful Geyser to erupt, with smoke plume in the distance, 1988. Visitation during the summer of 1988 was down, particularly in August and September, compared to previous years. However, as soon as the smoke cleared in October, visitors came to Yellowstone in record numbers, many to observe the fire's effects for themselves. The trend of higher-than-normal visitation continued in 1989 and into the 1990s, demonstrating that the fires caused only a temporary decline in the regional economy. NPS photo.

Meanwhile, the research coordination team was springing into action, recognizing a once-in-a-lifetime chance to improve society's knowledge of fire and its effects in a mostly natural wildland ecosystem. Even before the fires died out, Linda Wallace, a professor at the University of Oklahoma who was cooperating with the NPS, had already begun contacting colleagues and the National Science Foundation to gauge interest in a large research thrust. In October, the NPS and foundation hosted a four-day conference at Montana State University in Bozeman on fire ecology and the events of 1988. Despite the short notice, the subject's prominence attracted one hundred and thirty scientists, representing the fields of soils science, hydrology, wildlife biology, and economics. Conference attendees formed the Greater Yellowstone Fire Impact and Recovery Research Consortium (or "FIRE Consortium") to develop and guide a comprehensive investigation into the historic event.[33] Within one year, more than one hundred research projects were underway, directed by eighty-one scientists from thirty-five different institutions. The NPS funded over half the projects, totaling almost $6 million; the number of projects eventually doubled. The ultimate results of the studies would take many years to determine and synthesize, but scientists quickly hypothesized that Yellowstone was far from destroyed—instead, it was changed in ways familiar to nature.[34]

Although the scientific consensus regarding the positive role of fire in Yellowstone's wildlands would prove to be nearly unanimous, there were at least two critics: Thomas Bonnicksen, head of Texas A&M University's Department of Recreation and Parks, and Alston Chase, author of the recently published polemic *Playing God in Yellowstone*. Bonnicksen believed that the NPS should more aggressively set fires intentionally, to reduce fire danger and to replicate prehistoric conditions.[35] As fall turned into winter, he joined Chase in repeatedly criticizing park managers for their failure to reduce fire danger in this way. The two felt that Native Americans would have ignited fires more often than Yellowstone managers were permitting. More frequent fires, they believed, would have reduced fuel accumulations and so, in their minds, the regulation of natural fires was a failure because it had allowed too much fuel to pile up, producing conflagrations such as those seen in 1988.[36]

Bonnicksen and Chase, however, were alone among scientists in expressing such criticism; they were eventually silenced by their peers, by park managers, and by the environmental community, all of whom were excited about the fires and Yellowstone's future.[37] For example, Thomas Swetnam, of the University of Arizona's Laboratory of Tree-ring Research in Tucson, noted that Native American influence on Yellowstone's lodgepole-pine forests (the primary kind of forest that burned) was far from clear; William Romme believed the Native Americans' influence was probably minor; and Yellowstone chief of research, John Varley, stated that intentionally-set fires in those same forests would be difficult or impossible to ignite and keep under control. Lodgepole pines shed their lower branches as they grow, producing a forest with most foliage well off the ground and with little undergrowth. To effectively reduce fire danger in such forests, managers would have to ignite a crown fire—a fire that burns entire forests, from the ground to the tree crowns, usually wind-driven across hundreds of acres—and as the experience of 1988 sufficiently demonstrated, such fires are generally uncontrollable. Other researchers added their support and ecological explanations for allowing fires to play their natural role in the Yellowstone ecosystem, as did the noted fire historian Stephen Pyne.[38]

In addition, environmentalists continued to defend NPS and its policy, publishing more articles explaining the summer's events and Yellowstone fire ecology.[39] Similarly, the national press continued to increase its coverage of wildland fire ecology and its benefits, with articles appearing in the *Los Angeles Times* and *New York Times Magazine*. In the latter, Peter Matthiessen described visiting Yellowstone in the fall of 1988, and in a rebuttal of Alston Chase's comments he stated, "Far from being stunned by the destruction, I felt an exhilaration and relief, as if Yellowstone Park, for the first time in a century, had gotten a deep breath of fresh air."[40] Other papers around the country followed suit with their own post-fire articles, perhaps desiring to portray a more holistic view of wildland fire than they had the previous summer.[41]

As this suggests, park managers found an increasingly strong coalition of support in the scientific, environmental, and public press arenas. The latter two premised much of their arguments on the relevant scientific research, affirming that this research would be one of the most powerful determinants of NPS policy in this debate, just as it was in the Fishing Bridge debate (although in a more positive way). More and more concerned citizens were framing the fires as a form of natural rebirth, a view that was supported by the relevant research. Political opposition would mostly disappear, unlike the Fishing Bridge situation, when park managers faced such opposition. Yellowstone managers would enjoy tacit support over the fire policy review. (Politically, a lack of opposition often signifies support, at least for park managers.) However, before the political situation would become clear, park managers had a fire policy assessment to complete—and it needed refined estimates of the natural and human events that occurred in the summer.

Those assessments arrived over the winter. The first to report in was the Resource Assessment Committee, in October, revising the total acreage burned throughout the Greater Yellowstone Area (GYA), including the USFS lands around the park, from 1.6 million down to 1.38 million acres, with 988,975 acres burned in Yellowstone (or 44 percent of the park). The study results further indicated that just over half of this area was burned by a canopy or crown fire, just over a third was a surface fire (only the forest floor burned, with the trees above remaining alive and green), and the remainder was meadows or grasslands that would green up the following spring. Only a small percentage of the areas—less than 0.1 percent—were burned so hotly that soils were sterilized. By Christmas, the estimate of acreage burned dropped to 706,000 acres in Yellowstone; however, more refined mapping in 1989 increased the total burned area to 793,880 acres inside the park (only half of which was canopy burn).[42] All the estimates clearly demonstrated that much of Yellowstone remained unburned or was burned so lightly that evidence would soon disappear. These assessments were widely reported in the press, which furthered the dispassionate voice of scientific research in the ongoing fire policy debate.[43]

Similar reassurance that the fires were not as bad as commonly portrayed came from the Resource Assessment Committee's report on the wildlife that was actually killed by the fires. In making this report, the committee was countering the public's image of two popular, beloved fictional animals: Bambi (a white-tailed deer), of the well-known Walt Disney movie of the same name, in which deer escape a forest fire, and the USFS's Smokey the Bear, the iconic bear that advised generations of people that only they could prevent forest fires. The significance of these two characters in teaching Americans about wildland fire cannot be overstated; for decades a good portion of Americans grew up believing that wildfires were bad and killed or maimed beautiful, helpless animals like Bambi and Smokey the Bear.[44] Yellowstone's Resource Assessment Committee, however, found that in the Yellowstone fires of 1988 only 243 elk, four deer, two moose, and five bison were killed (and no bears), or about 1 percent of the total park population for each species. (Note that the dead animals would also help to sustain carnivores and scavengers like grizzly bears and coyotes). Additionally, visitors and park staff that summer and fall commonly observed park wildlife grazing placidly in sight of smoldering or burning forests, therefore belying the

FIGURE 16: Bison grazing near burning forest, 1988. Yellowstone's wildlife demonstrated that the fictional characters Bambi and Smokey the Bear were not necessarily correct about the influence of fire on native wildlife in national parks. In fact, very few animals in Yellowstone died due to the 1988 fires—of all large species, only 1 percent or less. NPS photo.

image of Smokey the Bear as well (figure 16). Finally, when studying the soils, water quality, and air quality the results were similar: short-term, localized impacts with expected long-term benefits.[45]

For a full fire policy review, accurate histories of each major fire in Yellowstone—the Clover-Mist, North Fork, Snake River Complex, Hellroaring, Storm Creek, and Fan—were needed; summaries of these fires arrived in early winter. The reports made many suggestions on how to improve communication effectiveness and supply delivery on fire lines, but otherwise there were no "smoking guns." Rather, the reports illustrated that park managers had done the best they could with the extreme weather conditions and unprecedented fire events of that summer. At least one review speculated that some of the firefighting tactics were "based mostly on the need to show local residents and critics that something was being done with what must have been a very frustrating situation."[46] The North Fork fire review report concluded that no amount of resources could have stopped the burn—even the bulldozers that park managers had declined to use. A more comprehensive Coordination and Management Review, issued a few months later, also exonerated park managers from any wrongdoing.[47]

In December, the report that would garner the most attention was released: the draft Report on Fire Management Policy written by the high-level Fire Policy Review Team. The team had met that fall with the Western Governors' Association, the National Fire Protection Association, members of academia, federal and local government officials, concessioners and outfitters, area business owners, and environmentalists. Most of these groups supported the continuation of a wildfire policy on federal land to varying degrees, as did scientists. Many NPS employees, in fact, supported a loosening of the policy to allow fires to burn free of prescriptions, as long as the fires did not cross park boundaries or threaten structures. With so much support from all these various sources, the Fire Policy Review Team affirmed the federal fire policy, specifically noting that land management agencies had sound objectives in allowing lightning-caused fires to burn unimpeded.[48]

Not only did the review team draw upon scientific research in their report, they also promoted the research opportunities afforded by a continuance of the fire policy. The team asserted, "[E]xtensive areas in which the achievement and maintenance of naturalness is a basic purpose are increasingly important to humankind. These areas are found primarily in national parks and wildernesses. They serve as invaluable scientific benchmarks; and the uniqueness imparted by their natural qualities is irreplaceable as a source of human inspiration and enjoyment."[49] The report's assertion that scientific analysis should inform policy making and was a reason to continue the existing fire policy was the strongest embrace of scientific research and its importance in NPS policy making to date.[50]

In addition to affirming park managers' use of naturally-caused fires, the team's report included several recommendations on how to strengthen federal fire policy and avoid further controversies. Specifically, they advised land management agencies to refine the weather and fuel conditions— called "prescriptions"—under which fires would be allowed to burn; those prescriptions should be based on place-specific research (especially in lodgepole pine areas) that includes details on fire behavior, fire history, and weather effects on fire. Further, hoping to add national context to fire decision making, the team recommended that fire managers assess the national and regional fire situation when a fire in the national park first ignites, and then determine what staff was needed and available to them. If such resources were not available, the team recommended that land managers suppress the fire immediately. To tighten decision-making lines of authority, the team advised that the park superintendent be held accountable for fires burning, by requiring him or her to certify daily in writing that any fires burning would not escape control, given such factors as foreseeable weather conditions and fire behavior. The team concluded that in the meantime no agency should allow fires to burn until their plans were revised accordingly.[51]

Upon releasing the Report on Fire Management Policy, the U.S. Department of Agriculture (USDA) and U.S. Department of the Interior (USDI) opened the policy to public comment for sixty days. Some fire experts criticized the report's implicit assumption that fires could be controlled. Comments from some residents in western states made the scientists' voices sound almost calm in comparison. For example, Bill Morris, director of the Wyoming Game and Fish Department, in a seventeen-page letter, argued that the entire report was premised on the unrealistic assumption that fires could always be controlled. Such an assumption seemed foolish to him, given that "all of the experts and resources available could not control [the Yellowstone] fires." He further argued that having the superintendent daily certify that any fires burning would not escape control was really just a search for a scapegoat. In conclusion, he gave a strong endorsement for allowing fires to burn: "Most wilderness areas had fire as a natural part of the environment before man [*sic*] developed any suppression tactics. If wilderness values are to be retained, fire must be part of the system. . . . We would like to see fire used more in the future, especially in wilderness areas."[52] Alaska governor Steve Cowper repeated many of the same concerns, noting specifically that he objected "to the recommendation that 'it is unprofessional and impractical for fires to be allowed to burn free of prescriptions or appropriate suppression action.'"[53] His state's fire managers had designated large portions of Alaska as places where fires were allowed to burn unimpeded, though carefully monitored. Such liberal opinions emanating from bureaucrats in relatively conservative states suggest the extent to which the 1988 fires had impressed themselves upon people of the West. Both research findings and personal observations from that summer endorsed allowing fires to burn. From this point forward, Yellowstone managers would coast to victory in their efforts to retain a prescribed natural-fire policy.[54]

The bureaucrats' comments were a good indication of the public's response to the report. In general, environmentalists liked it because it promoted the continued use of fires on federal land, something they feared would be prohibited completely based on the summer's rhetoric. For example, George Frampton of The Wilderness Society found the report to be "sound and well-reasoned" and generally supportive of a policy "based on solid science."[55] The Society of American Foresters (SAF), National Association of State Foresters, and the Environmental Protection Agency (EPA) agreed as well. Most NPS and USFS reviewers approved of the report, though some were concerned about its implication that all fires could be, or should be, controlled.[56] It should be noted that about forty-five respondents disagreed, feeling that the park was not large enough for extensive use of wildland fire. Nonetheless, four times as many respondents endorsed the report's findings, agreeing that fires should be retained in the parks.[57] In short, the balance of written opinion agreed that fires should remain a fundamental tool in park and land managers' toolboxes, with a substantial portion stating that the report did not go far enough in endorsing continued use of fire. The message for park managers was clear and agreeable: they had a strong and extensive support base.

In addition to accepting written input, the two federal departments held eleven public hearings around the country to solicit verbal input. The hearings reaffirmed the written comments, with the majority of speakers supporting the use of naturally-caused fire in public lands management. Again, environmentalists typically agreed with the Fire Policy Review Team's report; the Sierra Club made a special effort to have representatives at most of the hearings, focusing primarily on the scientific aspects of fire. Consistently, the club supported the ecological role of fire in wildland ecosystems. In contrast, the Farm Bureau Federation, which also had representatives at most hearings, consistently opposed unsupervised fires in Yellowstone (although they were not against the specific use of controlled fire in wild areas) and the creation of new wilderness areas. The bureau and others occasionally mentioned Alston Chase's ideas and logging as alternatives to fire. Finally, the only fire supporters to criticize the report strongly were experts whose testimony echoed that of Bill Morris and Steve Cowper.[58]

The last hearing, held in Cody, Wyoming, stands out because it produced twice as many pages of testimony as any of the others. It went on for almost four hours, with one person after another angrily ranting against fires and the NPS's actions in the summer of 1988. Cody residents expressed a deep resentment and suspicion of park policies; for example, Harold Davidson stated,

"God made man to have dominion over the earth and to subdue it. Man is not a slave of nature by this God-given mandate."[59] Gloria Hedderman, from the nearby town of Powell, believed, "Just like a girl, the whole Yellowstone ecosystem can never become a virgin again."[60] Yet another area resident, Reuben Bullock, not only criticized the NPS for the fires, but also for not reducing volcanic-explosion hazards through geothermal energy drilling (although few, if any geologists would agree that such drilling could reduce the chance of volcanic eruption). Some testimonials expressed at the Jackson, Wyoming, hearing echoed these statements, but none matched the intensity generated by Cody residents. The Cody hearing may have been more volatile because Senator Alan Simpson lived there, attended the hearing, and provided testimony and publicity. He continued the same bullying atmosphere toward Yellowstone's managers that he had expressed in his September 1988 Senate speech. Simpson's presence at the Cody hearing and the critical testimonials given by other attendees demonstrates that support for retaining fire as a policy tool was not unanimous; some political opposition remained—but it was on the wane.[61]

Indeed, the Cody hearing was the exception; those attending all the other hearings expressed widespread support for using prescribed natural fire to the maximum extent possible in federal wildland management. These hearings were the first time the government had gauged national support for its fire policy; one official at the Albuquerque, New Mexico, hearing confirmed that the support was extremely high—around 90 percent of those who commented. Support came not just from the public in general, but from many experts who again criticized the report for not going far enough in allowing lightning-caused fires. More and more the debate was not about *whether* humans should use fire in their public land management, but rather about *what level of control* people should exert over fire in wild areas and whether human-caused fires should be permitted to burn. Thus, consensus was clearly growing that the Yellowstone area was big and wild enough for fires to occupy a primary place in park managers' policy toolboxes.[62]

This consensus became clear in late January 1989, when Representative Ron Marlenee of Montana called to order a twelfth hearing—a congressional one. This hearing was dominated not by debate over whether fires should be allowed, but rather by a debate between those who felt people should actively manage fires (whether lightning-caused or human-ignited, intentional or accidental) or allow them to burn at will, naturally. Alston Chase and Thomas Bonnicksen both spoke and promoted active human use of, and control over, fire; they also suggested that land managers should actively ignite fires. Several forestry organizations took a more moderate stance, averring that people should use both kinds of fires. Opposing Chase and Bonnicksen were a variety of academics who believed that wildfires should be allowed to burn as naturally as possible, especially in places as wild as Yellowstone. For example, Professor Dennis Knight argued that by allowing wildfires to burn as naturally as possible, fires gave landscapes research value as controls against which to compare human-dominated landscapes. He stated: "To restrict fires unnecessarily is to diminish the wildness for which some parks and wilderness areas were established, and which is the reason for much of their scientific value."[63] The four other professors who spoke at the hearing, along with three environmentalists, all agreed with Knight and argued that the fires of 1988 were uncontrollable and inevitable. Outnumbered, Chase and Bonnicksen were increasingly isolated and ineffectual.[64]

In hindsight, these hearings were probably the turning point in the effort to preserve a fire policy based on allowing naturally-ignited fires to burn in national parks. An objective committee, as well as a majority of the public and most scientists, agreed with the plan. However, it was not yet entirely clear that the policy would be preserved. Indeed, Representative Marlenee still viewed the policy as "so misguided, so abusive, so wasteful, so destructive that no better definition could be drawn to describe the term 'scorched earth policy.'"[65] It would take more efforts by the NPS, scientists, and conservationists in the winter of 1988–1989 to cement the turn in the tide. In addition, attitudes on the fire policy hinged on the 1989 summer tourism flow at Yellowstone; large numbers of visitors were far from assured at that point.

As the winter progressed, Yellowstone's managers began a multi-faceted educational and outreach campaign. They reached out to local residents with a team of three NPS rangers (two men and one woman) who toured various communities. In fifty-four presentations given to forty-four different groups, the rangers talked about the summer of 1988 at Yellowstone; about fire ecology and nature's response to fire; and about the NPS's mission and the park's mandate. The rangers knew they might not convince everyone that fire was a natural, uncontrollable part of the Yellowstone ecosystem, but they hoped that putting a caring, sensitive face behind government bureaucracy would help emotions subside. These rangers were NPS interpreters, skilled at communicating with people in the language of nature and human experience. They admitted government mistakes and tried to empathize with their audiences as much as possible. The success of such efforts is hard to gauge, but the team provided something sorely needed for those residents living in the vicinity of Yellowstone—someone to whom they could vent their frustrations.[66]

Residents of the region also needed to hear from the person many saw as responsible for the fires getting out of control—Superintendent Bob Barbee. Consequently, in the winter and spring of 1989 he delivered numerous public presentations promoting future visitation to Yellowstone. He also gave a series of media and trade briefings, using videos and maps to illustrate that Yellowstone was indeed alive and well. Barbee even went on a two-week speaking tour of Europe to get the word out that the park was still worth visiting.[67]

As important as these efforts were, they were transitory and would not reach the many visitors park managers were hoping to see on their doorstep the next summer. Therefore, park managers installed a new museum exhibit on fires and fire ecology at the Grant Village Visitor Center (an appropriate choice, given that Grant Village had been evacuated twice during the summer). Called "Yellowstone and Fire," the exhibit included a twenty-minute film on the 1988 fires and fire ecology. At roadside areas where fire effects were particularly noticeable, park personnel also installed new wayside exhibits and opened two new boardwalks.[68] They compiled a fire "primer" and a special fire curriculum for school groups and teachers, distributing them to any educator or member of the public who desired to learn more about the fires. Over 2,300 teachers eventually requested the various materials. Yellowstone managers also sent the primer to all other national park units. And lastly, they included a special "fire insert" discussing the 1988 events and fire ecology with the welcome packet given to all visitors entering the park in the summer of 1989.[69] Environmental groups did their best as well to educate their members on the summer's events and fire ecology; most of the major national groups published articles on the fires in the winter of 1988–1989.[70] Such efforts not only helped to dispel the misconceptions about the 1988 firefighting season, but also drove home the point that fires were a natural part of the Yellowstone landscape. They were neither good nor bad, but simply a natural force that humans had to contend with in Yellowstone National Park. As summarized in the tourist brochure insert, the fires raised "deeper questions of just what we want from our parks, and just how far we are willing to let nature go in giving it to us."[71] Indeed, that was the crucial question of the winter of 1988–1989.

While the educational materials were being developed over the winter, park managers also commissioned economic analyses of the fires' effects.

The first of these confirmed that although some businesses were indeed hurt by the fires, few if any failed completely due to them. In fact, not only did some local businesses benefit from the $33 million that the federal government spent acquiring firefighting supplies in local communities, but Wyoming sales tax revenues (directly affected by the fires) actually increased 5 percent from the same period a year before. With that knowledge, concerns about the fires' impacts on the state's 1988 economy vanished.[72]

State officials did, however, continue to worry that summer tourism would not rebound in the future. As time went on, that fear subsided, in part because another recently completed study suggested that the fires had in fact stimulated Americans' interest in visiting Yellowstone, rather than subduing it. Residents in the region also felt encouraged by a series of articles that were published promoting the park's exciting new tourist and research opportunities.[73] The most visible of these was an article in *National Geographic* in February 1989. In the magazine's typical fashion, the article featured many colorful photographs demonstrating the fires' power, the firefighting effort, and nature's response to the fires. The magazine whetted the curiosity of its readers to see the park and the fire effects for themselves, with obvious positive economic implications. Politicians found increasingly less support for their earlier claim that the fire policy would lead to economic doom, so their influence continued to dwindle, though it would not disappear entirely.[74]

In May 1989, the Fire Policy Review Team issued its final report. Reflecting supportive public opinion and its strong initial analysis, the team made few changes to the draft. The team affirmed that fires, including lightning-caused fires, should burn on federal lands; they stated that fire management policies needed refining and strengthening; and they described how the inherent risks of fires could be reduced through careful planning and preparation. The team also suggested that managers should use planned burning more often, but they did not agree that fire plans be based exclusively on such fires, as Chase and Bonnicksen seemed to suggest. In the final report, the team retained the burdensome requirement that fire managers must certify daily in writing that fires burning on federal lands would not get out of control, and they must examine the national firefighting situation before deciding to allow a fire to burn. When he formally accepted the report, Secretary of the Interior Manuel Lujan (who replaced Donald Hodel when George Bush became President in 1989) ordered all Department of the Interior offices to suspend their fire plans until they could address the report's findings.[75]

Overall, the report was a victory for the federal managers, scientists, and environmentalists who wanted lightning-caused fires to continue burning naturally in national parks. Park managers had much work to do towards implementing the Fire Policy Review Team's recommendations, but the policy victory was basically in hand: managers would soon be able to reinstate a policy allowing naturally-caused fires to burn. The policy had some new caveats, most of which were ultimately intended to protect private property; these caveats reflected an economic concern, thus demonstrating that political influence over fire policy had not disappeared entirely. Motivated to protect their constituents' investments, politicians did succeed in making federal land managers more accountable for their actions. However, the larger victory was for the land managers: prescribed natural fires remained a viable management option. Yellowstone, and other federal lands where fires were permitted, would remain the wild, natural controls against which human impacts could be compared.

Over the next four years, park managers, greatly assisted by fire researchers and, to a lesser extent, by members of the environmental community, cemented into place this fire policy victory. A series of events, combined with NPS policy maneuvers, meant that by 1992 the NPS could substantially claim success.

The first event was the return of normal tourist flow to Yellowstone, starting in May 1989, when visitation was up 30 percent compared to the previous year. The 1989 total reached 2.68 million visitors, a 15 percent increase over 1988.[76] Visitors included dozens of reporters from all over the world, who authored many articles discussing fire ecology and promoting Yellowstone's new face. Such articles furthered the park's science-based, rebirth framing, which certainly helped stimulate further visitation and eventually garnered support for allowing future fires in the park.[77] One of the visitors was newly elected President George Bush, who went on a fire-ecology tour with Yellowstone's chief of research John Varley. (Bush apparently liked the tour so much he instructed his staff, including Manuel Lujan, to listen carefully to Varley.) Even though only 7 percent of the 800 Yellowstone visitors surveyed in July 1989 specifically came to see the fire effects, it was clear that visitation patterns had been restored. Visitation in 1990 was 2.86 million, and by 1995 over 3 million visitors were visiting Yellowstone annually; these numbers demonstrate that the resurgence in tourism was not transitory. As a result, all lingering concerns about negative economic impacts from the fires disappeared.[78]

Visitors to Yellowstone in the summer of 1989 found a park that was both black and green. Signs of the fires were obvious, and would be evident for decades, but it was not long before the burned areas began turning green, with new grasses and flowers seeding in from various sources. The amount of unburned area was a surprise to many visitors and illustrated that Yellowstone was indeed alive and well. By viewing firsthand the fire effects, visitors saw for themselves that the press had overblown the 1988 fire situation. Moreover, many of these visitors read the fire information rangers gave them and came to understand that the NPS did the best it could in a very trying situation. As the framing suggested, many learned that Yellowstone had not been destroyed, but rather renovated and reinvigorated thanks to the fires (figure 17).[79]

FIGURE 17: Seedlings of lodgepole pine near Madison Junction, early 1990s. Forests in Yellowstone predominantly consist of lodgepole pines (*Pinus contorta*). In addition to having cones that open without fire, many lodgepole pines in the Yellowstone area bear serotinous cones that open only through exposure to fire. Moving rapidly through a forest, fires scorch the cones but leave the seeds inside undamaged; later the seeds are released from the cone. Falling onto mineral soil that provides ideal germinating conditions for pines, the seeds germinate and encourage forests to begin anew after a fire. NPS photo.

Also, that summer park managers completed the reconstruction and replacement of burned boardwalks, road signs, and other damaged structures. In the backcountry, the Student Conservation Association mounted a Herculean effort to clear some 600 miles of trails, rebuild burned bridges, and install water bars to prevent erosion and protect the trails. The backcountry program continued for the next two summers, in 1990 and 1991, with both the NPS and USFS overseeing the work and providing additional funding. These efforts dispelled any lingering concerns that the fires would limit public access to Yellowstone.[80]

Several more conferences took place in 1989, each boosting scientific interest in and discussion about the fires. The University of Wyoming, Montana State University-Bozeman, Wyoming's Northwest Community College in Powell, and the Greater Yellowstone Coalition (GYC) all held conferences in April or May, at which many fire experts presented papers.[81] Illustrating how much public opinion had changed, Superintendent Bob Barbee received a standing ovation for his defense of fire policy at one of the conferences. Over the next four years, scholarly interest in the fires continued to increase and scientists completed many different fire-related studies.

The papers published within a year of the 1988 fires tended to dwell on the summer's events and fire management. Many of these papers, for instance, continued to debate the extent to which park managers could, or should, allow naturally caused fires to burn.[82] Articulating perhaps the strongest endorsement of allowing Yellowstone's forests to burn as much as possible by naturally caused fires was Norman Christensen, the professor who chaired the research assessment of the 1988 fires. In a paper published in 1989 he wrote, "To extirpate fire completely from a wildland ecosystem is to remove an essential component of that wilderness. . . . [T]here are those who would argue that chance is itself a value, that the unpredictable is the essence of the wilderness experience."[83] In stepping away from the normally subdued opinions scientists expressed, Christensen clearly lent support to the NPS's effort to retain wildfire. Certainly, scientists were strongly allied with park managers toward reinstating a policy allowing prescribed natural fires to burn as much as possible.[84]

Scholarly, in-depth research papers took more time but, by 1993, dozens of scientists had published papers investigating various facets of Yellowstone National Park's fire ecology. This tremendous response culminated in a 1993 conference on fire research held at Yellowstone. More than seventy scientists presented their post-1988 fire-research findings, collectively celebrating the opportunity to study how wildlands functioned with fire, on a scale rarely seen before. As with the previous conferences, this one demonstrated that nearly all scientists supported the NPS's plan to allow prescribed fires to burn in Yellowstone and other national parks.[85]

Having achieved support for prescribed fires, Yellowstone managers turned their attention to revising the fire policy in accordance with the Fire Policy Review Team's recommendations. In 1990, the managers began soliciting public input on the scope of these revisions. Only 154 people responded, with the majority supporting prescribed, naturally caused fires under specific conditions. A large minority, dominated by local residents, favored full fire suppression. This mix of public opinion hinted at the final policy outcome.[86]

Using the preliminary public input, Yellowstone park managers released the draft of their revised plan in the summer of 1991. The plan divided Yellowstone into three zones, with differing fire management practices designated for each zone. In most of the park, lightning-caused fires would be allowed as long as they met several measurable prescriptions: an energy release component (a measure of fuel intensity); a burning index (a measure of how difficult a fire would be to suppress); and a drought index (a measure of how dry and flammable fuels were). Fires located near all park boundaries and in areas upwind of two neighboring communities would be allowed to burn on a conditional basis only. Fires near all park villages would be suppressed. Additionally, the proposed fire policy plan specified staffing levels for the various levels of fire danger; chains of command; fire management and firefighting practices (including bulldozer use and use of management-ignited prescribed fires); public information distribution practices; interagency coordination practices; and smoke-management guidelines. Finally, the plan promoted research into fire ecology and behavior, as well as public education about fires.[87]

To solicit a second round of public input, park managers contracted local newspapers to insert 140,000 flyers advertising the revised plan's availability for review. As with the first round of public input, few persons responded—only 349.[88] Once again, the majority favored NPS's proposal to allow prescribed natural fires as much as possible.[89] By this time the issue had dropped off the radar screen for almost everyone in the region (only twelve people from the region wrote to express their thoughts) for several reasons. First, political concern was tempered by the proposed plan's focus on keeping fires controlled, on interagency cooperation, and on daily certification that fires would not escape control.[90] Second, the NPS's suppression of fires since 1988 assured residents that the agency's seemingly cavalier attitude toward fires had indeed changed—now, all fires would be controlled in some manner, at least on paper. Finally, the passage of time confirmed scientists' and NPS's assertions: seedling lodgepole pines grew tall enough to be observed by automobiles and tourists abounded at the park. Yellowstone was alive and well.[91]

The proposed plan seemed to strike a middle ground between allowing and controlling naturally caused fires in Yellowstone. Those interested in maintaining fire and those most concerned with putting limits on it were mollified. With this support, park managers had no problem getting the final fire policy plan approved and implemented in early 1992. That July the first prescribed fire—a small fire in Yellowstone's upper Lamar River Valley—was allowed to burn. Because the summer was wet, the fire burned only two acres and garnered little attention.[92]

After the rhetoric and amazing events of 1988, the fact that a policy allowing prescribed naturally caused fires was back on line was a notable policy success. Park personnel were duly proud of their efforts. Fire Management Officer Phil Perkins, for example, felt the plan still encouraged as much natural fire as possible. Chief of Research John Varley agreed, believing that these fires were solidly research based.[93] Scientific study had indeed carried the day—but the new plan's prescriptions for when to suppress fires bore the imprint of local politicians as well.

Over the course of the next decade, it became clear that the fire policy plan was solid, providing park managers with a broad range of options for deciding how to respond to different kinds of fires. Not surprisingly, in wet years, park managers were able to allow most naturally caused fires in Yellowstone to burn. Even in dry years, under the new plan, park managers had the flexibility to allow fires to play a substantial role in Yellowstone's landscape management. In some years, like 2001, most lightning-caused fires were permitted to burn (resulting in significant burned acreage), while in other years, like 2002 and 2003, most fires were suppressed—at least on paper, for in reality the fires were permitted to burn up to natural boundaries (a form of fire management called containment, which is allowed by the plan). In general, significant acreage in the park continues to burn, under somewhat controlled conditions, whether fires are declared wildfire or prescribed. Managers do not suppress all fires, even in dry years. Conversely, even in wet years they do suppress some wildfires. Such a record suggests that the plan provides great flexibility in deciding what fires to allow, how much acreage to burn, and what fires to suppress.[94]

Ultimately, the fire history of Yellowstone National Park makes it clear that not all "wildness" in the park is gone, for some fires still escape control and others are allowed to burn uncontrolled. Given the events of 1988, it is impressive that park managers are not worried about allowing significant acreage to burn. Although new burned acreages are but a small percentage of the park, they may be enough of an area that, over time, a fire regime approximating nature's own could be the result. Yellowstone park managers, with the help of scientists, have developed a plan that preserves as much natural fire and associated wildness as possible in the modern era. Political influence has meant a stronger commitment to control when needed, but the influence of scientists has allowed the most basic physical manifestation of wildness to remain, for fires still burn in Yellowstone.

And burn they will, whatever the policy may be on paper. As any observer of the 1988 wildfires (or those that have burned throughout the West since then) knows, a natural resource policy is only effective up to a point. When weather events combine to produce the hot, dry, and windy conditions that prevailed in 1988 in Yellowstone, the fire policy is no longer in control—nature is. While the fire policy review affirmed the strong role that scientific research can play in park management, the events of 1988 affirmed something stronger. As expressed by Montana Representative Pat Williams, "The fire did something else: it was nature telling people that in the end it will manage Yellowstone National Park and other wild areas."[95]

Reflections

In almost all ways, the fire policy review was influenced by NPS policy-making determinants that acted in vastly different ways than in the Fishing Bridge Village debate. Rather than contending with incomplete and indeterminate scientific data, for example, Yellowstone managers enjoyed an ample and preexisting scientific research base with clear implications for policy making. Research results were so clear and so unanimous, managers and the public could have phrased the scientific-base as answering a simple yes-or-no question: do fires belong in Yellowstone? While such a simple question was not (or rarely) explicitly asked, it was implicit in scientists' and managers' assertions in the years after the fires. Because scientists promoted the benefits of fires in the Yellowstone ecosystem, park managers were able to reinstate a fire policy that looked much the same as before, but one that allowed prescribed natural fires to burn in the park with minimal human influence. That such a broad scientific literature could be so succinctly summarized helped immensely with the press coverage of the fires and fire recovery after 1988. Reporters could—and did—portray fire as a natural and intrinsic part of the ecosystem. These reports and the preexisting and unified scientific research did more to restore the fire policy than any other influence.

Unlike the Fishing Bridge debate, during the fire policy review, Yellowstone managers enjoyed the support of both the scientific community and, to a lesser extent, the environmental community. Scientists, particularly Norm Christensen, were vocal supporters of a policy that would allow prescribed fires to burn as much as possible in the Yellowstone area. Members of the environmental community assisted as well, but their influence was less than what it would be in future controversies (especially the New World Mine issue). Scientists and environmentalists, along with park managers and the press, consistently framed the issue—naturally occurring fires burning in Yellowstone—as one of nature undergoing a cyclic and important rebirth, one that humans were fortunate to witness and that was well documented in the scientific literature. Overall, park managers were hardly alone in their desire and efforts to restore fire to Yellowstone's landscape; the coalition of support and compelling framing were clearly important factors in the eventual policy outcome.

Also, contrary to what occurred with the Fishing Bridge Village controversy, the concerns over restrictions on public access and threats to regional economies were absent once the fires of 1988 were extinguished. When visitors returned to the park in 1989, in large numbers, it became clear that both public access and the strength of the local economies would be protected. It was also clear to most visitors that the scientists and NPS managers were correct in stating that nature in Yellowstone was adapted to such fires (especially after the fire-germinated seedlings were tall enough to see from a moving car window). Yellowstone was not destroyed.

Again, in contrast to the Fishing Bridge situation, political opposition to NPS policy making concerning the fire policy was minimal. Fierce at first, the political opposition quickly abated to low-level pressure to ensure that some restraints were put on the fire policy to protect the private property of their constituents, as well as protect the tourist flow through neighboring communities. Most politicians lost interest in the policy outcome when they realized that the scientific research, coalitions, framing, public access issues, and local economies all appeared to favor the return of prescribed naturally occurring fire to Yellowstone.

Political opposition was also minimized, if unintentionally, by putting the fire policy review in the hands of a national policy review committee. In this way, the federal government succeeded in minimizing the often parochial interests of local citizens, neighboring communities, and the politicians who represented them. Additionally, Donald Hodel, Department of the Interior secretary, assisted by consistently deflecting criticism of the fire policy and NPS officials. In short, by giving the fire policy review to higher-level authority the government removed the policy from the seemingly tainted hands of Yellowstone park managers and gave the review an objectivity that these managers, no matter how impartial, could not achieve in the public eye.[96]

The outcome of this debate, then, was a complete line-up of the policy determinants in favor of restoring fire to the Yellowstone ecosystem and a fire plan with more workable restrictions. While some low-level political pressure remained through the end, park managers enjoyed nearly complete support from scientists and environmentalists, their associated and compelling framing, and a public not concerned about hampered public access or economic decline. The revised fire management plan allowed a large number of fires to burn, with substantial acreage, whether fires were declared "prescribed natural fires" or "wildfires." It was a plan that recognized both political and modern realities. The fire policy had some caveats, but it preserved park resources better than the results of the Fishing Bridge Village controversy.

Not long after reinstating the fire policy, Yellowstone managers found themselves with yet another significant controversy on their hands—the New World Mine project. That the mine was ultimately not built is a testament to many things, including the major policy determinants as well as the personal interest of an extraordinarily powerful person.

CHAPTER THREE

More Precious than Gold

You have the longest leash in the world.
—Secretary of the Interior Bruce Babbitt

These are not your normal bunch of crazies.
—Alex Balogh, of Noranda Minerals Corporation, in reference to
GYC staff members opposed to his company's proposed mine

VACATIONING IN JACKSON HOLE, WYOMING, FOR TWO WEEKS IN August 1995, President Bill Clinton took a day to travel to Yellowstone National Park with his family. To promote his environmental image, Clinton gave a speech at Old Faithful Geyser supporting protection "of our land, our water, our food, the diversity of our wildlife and the sanctity of our national treasures."[1] The comment about national treasures being sacred was an allusion to an environmental threat he had just learned of: a proposal to build a large gold mine just outside of Yellowstone. This mine promised a long list of problems for park managers if it were to be developed. With his interest piqued, Clinton, after watching Old Faithful Geyser erupt, boarded a helicopter and then traveled to the proposed mine site with Yellowstone superintendent Mike Finley. From there, Clinton returned to Jackson Hole for the rest of his vacation. His departure from Wonderland (the historic name for Yellowstone), however, was only temporary, for his influence would remain in the region and he himself would soon return.[2]

To have the president's interest—and soon involvement—in a national park's policy making is uncommon and partly a reflection of Yellowstone's high national visibility. And yet, the two previous controversies at Yellowstone did not achieve presidential attention, so something was different about this particular controversy. As the following discussion will reveal, Yellowstone superintendent Mike Finley and the NPS came to enjoy an extraordinary coalition with environmentalists and the press, who in turn used masterful framing of the issue (opposition to the gold mine) as a classic good guy versus bad guy contest to their advantage. With such strong assistance—and with eventual support (not just a lack of opposition) from the Wyoming congressional delegation—Yellowstone managers achieved a level of political support only seen in the wolf-reintroduction issue, which occurred at almost the same time. Because mines are commonly seen as offering a boost to local and regional economies, it would take such an alignment of support for park managers to succeed in defeating the New World Mine proposal.

Complementing the political support was an existing body of supportive scientific evidence regarding mining's environmental impacts; like the scientific research regarding wildfires in natural ecosystems, it was well established. Particularly clear was that most mines contaminated nearby waters with toxic minerals and acids. It was not immediately clear, however, that such would be the case with this gold mine, or that the waters in Yellowstone National Park would be impacted. Eventually, those doubts would be erased, enabling park managers and mine opponents to add scientific research as a powerful weapon in their arsenal against the proposed mine.

With both scientific studies and politics on board against the gold mine, this controversy's outcome may have seemed like a foregone conclusion. However, it was no easy task to apply the science to this issue successfully and it was an even more difficult task to reverse the typical political stance in favor of economic enhancement. Compounding the difficulties was a belated response by the National Park Service (NPS) itself against the proposed mine, a delay due largely to the evolving political situation at the time. The agency's delay could have cost the agency this battle, despite the scientific research base and support of the environmental community. The risk that the agency took by delaying its response to the mine threat is the reason that this chapter will suggest that national park policy-making outcomes often reflect political influences as much as they do the conclusions of the existing research base.

However, the NPS has considerable ability to influence the political context, as this story will illustrate. By methodically aligning the other determinants in its favor, the NPS was able to move the political determinant toward its desired goals.

The New World Mine:
Politics, Science, and Coalitions of the Unafraid

The roots of the New World Mine controversy date back to the 1870s, when two exploratory parties made very different discoveries in the Yellowstone region: one group was looking for gold and the other for natural wonders; both found what they were looking for and eventually received congressional blessing to pursue their ends. These two interests were able to exist harmoniously side-by-side for many decades, but this truce began to unravel in the 1980s, when a huge mine using new technologies was proposed to exploit a lucrative vein of gold—and by this time Yellowstone had become a national, even international, treasure.

The first of the exploratory parties was a prospecting trip by George A. Huston, who struck gold in an area of the Lamar River headwaters in Montana Territory. Within a year, miners had constructed an ore-grinding mill in the remote area, despite its location within the Crow Indian Reservation. Within another decade, miners had christened their primitive camp "Cooke City," in the hopes of convincing Jay Cooke Jr. of the Northern Pacific Railway to finance a spur line to the town. A crash in the eastern financial markets stymied that hope, but the name stuck. The historic American pattern of Indian dispossession soon occurred in Cooke City, for in 1882 the federal government converted the area around the new town from Crow reservation lands to public domain lands. Prospectors poured in to lay their claims; before long 1,450 claims had been filed and the gold rush was on.[3]

The Washburn-Langford-Doane expedition was the second exploration; its members sought natural wonders in the region, a little farther south and west from the prospectors in Cooke City. They discovered many of the fabulous resources that would soon become the centerpieces of Yellowstone National Park. According to modern legend, they came up with the idea of preserving those natural wonders in a national park. Upon their return to civilization, members of this expedition publicized their discoveries and helped popularize the national park idea for the Yellowstone area.[4]

These twin discoveries of treasure both received congressional blessing and legal validity in 1872, when Congress passed both the Yellowstone
National Park Act and the General Mining Law. As famous as the first act
is, the second often seems more infamous today, at least from a conservation viewpoint. In keeping with the Manifest Destiny thinking of the era,
the General Mining Law encouraged the settlement and development of the
then-unsettled American West by allowing any prospector to stake and lay
claim to mineral-bearing lands (a process called "patenting"). After some
modest improvements and payment of five dollars per acre, the prospector
could own the land and the minerals under it outright. The law made no
provision for royalties or reclamation once mining ends, a situation that has
not changed to this day and that encourages the law's infamous reputation.[5]
These two acts of Congress set the stage for the conflict that would develop
between mining proponents and Yellowstone defenders one century later.

Mining prospered in Cooke City through the 1880s, with later spurts
of activity in the 1930s. Meanwhile, in 1935, the Beartooth Highway opened,
connecting Cooke City to Red Lodge, Montana, via the 10,947-foot-high
Beartooth Pass. One of the outstanding scenic roads in the United States,
the new highway offered visitors a new route to Yellowstone. With most
mining ending in the 1950s, the increasing number of tourists traveling the
scenic highway helped shift Cooke City's economy toward tourism. Most
visitors passed through in summer, but some waited for winter when the
town had the opposite attraction of being at the end of a plowed road (the
Beartooth Highway is not plowed in winter). Visitors drove 50 miles through
Yellowstone's wildlife-rich northern range to get to Cooke City, where they
strapped on skis or hopped on snowmobiles to enjoy the area's abundant
snowfall. Catering to their needs were about seventy-five hardy year-round
residents, whose numbers swelled to a few hundred in the short summers.
By the 1990s tourism was the economic mainstay of the town (figure 18).[6]

By the time mining played out in the 1950s, the New World Mining
District (the name of the actual mining area just north of, and about 2,000
feet higher than, Cooke City) had produced about 60,000 ounces of gold,
about 700,000 ounces of silver, and large amounts of copper, lead, and
zinc. Although profitable, these amounts are small compared to the minerals extracted in the more famous gold rushes in California, Alaska, and
Colorado. However, prospectors completely missed the largest, single gold-
ore body in the area, one that would put Cooke City on the map of large,
modern gold-producing regions. In 1987, a Canadian mining company, the

FIGURE 18: Cooke City, Montana, 2011. Cooke City had its origins in mining, but has gradually transformed into a town mostly dependent on tourism. The New World Mine proposal divided the town's residents into those who supported the mine, those who opposed it, and a small number who were ambivalent. Some proponents changed the name of their business to reflect their support of the mine, such as the Prospector Restaurant on the right side of this photo. Author photo.

Noranda Minerals Corporation, renewed prospecting operations in the mining district, hoping to use new techniques for extracting bullion from low-grade ore or former mine tailings. Noranda was part of the largest natural resources conglomerate in Canada, with annual sales of $8 billion (Canadian dollars) or more. Its mineral-exploration branch was the second largest in the world, and its holdings were global.[7] In its explorations above Cooke City, the company discovered the overlooked ore vein—a vein so large that the company's geologist believed more than 2.5 million ounces of gold were present, along with 10 million ounces of silver and 179 million pounds of copper, with the possibility of even more discoveries once extraction began. Consequently, in July 1989, Noranda announced its intention to develop a mine in the area.

The company knew that its proposal would likely touch off a controversy—but it seemed to have little idea that the proposed mine's proximity to Yellowstone meant the level of the controversy would be heightened.[8]

In Montana, the state's Metal Mine Reclamation Act requires mining companies to develop a mine application that includes an operating plan, baseline studies showing existing environmental and socioeconomic conditions, and a reclamation plan. Applicants then submit the application to the Montana Department of State Lands, which reviews it for completeness and requests any necessary revisions. The applicants then may revise and resubmit the application, with further rounds of review and revision as needed, until the plan is deemed complete. At that time, the state commissions an environmental impact statement (EIS) on the application pursuant to the Montana Environmental Policy Act. Once the EIS is complete, applicants can develop their mine, assuming the state has approved it. Authorities in Montana, known as the "Treasure State," were not known for turning down applications to mine.[9]

Believing its odds of a successful application were good, Noranda spent the next few years drafting its application to mine above Cooke City. Throughout 1989 and 1990, the company conducted further exploratory activities and defined the ore body. Because a portion of the mine would fall on U.S. Forest Service (USFS) lands, Noranda also had to submit its application to the Gallatin National Forest, which meant that the USFS would share permitting authority with the State of Montana and that the EIS would have to comply with the National Environmental Policy Act. Due to its potential impacts on nearby Yellowstone National Park, the NPS was invited to be a "cooperating agency," allowed to review the application and provide technical expertise on its completeness and the potential impacts upon the park. However, the NPS did not have the authority to approve or deny the application; such authority rested with the State of Montana and the USFS. Due to this situation and the political climate under the George H. W. Bush administration, which did not allow Yellowstone superintendent Bob Barbee (still at Yellowstone's helm) to take a strong stand against the mine, the NPS was not initially a major player in the mining controversy. That would begin to change in 1993, after Bill Clinton was elected president and Mike Finley replaced Barbee as Yellowstone's superintendent.[10]

On November 14, 1990, Noranda submitted its first application to mine—a mammoth document of fourteen volumes, three feet thick. The company proposed to mine gold-, copper-, and silver-bearing ore from several areas centered around Henderson Mountain, about 3 miles north of Cooke City and 2 miles east of Yellowstone's northeast corner (figures 19, 20). Two open pits would be necessary, one on each side of the mountain, along with an underground mine to access the main ore body under Henderson Mountain. These operations would cover 1,720 acres, most at or near timberline (around 10,000 feet above sea level). Processing the ore would necessitate a mill in upper Fisher Creek, in which a cyanide vat-leaching method would be used to process between 1,000 and 1,800 tons of gold ore per day, producing gold bullion. Upon completion, coarse tailings would be deposited as backfill in the mine, while 5.5 million tons of fine tailings would be wasted to a nearby impoundment. A high-density, polyethylene (plastic) liner would prevent the tailings from seeping into the groundwater. The mill would run around the clock, year-round, from twelve to twenty years, and require one hundred and forty workers during operation. Construction of the mine would require another one hundred and eighty or so employees. To house the workers, the company proposed constructing a work camp between the mine and Cooke City. Finally, Noranda proposed significant improvements to the rough roads over Daisy and Lulu Pass to facilitate mine-related travel.[11]

Outside of the New World Mining District, several other significant changes would be necessary for the mine. To power its operations, the company proposed building a new 68-mile-long, 69,000-volt transmission line from Cody, Wyoming, to the mine. The company also proposed to expedite ongoing highway improvements to the Chief Joseph Highway, the main route by which it would haul materials to market in Cody. (The NPS prohibited such hauling through the park.) Because 8 miles of that route were not then being maintained in winter, the company also proposed to shoulder the expense of snow plowing. With these improvements, the company would send one or two heavy truckloads of copper mill concentrates to Cody daily for smelting, along with occasional shipments of gold bullion. Other new traffic would consist of mine employees traveling to their homes, recreating, or procuring groceries and other supplies. This other new traffic would not only go to Cody, but also through Yellowstone National Park to Gardiner and beyond.[12]

Watching the company move its proposal forward were many residents of Cooke City. Some welcomed the potential infusion of extra dollars into their relatively quiet economy, while others feared the influence of a large outside corporation. Stirred by the company's seemingly rapid application submission and the mine's potential environmental and social impacts,

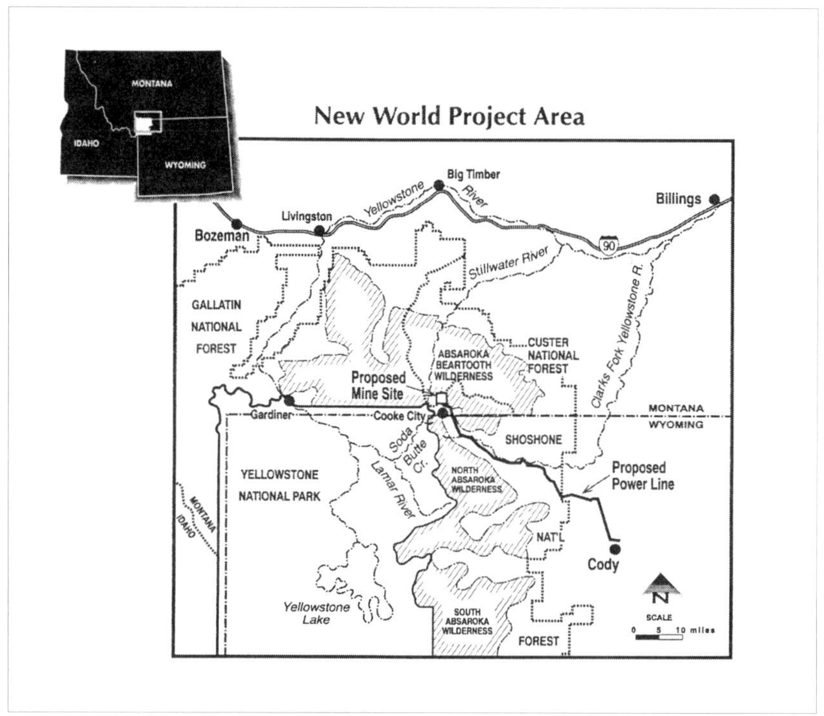

FIGURE 19: The Yellowstone-Cooke City area, including the proposed site of the New World Mine. Source: United States Department of Agriculture, U.S. Forest Service, and Montana Department of State Lands, "New World Project Newsletter," June, 1995, Yellowstone Center for Resources, National Park Service, Mammoth Hot Springs, Wyoming.

some concerned townspeople formed the Beartooth Alliance. With an initial membership of seventy-five people (primarily local business owners, summer residents, and guides), the alliance asked to provide input on the mine application, initially hoping mostly to mitigate the mine's potential impacts. As the application process progressed, however, the Beartooth Alliance came to oppose the mine.[13]

Members of the alliance had many reasons for concern. Although the New World Mining District was already degraded by past mining activity, forty years without mining had allowed some scars on the landscape to heal. Some feared the new mine would reverse the healing that had occurred

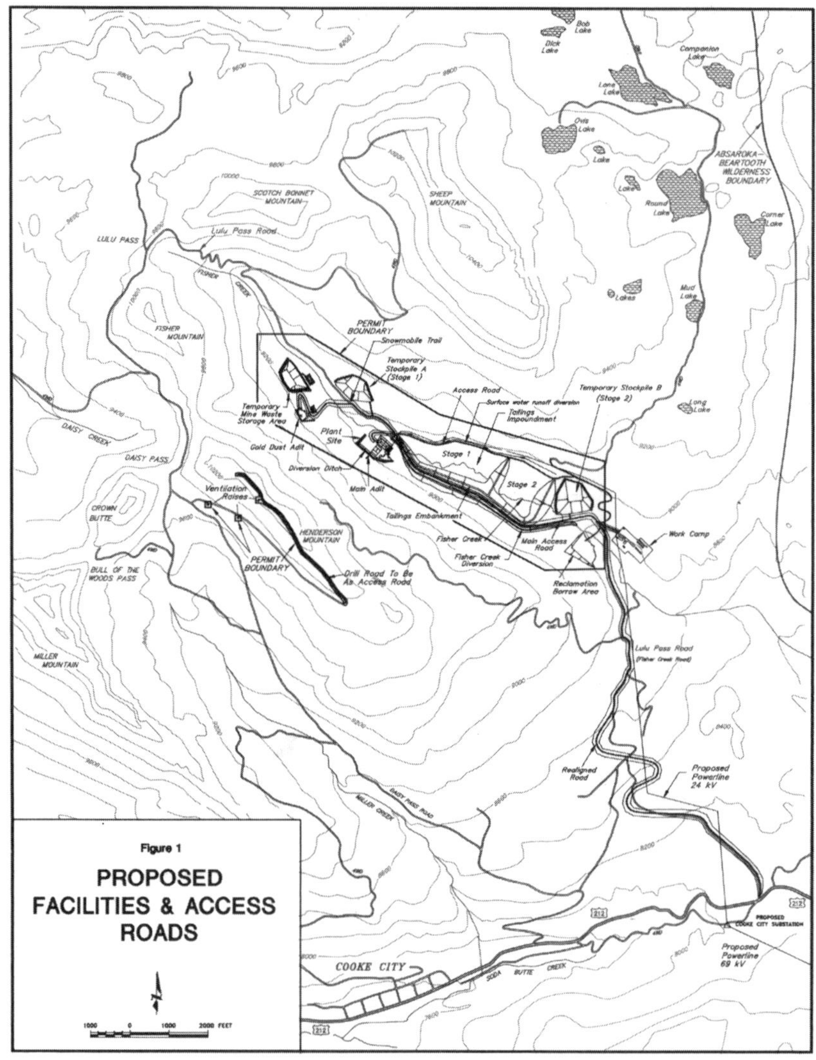

FIGURE 20: Detail of the New World Mining District and proposed mine facilities. Note that this map omits the two open pits that were originally proposed for the site, reflecting a change in the Noranda Mineral Corporation's proposal in 1992. Source: United States Department of Agriculture, U.S. Forest Service, and Montana Department of State Lands, "Scoping Document: Crown Butte Mines, Inc.'s New World Project," May 1993, Yellowstone Center for Resources, National Park Service, Mammoth Hot Springs, Wyoming.

there, or create new resource impacts. For example, many gold-bearing ore bodies are rich in iron sulfides (iron pyrite, or "fool's gold"), which, when exposed to air, emit acid leachates and dissolved heavy metals into local water bodies. Miller and Fisher creeks had already been degraded through such leaching by earlier mining activity; the new mine presented the threat of amplifying that contamination. Moreover, the high elevation and harsh climate of the mine's location would make efforts to reclaim the impacted land, when mining was completed, challenging. It would be equally difficult to build mine structures, especially the tailings impoundment, that would have to withstand blizzards, avalanches, subzero temperatures, and earthquakes, all possible occurrences in the region. Much of the proposed mine site contained stands of whitebark pine, a tree whose nut-bearing cones are crucial to the nutrition of grizzly bears that live in the region. Then still listed as threatened under the Endangered Species Act, the grizzly bear's survival depended on these trees, as well as on the widespread availability of wildlands unaltered and unoccupied by people. The proposed mine would take out many whitebark pine trees and introduce high levels of human activity in the mining area and beyond—including habitat of the endangered grizzly bear. Finally, the proposed power line threatened to mar the wild character of the undeveloped landscapes through which it would be built.[14]

Equally motivating members of the Beartooth Alliance were the mine's potential social impacts. Many town residents treasured Cooke City's quiet, rural character and feared that the mine would create an industrial, polluted, and noisy atmosphere. Others feared that the proposed mine would curtail their access to a favorite backyard playground: the New World Mining District. Improvements to the Chief Joseph Highway virtually guaranteed increased traffic through their area, with regular snow plowing particularly threatening the town's deep winter solitude, as it would no longer be the end of the road.[15] Once it was proven (in a few more months) that the mine posed a direct threat to nearby Yellowstone National Park, Cooke City residents also defended the park.

During the application review process in 1991, Beartooth Alliance members grew increasingly concerned about the mine's threats to their way of life and the local environment. Noranda was an outsider and seemed insensitive to their concerns, at least in the opinions of some. These worries, along with the knowledge that the alliance lacked experience and power in dealing with a large intruder, made the group seek assistance from other likeminded organizations. Soon, the alliance began working with the Greater

Yellowstone Coalition (GYC), a conservation group based in Bozeman, Montana, devoted to the protection of the entire Yellowstone area. GYC employees had been watching the developing controversy since 1989 and were increasingly worried about the potential threats to Yellowstone. Once Noranda finalized its first application, the GYC's concerns about the mine crystallized into direct opposition. For the GYC, the collaboration with the Beartooth Alliance offered local legitimacy; for the alliance, affiliation with the larger group offered more advocacy skills and broader networking capability.[16] Just as these groups began to realize that they would soon have a major effort on their hands, they also came to realize that their collaboration would serve them well. It would take more time for the NPS to join the team.

As noted earlier, Noranda did have some supporters in Cooke City. Some town residents hoped to profit directly from the mine by working for it, or indirectly by providing goods and services to its workers. Some residents went so far as to change the name of their businesses to promote the mine, such as the "Prospector Restaurant" (see figure 18). While Noranda acquired some local legitimacy from such supporters, the fact that it was based in Canada still meant it would be seen as an outsider, more so than the GYC based in nearby Bozeman. Furthermore, the bullying tactics used by the company—such as offering a local landlord four times the usual monthly rent for the residence of local Beartooth Alliance volunteer Wade King when his lease came up for renewal—did nothing to improve Noranda's public face. For many in the region, it was a portent of things to come.[17]

Throughout 1992, the company's application proceeded through the review phases. Combining the comments from the various concerned agencies and interest groups, the Montana Department of State Lands and the Gallatin National Forest sent the first application back to Noranda with about eight hundred questions for the company to address, in a document more than one hundred pages long. Later that year, the company significantly amended its proposal by dropping the two open pits and the associated cyanide vat-leach extraction, largely because it found that the ore in the pit areas was not as rich as expected. Instead, the company decided to focus its application on the rich, underground ore body, where more than 90 percent of the recoverable gold occurred. This significant change meant that application reviews would take the better part of another year.[18]

Many of the questions about the application came from NPS staff members in Yellowstone, who were themselves growing increasingly worried about the mine. Still operating under the first Bush administration, the

NPS staff was under the gag order not to oppose the mine directly. Instead, they were limited to more general "concerns" about the mine. To that end, Yellowstone superintendent Bob Barbee and his staff carefully examined each of the applications and submitted extensive comments and questions about them. Moreover, they exchanged information with the environmental community in an effort to share precious technical expertise, particularly from experts in the NPS's Mining and Minerals Branch in Denver. Such efforts both helped the small interest groups (the GYC and Beartooth Alliance) and also laid the groundwork for a stronger, more public coalition in the hoped-for time when the political climate would change (which it finally did after Clinton defeated Bush in the 1992 presidential election). Such NPS efforts were made possible by the fact that the Yellowstone park staff was growing and becoming increasingly professionalized. The Yellowstone Center for Resources (YCR), for example, was created in 1993; the center employed many of the staff specialists that scrutinized the mining proposal.[19]

The application review delays gave the environmental community more time to organize with each other and to strategize against the mine. Although the GYC had already decided to oppose it, the group knew that a successful campaign—if that were even possible—would require a Herculean effort, necessitating far more staff, expertise, and funding than it could spare. At that time, the GYC was the largest conservation group with an organizational commitment against the mine; other such groups had made statements of opposition, but were too extended for a lengthy, tiring battle. As the GYC staff knew, a successful campaign would require a large amount of publicity and involvement from other conservation groups—especially at the national level. While such a campaign was daunting, members of the GYC knew that their group would become stronger and its message—to preserve the ecological integrity of the "Greater Yellowstone Ecosystem"—more visible if it piloted a large campaign against the mine.[20]

At their fall 1991 meeting, the GYC's board members debated the merits of entering a full campaign against the mine. Rather than jumping in head first, they instead directed their staff to gather critical data about the proposal over the next six months. Specifically, the group was to seek out natural-resource and legal expertise to help those concerned about the project better understand mining technology and the mine's probable impacts. The group quickly hired Robin Patten, an ecologist familiar with mining issues, to compile hydrological, wildlife, reclamation, and geological data.

Similarly, it began working with Doug Honnold of the Sierra Club Legal Defense Fund (today known as Earthjustice), a conservation group specializing in legal action toward conservationist ends, to examine the mining company's legal liabilities. These would prove to be astute moves that would strongly influence the GYC's strategy, Noranda's eventual willingness to compromise, and the ultimate outcome of the controversy. At the time, however, these results were mere hopes.[21]

As the winter of 1991–1992 progressed, GYC staff developed ideas on a media campaign and increased their political lobbying and grassroots organizing. The GYC also expanded the scope of its activist network, by involving more regional groups and by gaining the attention of some national groups, especially the National Parks and Conservation Association (NPCA) (opposed to impacts on Yellowstone), the Mineral Policy Center (which saw the proposed mine as an example of the problems with the 1872 General Mining Law), and American Rivers (worried about the possible pollution of the Yellowstone River, especially the Clark's Fork of the Yellowstone River in Wyoming, the state's only designated Wild and Scenic River). Through these efforts, GYC staff gradually realized that their group had little choice but to embark upon a full-fledged battle to defeat the mine and its potential threats to Yellowstone. Of the conservation groups interested in Yellowstone matters, they were uniquely positioned to take on the mine because they were, by nature and name, a coalition of local and regional conservation groups focused on stewardship of the Yellowstone area. (The NPS was still constrained against direct mine opposition, so the baton was still in the environmental community's hands.) By spring of 1992, the GYC had made the commitment.[22]

The mine's location close to the Wyoming state line presented additional angles of opposition. Although it was to be located in Montana, many of the mine's physical and social impacts would literally and figuratively flow downhill into Wyoming. Two of the three streams draining the project area flowed into Wyoming, posing a greater contamination threat to Wyoming waters than to Montana's. Similarly, if the tailings impoundment should collapse (a possibility many viewed as likely, due to the avalanche and earthquake potential of the mountainous area), Wyoming would suffer the brunt of the flood impacts. Furthermore, Wyoming would not receive the severance royalties that Montana would (Montana state law required such payments, unlike the national mining law), even though most mine employees would likely depend on Cody in Park County, Wyoming, for social services such as schools for their children (as Cooke City offered no such services). Capitalizing on these geographic nuances, the GYC soon found the Cody Country Chamber of Commerce, ordinarily a body that consistently promoted economic enhancement (as it did in the Fishing Bridge Village controversy) receptive to discussions about a movement to oppose the mine. As a result, one Park County commissioner adopted a position opposing the mine and the Cody Economic Development Council requested a study examining the mine's socioeconomic impacts on their area. Indeed, the geographic location of the mine and the areas it would impact offered unique conservation alliances in the otherwise pro-development Cody area. These weaknesses in the mining project would haunt mine advocates and eventually present possibilities for public framing of the issue in ways that compelled many in Wyoming to react against the mine.[23]

With the mine application nearing completeness in late 1992, members of the GYC took the initiative to travel to Noranda Minerals Corporation's headquarters in Toronto, Canada, to meet directly with the company. Although they found the company receptive to their concerns and committed to environmental stewardship, Noranda would not back down from its lucrative proposal, despite threats of opposition. The company was indeed concerned with its environmental image—it no longer planned to develop the two open-pit mines and it was continuing to plan for the area's reclamation from earlier mining. According to U.S. law, the company had a valid right to mine. Furthermore, the mining history of the Cooke City area seemed to some to confer legitimacy to the company and its proposal. The company firmly believed it could develop the mine while protecting Yellowstone, a position it would hold throughout the brewing controversy.[24]

Montana approved the company's application to mine in April 1993, a step that heightened the battle between preservation and exploitation. Funded by Noranda, the state began preparing the EIS by soliciting public input on the scope of the plan. By law, the state had only one year to prepare the EIS (a timeline that would prove to be impossible in this instance). Meanwhile, fueled by the heightened immediacy of the threat to Yellowstone and Cooke City, the conservation community redoubled its efforts to find weaknesses in the mine proposal and to motivate citizens and the NPS (still unable to directly oppose the project) to work against the mine. For all parties, 1993 proved to be a critical year in the controversy's development.

Not subject to the NPS's political position, GYC decided to move forward with a major "World War III Noranda campaign."[25] To the group, such a campaign presented an unparalleled (if unfortunate) opportunity to highlight two significant environmental messages. First, the group believed that the various federal land management agencies in the Yellowstone region (including six national forests, two parks, and several other state and federal agencies) had conflicting missions that made long-term conservation of the nationally significant area problematic. The USFS, for example, had allowed substantial logging in the Yellowstone area in the 1980s, just at the same time that the grizzly bear population was bottoming out. If the federal land management agencies in the region were more committed to coordinated management of the Yellowstone area, they would have looked dimly upon such logging. In this case, they should have been more skeptical of a mine that promised so many impacts upon the area's resources (including the threatened grizzly bears). Instead, the Gallatin National Forest and State of Montana seemed poised to approve this mine and all its impacts.

The proposed mine and its possible impacts were also an illustration of the problems with the 1872 General Mining Law: if Congress amended the law to require reclamation of mined areas, the New World Mine might not be such a potent threat to Yellowstone.[26] Congress was actually considering reforms at the time; on November 18, 1993, the reforms passed both houses. The House passed a reform bill calling for royalty payments, an end to the patenting of government lands, and requirements for prevention of environmental damage and reclamation thereof. The bill also established standards to classify certain lands as "unsuitable" for mining. The Senate passed a very different reform bill, calling for royalties of only 2 percent, along with a few other changes. The bills were referred to a conference committee, where they languished throughout 1994.[27]

Watching the progress of the reforms, new Secretary of the Interior Bruce Babbitt held his breath. Reform seemed so close, with bills passed in both houses. Babbitt, however, knew that the constituency for and against reform was closely balanced and that negotiations between the two fairly different bills were sensitive. He also knew that western congressmen, especially Wyoming's senator Alan Simpson, opposed significant reform of the law. Simpson was ambivalent about the New World Mine, even though he had worked at a ranch (the B4) near Cooke City early in his career and was therefore familiar with the resources at stake. A high-profile battle by the NPS against the New World Mine could backfire, leading Simpson to oppose substantial reform of the 1872 law more strongly. Consequently, Babbitt had Superintendent Barbee continue the moderate stance he had been holding.

Focusing on the long-term war over the issue, not the immediate battle, became Barbee's and Babbitt's approach while the conference committee did its work—or tried to do so. For the time being, the conservation community had to lead the charge against the mine, with the General Mining Law continuing to be in effect as it had been for one hundred and twenty years.[28]

While there is no record of communication between the NPS and the GYC about NPS's formal position on the mining project, it is almost certain that Barbee conveyed in some way the reasons for his agency's stance (sitting on the sidelines) to the GYC. Realizing it would have to lead the way for now, GYC redoubled its efforts to broadcast word of the mine and gain support for the cause of protecting Yellowstone. The group soon gained its first national ally, American Rivers, a national organization devoted to river conservation. When writing to Gallatin National Forest officials about the scope of the EIS, American Rivers noted that the Yellowstone River was the longest free-flowing river remaining in the contiguous forty-eight states and pointed out that every one of the streams emanating from the proposed mining area drained into various forks of the Yellowstone River. Any toxic releases, such as from a collapsed tailings impoundment (a distinct possibility), were certain to harm the Yellowstone River in some way. Expressing the fears of most mine opponents, American Rivers stated, "We are unaware of any mine developed in such a sensitive, alpine environment that has not resulted in environmental degradation."[29] In this way, American Rivers became the first of several national environmental groups to elevate the visibility of the mine and its threat to Yellowstone.

Even if they could not oppose the New World Mine directly, Yellowstone managers could still make things difficult for the mining proponents. With this in mind, park staff compiled a detailed list of impacts the mine could potentially have on Yellowstone National Park and the Yellowstone River.[30] The NPS list, which was provided to the Gallatin National Forest as subjects to consider in the EIS, encapsulated most of the dominant issues of all mine opponents:

The proposed New World Mine has the potential for significant direct and indirect impacts to Yellowstone National Park. Potential impacts include degradation of surface and groundwater quality, increased traffic through the Northeast Entrance of Yellowstone which is presently accessible by motor vehicle less than six months of the year, and the cumulative effects of this development on what is presently the least-visited entrance of the park; changes in quantity of water flowing into the park; increased occupation and disturbance of grizzly bear and other wildlife habitat; loss of scenic and recreational values in and adjacent to Yellowstone Park; noise and light intrusion associated with the mining activities; degradation of air quality including scenic vistas from and into Yellowstone; socioeconomic changes to the gateway towns of Silver Gate and Cooke City which currently have very small numbers of permanent residents, and the potential for increased demand for park-provided emergency services, waste removal, year-round snow plowing, and visitors services within the park.[31]

While such a list was comprehensive and the items on it cause for worry, it was not a direct statement of opposition and some park staff understandably felt muzzled. NPS staff member Stu Coleman, for example, urged Barbee to take a stronger stance, but to no avail. Both Superintendent Barbee and Interior Secretary Babbitt felt they needed to stay focused on the larger goal: if the congressional conference committee did succeed in forwarding the reformed General Mining Law to the president for signature, they would then have a strong tool to use against the New World Mine and all mines. Nonetheless, Yellowstone park representatives were getting stronger and stronger in their statements.[32] Coleman, for example, was quoted as saying, "I guess if you threw a dart in a map of the United States, and decided to put a gold mine there, it's probably the worst place possible—high elevation, next to Yellowstone, grizzly bear habitat, three drainages. . . . It's just a bad deal all the way around."[33] The Noranda Minerals Corporation complained about Coleman's forthrightness, but Barbee defended him.[34]

Rhetoric was abundant and easy to generate, but stronger action was necessary to oppose the mining project. Court action could stop the mine cold, so mine opponents began looking for a legal stick to use. Until this time, the most promising possibility seemed to be the mine's impacts on grizzly bears, still a threatened species under the Endangered Species Act. Worried about the mine's potential impacts on the bear, the NPS had its scientists study grizzly bear use of the mining district (another example of the agency providing research expertise, even though it was standing on the sidelines for now). The researchers found that bears did indeed use the whitebark-pine groves on Henderson Mountain, but they avoided the existing roads there. Mining might further displace the bears from this high-quality food source, but their use of the general area was not critical to their survival. The report did not offer the conclusive evidence needed to prove the company would violate the Endangered Species Act. Given the NWF's failure to succeed on the same grounds in the Fishing Bridge Village controversy that had just ended, opponents in the mining controversy began to look for other ways to stop the project.[35]

High on the list of other laws potentially being violated was the Clean Water Act (CWA), which required a company discharging pollution into bodies of water to obtain a "national pollutant discharge elimination system permit" (NPDES permit) from the EPA *before* it could in fact discharge that pollution. Noranda's own mine application had identified three historic adits (mine tunnels) that were leaking acid or contaminated water with heavy metals from earlier mining. Although the EPA would soon argue that such old adits were included under the NPDES requirement, courts had not yet made the same determination. Noranda had obtained a permit that it believed covered such discharges, but the GYC's lawyers believed the permit actually covered only general, surface, storm-water runoff from construction activities, and that the company instead needed specific permits for each of the three adits. Recognizing the same vulnerability, Noranda had petitioned Montana to reclassify Miller and Fisher creeks as "industrial" streams, which would waive the necessity to obtain the NPDES permits and remedy the existing pollution. The company wanted to take the easy way out, an action that compelled the GYC (and soon, the NPS) to prove that Noranda needed NPDES permits for the adits.[36]

Although there certainly seemed to be a potential CWA tool to use, the GYC had several things to prove before it could win in court. First, it would have to show that the CWA did indeed apply to old mining adits. Second, it would have to demonstrate that Noranda's existing permit did not, in fact, cover such discharges. Third, it would have to prove that the discharges reached a body of water and degraded it. Miller and Fisher creeks were already degraded streams, but the GYC had to discover whether the adits were responsible for that degradation, or whether the streams were naturally degraded. Essentially, this was another way of saying that the scientific research regarding acid mine drainage was well established and accepted, but whether it applied to this case was the question. Finally, the GYC would have to prove that the polluting sources were on land Noranda owned or controlled. Separately, the GYC would have to ponder its own risks—if it were to lose the lawsuit, it would be liable for Noranda's legal and court costs, which could easily total several million dollars. Gambling that the legal process would offer time to research these questions and anxious to find anything that would give Noranda pause, the group decided to take the risk. In September 1993, GYC and eight other conservation groups (all but one of which were based in the Greater Yellowstone area) filed suit against Noranda, alleging CWA violations.[37]

The tailings impoundment was another important issue and legal vulnerability. Behind a new hundred-foot-tall dam, Noranda would submerge the fine tailings under water, a technique that prevented them from oxidizing and producing acid waste. At the bottom of the lake would be a high-density polyethylene (plastic) liner intended to prevent tailings waste from entering groundwater. Besides the lake's unsightliness, such liners were still a relatively new technology lacking a long-term record of success. In fact, a similar tailings impoundment had recently failed at Summitville, Colorado, destroying all life in a 17-mile stretch of the Alamosa River (a tributary to the Rio Grande) and sticking the federal government with a $100 million cleanup. With this collapse on their minds, it was hard for the EPA or mine critics to believe that something only the thickness of a heavy-duty plastic garbage bag could withstand the earthquakes and avalanches in the Yellowstone area.[38]

Yellowstone staff, who felt the same way, used their graphics expertise and publication abilities to aid the cause in a not-so-subtle way. They produced and distributed a full-color, bound booklet that ostensibly detailed the mine and its potential impacts on the park. However, an underlying message of opposition was clear from the first page, which featured a picture of a lovely mountain meadow with snow-capped peaks in the distance (the threatened Fisher Creek wetlands and Henderson Mountain). The caption below it read, "Centered in the rugged Beartooth Mountains of south-central Montana, the proposed New World Mine is surrounded by national park and U.S. Forest Service Wilderness at elevations of 8,800 to 10,300 feet. If Crown Butte Mines' proposal is approved, this high mountain meadow, which drains into a Wild and Scenic river, would be buried under nine stories of toxic mine tailings."[39] The booklet's message and NPS's position were clear.

Perhaps due in part to this booklet, the tailings impoundment soon became a focal point of criticism and garnered the first potential ally in the political world. U.S. Senator Max Baucus, a Democrat from Montana, highlighted the concerns with the tailings impoundment in a letter to Noranda Minerals Corporation CEO Alex Balogh that fall. Baucus made five demands, one of which was that "[n]o tailings pond should be established at the site," because if it were, and it failed, "the impact to the greater Yellowstone ecosystem would be cataclysmic and the damage irreversable [*sic*]."[40] He asked Balogh instead to develop a plan that did not require an on-site tailings pond. Coming from a highly visible public figure in the state that most stood to benefit from the mine—and from a politician not known for his strong environmental positions—the letter buoyed mining opponents. They widely distributed it, including to NPS director Roger G. Kennedy, who actually replied by "wholeheartedly" agreeing with Senator Baucus.[41] This was another indication that the NPS's response to the mine might be moving away from neutrality, toward overt opposition. Baucus's letter also highlighted the growing visibility of the issue. Indeed, when President Clinton toured the mine site in 1995 he referred to and concurred with Baucus's letter.[42]

Knowing that support from the Wyoming congressional delegation would be even more crucial, GYC staff began lobbying Wyoming politicians to oppose the mine. In September, GYC staff led Wyoming governor Mike Sullivan and Park County commissioners (as Cody is the county seat) on a tour of the mine site. Seeing firsthand the potential problems the mine could bring to his state, Sullivan soon directed the Wyoming Department of Environmental Quality (DEQ) to study the mine's potential socioeconomic impacts on Park County. Moving quickly to complete the study, the DEQ concluded that the mine would cost Wyoming state and local governments $500,000 or more annually, while only returning $50,000 to $80,000 in sales and property taxes. Such estimates demonstrated that the mine might not be the economic boost many originally thought. One study by itself, though, is not always that influential; recall the failure of the Fishing Bridge economic study to sway Wyoming opinion. Even though this particular study came from Wyoming's DEQ, it would still take more proof that Wyoming's economy would be harmed before the state's politicians felt comfortable taking strong positions against the mine.[43]

Rolling up their sleeves, GYC staff continued gathering the necessary data to prove the New World Mine adits were indeed polluting local streams, and thereby win their case in court. Working with the Beartooth Alliance, they gathered samples of all known springs and adit flows in the mining district. They found most springs to be neutral, but those closer to historic mining areas tended to be more acidic, especially in the headwaters of Fisher Creek, where the historic mining activity was concentrated and where Noranda wanted to mine. These sampling efforts proved that historic mining did contribute to the acidity of springs near the mine, but more research quantifying the level of acid contribution was still needed to convince a judge that Noranda was responsible for polluting the creeks and therefore responsible for cleaning them up.[44]

Early in 1994, the GYC's active and direct efforts (as well as the more subdued efforts of the NPS) to get national attention began to pay off. Several national conservation magazines carried articles critical of the mine proposal, including *Backpacker, National Parks,* and *Trout.*[45] Bob Ekey, GYC's press director, in writing for Trout Unlimited, cleverly stated that "Montana gets the mine . . . while Wyoming gets the shaft."[46] Additionally, American Rivers, which published an annual list of the country's most endangered rivers, placed the Yellowstone River at the top of that list in 1994 and used the national fame of its board member, Michael Keaton, to publicize the announcement. This organization had just finished a successful campaign against the Windy Craggy mine in British Columbia, Canada, so it helped GYC by networking with its contacts in Canada and in Washington, D.C. to build more opposition to the New World Mine. Additionally, the NPCA, effective at working with the NPS's internal culture, began pushing the agency to take a strong public position on the mine (as mining reform was still stalled in the congressional conference committee).[47]

Working with national groups brought a broader vision to the mining opponents and pushed the NPS to emerge from the sidelines. Rather than focusing on the threats to Cooke City or the Clark's Fork Wild and Scenic River, these groups began emphasizing the threats to Yellowstone, a name much more familiar to most Americans than the other two. The groups also began to exploit the fact that Noranda was not an American company, by stating that it would not be the American public that would benefit from the mine. In so doing, they began framing the issue so it was more compelling to most Americans, as a classic good guy versus bad guy issue: a large and foreign invader threatening a national treasure. Yellowstone staff, still working with the activists behind the scenes, also suggested that the groups look into whether the mine threatened Yellowstone's status as a World Heritage Site—places that are of universal natural or human value, formally designated as such by the United Nations Educational, Scientific and Cultural Organization (UNESCO). If it did, Noranda's threat could be framed as a global one, to all humanity.[48]

The mining issue soon received national recognition from the conservation press. Howell Raines, the *New York Times* editorial-page editor, enjoyed fishing in the Yellowstone area and heard about the mine from some of his friends there. On one of his visits, he had lunch with Mike Clark, the new executive director of the GYC. The two not only discussed the mine, but realized they had mutual friends. Enjoying his meal with Clark, Raines promised the support of his influential newspaper. Shortly thereafter, his employee Bob Semple called Clark's employees, Louisa Willcox and Bob Ekey, to put together an editorial. Published on August 29, 1994, Semple's editorial in the *New York Times* began strongly: "A calamity threatens Yellowstone, the crown jewel of the American park system." The editorial continued, "Noranda promises a pollution-proof project. The company says it can pull eight million tons of ore out of the mountain, fill a 77-acre lake 10 stories deep with waste and seal it for eternity. That sort of technological confidence chills the blood."[49] Semple concluded with a call to President Clinton to stop the mine by buying out the mineral claim from Noranda. He reiterated his call for a buyout in another editorial three weeks later. As time would tell, his calls for a buyout—estimated to cost $35 million—were less idealistic than they first appeared.[50]

Still, Noranda Minerals Corporation had the upper hand; it controlled the land where the gold deposit occurred and had the 1872 General Mining Law on its side. Recognizing the growing opposition, however, the company hired media consultants to defend its position. Noranda and its consultants downplayed the threat to Yellowstone, emphasizing that the proposed mine was outside of the park and in a drainage flowing away from the park. Knowing how resonant economic enhancement was to Americans and their politicians, Noranda promoted the economic benefits that the mine would bring to the Cooke City area. Understanding the importance of politics as well, the company urged its shareholders to write their congressional representatives to temper or discard the reforms to the 1872 General Mining Law that Congress was currently considering. All told, the company consistently presented the view that it could develop its mine in a manner that would protect Yellowstone while stimulating the local economy—especially if it could convince politicians to jump on board.[51]

By the end of 1994, it appeared that Noranda's efforts were paying off, if the lack of progress on the General Mining Law reforms was any indication. With the two versions produced by the House and Senate so different from each other and lacking a strong consensus, the congressional conference committee was unable to reconcile the two bills before the November mid-term elections. Those elections turned control of the U.S. House to the Republican Party, which had several members opposed to any mining act reform. Interior Secretary Babbitt realized that the opportunity to reform the law had passed by unsuccessfully.[52] About the same time, Superintendent Bob Barbee left Yellowstone, moving to Alaska to become the NPS regional director. Replacing him was Mike Finley, arriving at Yellowstone from Yosemite National Park, where he had grown accustomed to controversy. Finley had begun his career in Yellowstone many years earlier as a firefighter. He was more outspoken than Barbee, so when the election returns were in, he called Babbitt to request permission to more directly oppose the mine. According to Finley, Babbitt gave him "the longest leash in the world."[53] This change of direction would come to strongly influence the battle against the mine; finally, those in charge of the national treasure most threatened by the mine—an organization more familiar to Americans than the conservationists—could voice their opposition publicly.

Finley was not the only important change of staff in 1994; the GYC also hired a new executive director—Mike Clark, mentioned above. Having worked previously in environmental and social justice issues in the American South and Washington, D.C., Clark brought with him a familiarity with the political workings of the nation's capital that was new to the young group. He had and continued to cultivate an extensive network of friends and colleagues on the East Coast. Later in this battle, he would spend weeks at a time in Washington, D.C., hanging out in the hallways of the Senate, House, and Department of the Interior office buildings, waiting patiently for an opportunity to chat with Babbitt or other congressmen and women, even if only for a minute or two. Politicians became used to seeing him, and eventually they trusted him to provide answers to detailed questions about the mine proposal. Clark eventually developed a close working relationship with Finley as well.[54]

The arrival of Finley and Clark, along with Interior Secretary Babbitt's permission to oppose the mine directly, were timely. Late in 1994, the Gallatin National Forest and State of Montana called a meeting of the many different federal, state, and local agencies (over twenty in total) involved in the EIS to begin working on developing alternatives to be analyzed in the statement. After several delays in getting to this crucial point, the process appeared to be picking up steam.[55]

Public dialogue during the first half of 1995 mirrored that of 1994, but with more intensity. With most state officials in Montana on record supporting the mine, opponents escalated their publicity and lobbying efforts.

Joining the influential *New York Times,* which published another editorial criticizing the mine in March 1995, was the Greater Yellowstone Area's largest newspaper, the *Billings Gazette,* which printed an editorial critical of the mine.[56] Conservationists kept up pressure in the press as well, with American Rivers again designating the Clark's Fork of the Yellowstone River as the country's most endangered river.[57] Lobbying efforts also achieved several successes. In March 1995, new Wyoming governor Jim Geringer became the first Republican to air concerns about the mine. Writing Montana governor Racicot, his position was clear and strong: "I will say unequivocally that operation of the mine and the resultant permanent tailings impoundment must result in zero environmental degradation on the Wyoming side," including Yellowstone Park.[58] Geringer also supported Park County, Wyoming, in its efforts to have its economic concerns fully addressed by the mine. Certainly, the prospective impacts upon Wyoming were becoming an Achilles' heel for Noranda, as well as for Montana.[59] Finally, conservationists reached out for new allies and found an unlikely one—the Montana Snowmobile Association, whose members had enjoyed touring the New World Mine District for years and who feared that the mine would curtail their access to the area. Snowmobilers and environmentalists would not ordinarily be allies, but with a common enemy to fight, they dropped their prejudices and joined forces against Noranda.[60]

Once the winter snows melted, things really began to heat up. The leading concern with the proposal was still the mine's potential effects on water quality, both through probable acid mine drainage and possible tailings pile failure. New testing and modeling of the proposed mine demonstrated that even though its entrance would be in Fisher Creek (away from Yellowstone), the ore body itself was much closer to the surface—as close as 120 feet—of the Miller Creek side (facing Yellowstone). Should the mine be developed, a growing number of scientists feared that springs feeding Miller Creek would be acidified, and thus the streams flowing into Yellowstone. While conclusive proof was still lacking, the writing on the wall was becoming clear. For now, the scientific data regarding mining impacts seemed increasingly applicable to the New World Mine and Yellowstone situation.[61]

Noranda fought back, hiring former Senator Birch Bayh and former Montana governor Tim Babcock to lobby on its behalf. Regarding acid mine drainage, these lobbyists and the company promised that Noranda would restore the 3 miles of Fisher Creek that were already degraded. The company also stated that it planned to move 250,000 tons of inadequately stored acidic rock from earlier mining into its proposed impoundment, thereby improving water quality in Soda Butte Creek, which flowed to Yellowstone after picking up Miller Creek. The impoundment facility would be designed to withstand climatic and seismic activity (greater than anything the area had seen in the last one hundred and fifty years) by using state-of-the-art technologies that had already proven successful elsewhere in the world. If the impoundment somehow did fail, Noranda claimed it would take two years for the tailings to even begin acid drainage—an adequate time to rectify the dam failure, in the company's opinion.[62] To drive home the point that the impoundment would be in Fisher Creek and not endanger the park, Noranda emphatically stated, "Water from our facilities would have to flow uphill to reach Yellowstone."[63] Finally, the company repeated the economic benefits the mine would bring to the community: about $45 million in taxes over the life of the mine and an annual payroll of $7 million or more.[64]

Such claims rang hollow to mine opponents. Not only had Noranda petitioned the State of Montana to downgrade stream quality in the New World Mining District to "industrial," the company had also petitioned the state to double the amount of pollution that mines were allowed to discharge into such streams. To make matters worse, the company then colluded behind closed doors with the state to draft a consent decree to that end. It was only after the GYC had filed another lawsuit (against the State of Montana alleging violations of the state's open government law) that the state backed down from issuing the decree. In researching Noranda's past environmental records, mine opponents also found numerous violations at its facilities elsewhere in North America, including at two existing mines in Montana. In what seemed to be a pattern, Noranda also underplayed the fact that the percentage of acid-producing sulfides in the New World Mine ore body was many times that of typical gold-bearing ores—in fact, up to twenty-five times higher than the typical amount. All told, Noranda's track record in this and other locations gave mine opponents plenty of reason to doubt the company's assertions, plenty of fodder for public criticism, and plenty of material to make portraying Noranda as the bad guy easy.[65]

Finally stepping out from the sidelines, Yellowstone park managers began to assume a leadership role against the mine, alongside the GYC. Superintendent Finley sparred openly with the two agencies directing the EIS, asserting that they were unresponsive to Yellowstone's concerns. Finley had good reason for his actions, as officials at both agencies had recently been quoted downplaying the risks of the mine to Yellowstone. USFS regional forester Hal Salwasser dismissed concerns that the mine could harm the park as "nonsense," echoing the pervasive attitude of Gallatin National Forest staff (particularly its geologist, Sherm Sollid) that the mine should be developed.[66] Others agreed, including Mike DaSilva, an environmental impact specialist assisting the State of Montana in preparing the EIS. DaSilva stated, "I doubt there would be much impact at all on Yellowstone National Park."[67] Such remarks made Mike Finley believe that these officials had already made up their minds, and that the EIS would not seriously examine the mine's impacts on Yellowstone. Finley responded by sharply criticizing the EIS's lack of depth, comprehensiveness, and range of alternatives, and publicly asked: "How can the logical mind approve this?"[68] Not finding allies in the USFS or the State of Montana, he turned to his colleagues in the Geologic Resources Division in Denver to examine the potential of a mine buyout (thus, possibly doing an end run around the two permitting agencies). They estimated it would cost less than $50 million to adequately reimburse Noranda. While that figure was within the realm of possibility given contemporary federal government spending, it was still a large sum. Finley would need the best scientific data and the most powerful political allies to make the buyout happen—and it would not be long before he would have the support of both.[69]

Events reached a crescendo late in the summer of 1995, as mine opponents enjoyed three major victories, each about a month apart. First was President Clinton's visit in August, signaling the arrival of powerful political support. Second was a decision by the World Heritage Committee to place Yellowstone on its list of World Heritage Sites in danger. The third victory was a judicial decision on the CWA lawsuit. These events made 1995 the turning point in the battle against the New World Mine; the stories of how each came about follow.

The president had first learned of the New World Mine earlier that summer, at a town meeting he had held in Billings, Montana. There, Cooke City resident Sue Glidden asked him about the mine and invited him for a tour of the mining district. Clinton did not immediately accept the invitation, but did express concern about the mine and stated that "no amount of gain that could come from it could possibly offset any permanent damage to Yellowstone."[70] Once the president's plans for his Jackson Hole vacation in August firmed up, the *New York Times* printed two more editorials, calling for him to tour the mine site. After he arrived in Jackson Hole, the local press took the torch from the *New York Times* and continued to urge Clinton to take the tour. Bob Ekey, communications director for the GYC, led the local efforts, staying at the same hotel as many of the press members who were following Clinton's visit and taking the liberty of sliding daily press releases about the mine under their hotel room doors. Many press members followed up with requests for more information.[71]

His curiosity piqued, Clinton did finally tour the New World Mine District by helicopter with Superintendent Finley. Following the green ribbons of willows that were thriving alongside Miller and Fisher creeks (the area having begun to heal from the earlier mining), Finley told Clinton that acid mine drainage from the mine would turn those streams back into orange stripes of acid water, if they weren't buried by massive piles of tailings. Dodging summer thunderstorms, Clinton's helicopter turned back toward Yellowstone and landed in nearby Lamar Valley where Clinton met with area conservationists, including Mike Clark.[72] Persuaded that there was indeed a serious threat present, Clinton announced a two-year withdrawal of 4,500 federal land acres in the New World Mining District from new mining claims. The ban had a two-fold message: the EIS needed to be more detailed and exhaustive and Noranda Minerals Corporation needed to take the New World Mine's threat to Yellowstone National Park more seriously. Promising that he was "going to take care of this," Clinton then left and returned to Jackson Hole.[73]

Noranda, however, took away a different message from the president's announcement. Before the federal government could finalize Clinton's announcement with publication of the temporary withdrawal in the *Federal Register*, Noranda filed thirty-eight new claims on the very land Clinton had proposed withdrawing. Even though this circumvention was clearly a hostile response to the president (see figure 21 for a "pointed" view of Noranda's action in a local newspaper), Noranda probably felt that Congress's failure to reform the General Mining Law meant it still had the upper hand and would get its mine, even if it had to wait an extra year or two. The move, though, was a serious tactical mistake, for it galvanized mine opponents to make the buyout happen like few other actions. It was easier than ever to portray Noranda as the bad guy, audacious enough to play hardball with the president himself. Within a year, the company would find that Clinton also knew how to play that game.[74]

Clinton's visit was barely old news before the press had another reason to highlight the mine's threat to Yellowstone. Following up on the suggestion from Yellowstone staff, mine opponents had researched the potential for declaring the Yellowstone World Heritage Site as endangered. Corresponding

FIGURE 21: One opinion of the claims filed by the Noranda company after President Clinton's announcement of the withdrawal of these lands from mining, printed in the *Jackson Hole News and Guide*. Drawing by cartoonist P. W. Jim. Used with permission.

with a consortium of fourteen environmental organizations (most of the major national groups, as well as the GYC and Beartooth Alliance) throughout 1995, Dr. Adul Wichiencharoen, chairman of the World Heritage Committee, agreed to send a delegation to Yellowstone to investigate the threat posed by the mine. Formally invited by Department of the Interior assistant secretary for Fish, Wildlife and Parks, George T. Frampton, the four-member delegation joined NPS representatives, key conservationists, and mine personnel on a tour of the New World Mining District and Yellowstone for three days in September 1995.[75]

The committee members arrived in Yellowstone to find a letter signed by thirty-five prominent Americans urging them to consider the threats to Yellowstone seriously. Signatories to this letter included former president Jimmy Carter, actors Robert Redford and Harrison Ford, philanthropist Laurance Rockefeller, conservationist David Brower, and wilderness historian Roderick Nash. Persuaded by that letter, their mine-site tour, and the discussions in Yellowstone, the delegation reported to the World Heritage Committee at its annual convention in Berlin, Germany, in December, with a recommendation that Yellowstone be placed on the endangered list. The committee in turn accepted the recommendation, declaring Yellowstone endangered based upon "ascertained . . . and potential dangers."[76]

Reaction to the World Heritage Committee's announcement was mixed. Mine opponents found it a bittersweet victory—good for their cause, but unfortunate given the magnitude of the environmental threats to Yellowstone.[77] Noranda president Joseph Baylis responded by reiterating the company's theme: the proposed mine "has not, does not, and will not in any way threaten Yellowstone."[78] Others, like Montana senator Conrad Burns, reacted more negatively, criticizing the United Nations (UN) and "extreme environmentalists" for attempting to kill the mine.[79] Burns's reaction was tame compared to that from groups like the American Policy Center, a nonprofit foundation dedicated to the "promotion of free enterprise and limited government regulations over commerce and individuals," and Alaska congressman Don Young.[80] Fearing the UN was assuming management authority over Yellowstone from the U.S. federal government, Young introduced a bill into the next several sessions of Congress called the American Lands Sovereignty Act, which would have eliminated World Heritage Site designations except when specifically approved by Congress.[81] NPS staff in Yellowstone and Washington, D.C., reassured the public that the World Heritage Committee's designation was only symbolic and that the U.S. federal government retained exclusive jurisdiction over Yellowstone and all other World Heritage Sites in the country. More significantly, Superintendent Finley quickly learned not to advertise the endangered designation too widely or strongly, to avoid triggering a reaction that would backfire against his cause.[82] Conservationists, because they were not in the position of defending Yellowstone autonomy, continued to use the endangered-site designation, generally to their advantage. Therefore, through the conservationists, the NPS as their ally could indirectly use the designation to frame Noranda not just as a neighborhood bully, but as a threat to an international treasure.

The third and final victory, like Clinton's interest, would prove to have an immense influence over the controversy's outcome. On October 13, 1995, Judge Jack Shanstrom of the U.S. District Court in Billings, Montana, ruled in favor of the GYC and Beartooth Alliance in their CWA lawsuit against Noranda. Shanstrom found that local streams were indeed being degraded by discharge from three preexisting mines; that the discharges were covered under the CWA; and that Noranda had failed to obtain the proper permits for such discharges. He noted that Noranda had stated more than once that the pollutants in the streams were not entirely natural but in part caused by previous mines. Using words the mine opponents relished, Judge Shanstrom concluded, "This Court finds defendants liable for violations of the CWA for discharges occurring at New World."[83] He also ruled that the tiers of Noranda corporate subsidiaries did not confer legal and financial immunity upon the higher-level companies. Those with deep pockets were responsible and would have to pay up to $25,000 per day per adit. Noranda appealed but lost again, making it liable for as much as $135 million in civil penalties (the exact amount was not determined at the time of Shanstrom's judgment).[84]

Mine opponents rejoiced, not expecting their legal action to be this decisive. Now they had most policy-making determinants on their side, with the most powerful one, political support, also looking likely. They had a strong coalition opposed to the mine; the international threat posed by Noranda made the company look like a real villain; the mine threatened both recreation access and local economies; the scientific data regarding mine impacts was increasingly clear and helped provide the foundation for the legal decision; and President Clinton's strong interest in the issue indicated high-level political support. Realizing how much the playing field had changed, Mike Clark said, "We've got them on the run."[85] Much work remained to be done, but Noranda was probably going to be more receptive to a buyout.

Discussions of a buyout faded into the background that fall while the draft EIS ground forward. Allowed to review the draft before it went public, Superintendent Finley and his staff found it to be inadequate and pro-mine in tone, which was not surprising given the evident biases of the USFS and State of Montana. For example, the EIS commonly used the word "might" to describe the mine's water quality impacts; Finley felt the word "will" would be more accurate. Park staff feared that the draft EIS would not be the impartial look at the proposed mine that it was supposed to be.[86] In spring of 1996, Finley spoke at the GYC's annual conference and made clear his feelings about the EIS: "The [EIS] product is time- and deadline-driven; it's not quality-driven. I've said it before and I'll say it again, this process is flawed. . . . You deserve a factual analysis and you're not going to get it. It's politically driven . . . ."[87] His remarks, reported throughout the region, were sharply disputed by Montana governor Marc Racicot, a mine supporter to the end. Finley's superiors in the regional NPS office responded by defending him and the agency's position.[88] Clearly, by this time, Finley and his NPS associates were presenting a united front against the mine. Indeed, they were pushing their agency's limits in responding to a threat originating outside the park—more strongly than in virtually any other environmental threat in the late twentieth century.

Superintendent Finley's vocal opposition, along with continued articles in the conservationist press (like that of American Rivers, which again designated the Clark's Fork River of the Yellowstone as the nation's most endangered river for the third year in a row, an unprecedented action for the group), were by now having an influence on public opinion.[89] Several polls in 1996 found strong public opposition to the mine; one poll found that two-thirds of the Cody Country Chamber of Commerce members were opposed to it. Recognizing that it was now safe to show opposition publicly, Senator Craig Thomas, a Wyoming Republican, announced in late July, "Folks have been asking me for more than six months about this thing. There is only so long you can withhold your opinion when in fact you have a strong conviction that this . . . might be the worst place to site a mine. . . . [T]his proposal should never happen."[90] Similarly, the Wyoming legislature passed a law in March 1996 imposing a ten dollar per-ton-fee on any solid waste, including mining waste, stored in the state but created in another. The law was a shot across the bow intended to tell Noranda in no uncertain terms how the State of Wyoming viewed its mine proposal.[91]

Having Wyoming on board against the mine was a big catch for the NPS and its conservationist allies, but the biggest catch still needed some finessing. After Clinton's visit to Yellowstone, Mike Clark, executive director of the GYC, continued lobbying Clinton—through Kathleen McGinty, Clinton's director of the Council on Environmental Quality—to revisit the issue, since the land withdrawal had not succeeded in stopping Noranda from proceeding with its mining proposal. Clark pointed out that not a single elected federal politician in the region criticized Senator Thomas's stance or spoke in favor of the mine. Nor had a single newspaper editorialized in favor of the mine, regionally or nationally. With Yellowstone National Park being such a well-known and beloved place for Americans, Clark was able to persuade McGinty that this was a safe issue on which Clinton could take a stand and to move forward on negotiating a buyout. In so doing, Clinton could boost his reputation among environmentally-conscious voters. With the 1996 elections less than a year away, Clark knew that Clinton needed such a boost, because he had taken few environmentalist stances thus far in his administration.[92]

Clinton's interest remained strong and Noranda's failure in court did indeed make the company receptive to buyout negotiations. Thanks to a belated but strong alliance between conservationists and the NPS; to good issue framing; to concerns about harmed—not enhanced—economies and park access; and to solid scientific research, mine opponents got the strongest of all political allies: President Clinton. In February 1996, Ian Bayer of Noranda and Mike Clark met with McGinty and Ray Clark of the president's Council on Environmental Quality to begin working towards a solution that benefitted everyone. They continued to meet throughout the winter and spring of 1996, focusing on the mine's monetary value, cleanup and restoration of the New World Mining District, and resolution of the CWA lawsuit. In addition, the Clinton Administration formed a special task force to represent the federal government, with officials from the Attorney General's Office, the Department of Agriculture, and the Department of the Interior participating. Discussions proceeded fitfully, although Mike Clark's quiet, businesslike approach and Senator Birch Bayh's influence kept the suite of Noranda mining companies (whom he continued to represent) at the table. By late summer 1996, participants sensed a compromise and engaged in some all-night sessions toward that end.[93]

On August 12, 1996, the discussions culminated with another trip by President Clinton to Jackson Hole and Yellowstone. In a beautiful mountain meadow near Cooke City, Clinton presided over a ceremony at which all parties in the dispute signed an agreement to buy out the mine (figure 22). In his remarks, Clinton explained that he had directed Vice President Al Gore, Kathleen McGinty, and his Cabinet to work toward a resolution, and had followed the discussions personally and closely throughout the winter. As Clinton stated, "[M]illions and millions of people . . . will directly benefit from the decision we announce today. Yellowstone is more precious than gold."[94] Clinton, Ian Bayer of the Noranda companies, and Mike Clark then signed the agreement. In exchange for $65 million in federal government property, Noranda would cease pursuing its mine in the Yellowstone region forever and surrender title to its land there to the federal government. The company would deposit $22.5 million of those funds in an escrow account for cleanup and rehabilitation of the New World Mining District. The GYC agreed to drop the CWA lawsuit. The government pledged not to pursue penalties against Noranda relating to this same lawsuit and agreed to remove Noranda's surrendered land for twenty years from further mineral patenting. All parties promised to work expeditiously within the next year to identify the federal government property to be offered for exchange and to bring the agreement to a final resolution.[95]

The immediate threat of the mine was gone; conservationists and NPS personnel were euphoric. In a statement about the event, Clark wrote: "Beneath the craggy peaks of Yellowstone, we paid tribute on August 12 to one of America's most glorious legacies—the belief that wild places have their own special value in a democracy that looks not just to the present and the past, but into the unknown future."[96] Superintendent Finley remarked that "[the agreement] preserved two sacred cows. We advocated and protected private property rights, and we saved the natural character of our mother park."[97] Beyond the words of reflection and recognition, it was clear that conservationists and the NPS had formed a mutually supportive coalition, one that did not suffer from the absence of the USFS. The coalition had

FIGURE 22: President Bill Clinton celebrating the buyout of the New World Mine, 1996. After visiting Yellowstone in 1995 and touring the mine site, Clinton and his staff worked diligently to arrange a buyout of the mine. Clinton returned a year later to celebrate the agreement. To Clinton's right is Mike Clark, of the Greater Yellowstone Coalition; at his left, Kathleen McGinty, director of the Council on Environmental Quality; and at her left, Alex Balogh, of Noranda Minerals Corporation. In the background is Superintendent Mike Finley. NPS photo.

brilliantly played Noranda's Canadian origin and the company's suspicious actions against Yellowstone's sanctity and renown, toward their own goals. They had worked tirelessly to assemble research findings to support their cause. They had clearly demonstrated the potential harm to local economies and public access. Perhaps most importantly, they had garnered political ally after political ally, eventually culminating in the support of the president himself. No wonder they won—and, as would become evident, of all the issues Yellowstone managers have dealt with in the last thirty years, their victory in the mining controversy was almost unilateral and the outcome went the farthest in protecting Yellowstone's integrity.

Learning from the events of the year before, the federal government moved quickly to withdraw the New World Mining District from further patenting or mineral purchase. Again, this land withdrawal was only valid for twenty years, a worrisome compromise that mine opponents would not forget. For now, they accepted it as a way to buy the time needed to work out the federal property transfer and a more permanent mineral withdrawal.[98]

Identifying the $65 million in federal government properties for the exchange with Noranda proceeded in fits and starts. Efforts to get the money by selling federal property quickly became controversial, so the Clinton Administration abandoned the idea. Efforts to use royalties that the federal government collects from coal, oil, and gas leasing in Montana (the federal government does collect royalties on those forms of resource extraction) also became controversial, so that idea too was tossed. Casting about for other solutions, the Clinton Administration next proposed tapping into the Land and Water Conservation Fund (LWCF), which uses royalties from off-shore oil and gas drilling to fund conservation and land acquisition in the Unites States. The Senate approved the LWCF funding for the buyout, but it stalled in the House because House Republicans felt that the president should not tell them how to spend LWCF funds. However, Representative Rick Hill, a Republican from Montana, introduced House legislation that he hoped would allay some of his colleagues' concerns, with provisions for a $12 million reconstruction of part of the Beartooth Highway and a $10 million transfer of federal coal properties to the State of Montana.[99]

These provisions helped, but one snag remained: Margaret Reeb, a retired schoolteacher, still owned 30 to 60 percent of the recoverable gold in the New World Mining District. She had leased her property to Noranda to mine the gold, but was not included in the buyout agreement and was understandably displeased with it. Noranda Minerals Corporation had been unable to work out an arrangement with her. Zeroing in on this last hurdle, Representative Hill, Noranda, and Reeb agreed to put a conservation easement on her land while retaining the title in her name. Hill also included a provision allowing future mining on Reeb's land subject to approval by Reeb, Congress, and the president. With this last issue settled, the House passed the bill in September and Clinton signed it into law on November 14, 1997.[100]

Resolution of the twenty-year mineral-withdrawal deadline took a different twist. Reeb, who died in 2005, believed to her final days that the lands she owned should have been mined. Her heirs felt differently and, three years later, worked out a deal with the Trust for Public Land and the USFS whereby the USFS agreed to keep the land undeveloped in exchange for $8 million in cash paid to the heirs.[101] With that, the New World Mine issue was put to bed. Full protection against the mine was achieved, without any compromise to Yellowstone's integrity. The gold remains underground; aboveground, the formerly toxic streams flowing from the New World Mining District into Yellowstone have been restored (figure 23). Happily, in this case, politicians of all stripes—persuaded by the NPS and its allies that the mine would have had unacceptable impacts on the park— banded together to protect the park known as Wonderland.

Reflections

Why were park managers so successful in this case? In a word, because all the policy-making stars were powerfully aligned. Every single one of the major contemporary policy-making determinants went in favor of the NPS: the scientific research was completed, easy to understand, and supported mine opponents' intentions; politicians expressed not just ambivalence but actual support for the mine opponents; the issue could be and was compellingly framed; the environmental community offered an intimate and powerful alliance with park managers (if covertly in the controversy's earlier years); defeating the mine protected existing public access; and, similarly, defeating the mine did more to protect the regional economy than approving the mining project would have. This policy-making endeavor was a slam dunk for the NPS.

By reviewing the role of each determinant in more detail we find that environmentalists led the fight against the mine from the beginning;

FIGURE 23: Henderson Mountain reclamation site, 2011. The New World Mine would have been located under this mountain, the site of mining in the early 1900s. Part of the 1996 agreement required Noranda to reclaim the damage from the earlier mining. Shown is the mountain in 2011, with extensive reclamation underway or complete. Author photo.

without their leadership, mine opponents would never have succeeded. This battle, in fact, was such an endeavor and a success for the GYC that it became the defining moment for the coalition, transforming it from a local group few had heard of into *the* regional environmental group, the "Sierra Club" of Yellowstone in the way that that group has been for Yosemite National Park in California. NPS leaders and Yellowstone park managers eventually stood beside the conservationists, but they never stepped out in front as the policy-making leader; their coalition with the environmental community, one that was hidden from public view initially, became more obvious after 1994. That coalition was crucial to the controversy's outcome; given NPS's political reality (being constrained from expressing direct opposition early on), the mine could have become reality without such a powerful coalition (particularly since both permitting agencies so clearly favored the mine).[102]

Coalitions rest their strength as much on the charisma of the key personalities at their helms, as they do on their member groups. In this case, Mike Clark and Mike Finley deserve substantial credit for leading their coalition to victory. Superintendent Finley had the guts to stick his neck out (granted, he enjoyed a favorable political climate for doing so) much more than his predecessor. He also enjoyed an unusual ability to work directly with Interior Secretary Bruce Babbitt, stating later: "I conspired with the Secretary a lot. . . . And that's something that happens in Yellowstone and Yosemite and some of the bigger parks, where you can have the direct relationship with the Secretary."[103] His willingness to stick his neck out and ability to work directly with powerful players helped the public and regional politicians both see that it was not just the liberal environmentalists fearing the mine and its impacts on Yellowstone; the normally staid agency in charge of Yellowstone, the NPS, was strongly opposed to it as well. On the conservation side was Mike Clark, executive director of the GYC, who brought Finley's adeptness at working within political circles to the conservation community. Finley minced no words in describing Clark's influence: "Mike Clark, the former director of the Greater Yellowstone Coalition, is probably one of the most prominent leaders in terms of protecting Yellowstone."[104] Without the vision and political savvy of Finley and Clark, this mining controversy might well have had a different outcome.

Indeed, of all the controversies described in this book, this one was perhaps most influenced by two key individuals, thus raising the question of whether such key personalities are a seventh major determinant of contemporary NPS policy making. Key personalities are indeed important, but their policy-making influence is generally covered by the "politics determinant," because most are elected or appointed politicians. For example, in this controversy Bill Clinton and Interior Secretary Babbitt created the supportive political atmosphere that encouraged Finley to advance his bold agenda. Similarly, the Fishing Bridge Village debate had Senator Alan Simpson playing the dominant role, and in the fire policy debate Superintendent Bob Barbee and Interior Secretary Donald Hodel played the key roles. Because all key personalities are elected or appointed officials, or park superintendents taking their cue from such officials, it is clear that the influence on policy making from such key persons is attributable to the country's current political climate and the political construction of the NPS.

Also important to the mine opponents' success was the ready ability to frame the issue as being the good guys (Yellowstone National Park and its defenders) versus the bad guys (Noranda Minerals Corporation), or the treasured icon threatened by the evil foreign corporation.[105] Noranda seemed unable to understand the power of such imagery, instead providing a concrete example of itself as a bad guy when it intentionally subverted President Clinton after his mineral withdrawal. By framing the issue in such a way, and by pointing out the vote-acquiring advantages in opposing the mine, the anti-mine coalition was able to get widespread public support and eventually the support of the president.

Research and monitoring data played an important role in the mining controversy as well. Already established was the research regarding the effects of acid mine drainage on streams and aquatic life. Applying it to the New World Mine situation took some time and effort, but was still effective, helping to win the CWA lawsuit and thereby making Noranda willing to compromise. Moreover, the scientific data was easy to understand and summarize in yes-or-no questions: is past mining degrading streams and is Noranda responsible for that? The answers were yes and yes. While research proving that the mine would have contaminated the very streams flowing toward Yellowstone was not complete at the time of the controversy—research did confirm this link two years later—participants in the debate knew that it was almost certain to happen. It was known that even though Miller Creek would not be disturbed on the surface, the springs feeding it would be affected by the underground mining. Consequently, mine opponents essentially had a third yes-or-no question being answered in the affirmative: development of the mine would impair Yellowstone's waters. Even without that affirmative scientific link, the research base was still pivotal in the lawsuit's outcome.[106]

Politicians were probably *the* most powerful influence at play in the New World Mine controversy. For the NPS, critical to obtaining political support was demonstrating that the mine would have harmed the Wyoming economy. Gradually, Wyoming's politicians—who typically would have favored a mine like this—came to oppose the mine. Such opposition seemed to outweigh Montana's support of the mine (which would have stimulated that state's economy). The fact that development of the mine would have threatened snowmobile access to a favorite recreation area also helped NPS's cause.[107] What carried the day, in the end, was the personal and ongoing interest of President Clinton. With that support, the controversy wound its way toward a relatively fast resolution in 1996.

Politics also heavily influenced the role of NPS in the mining issue.

Located in a department with a presidentially appointed executive, the agency was initially constrained against a direct role in the battle. Superintendent Finley bristled under such muzzling and, after he retired, lamented the agency's weakness: "The NPS has disappointed me many times in its decision not to protect park resources and in its lack of vision. That's just the nature of bureaucracy and the changes in personality and leadership, or lack of it, in the organization."[108] Once he had the political climate necessary to express his vision, Finley was able to parlay NPS's political vulnerability into a successful movement against the mine. While he could celebrate the mine's defeat with conservationists, Finley and others knew that the political climate could—and would—change, making it more difficult for them to use the park's political vulnerability to their advantage in the future. Such is the nature of American politics: the pendulum swings back and forth over time, subjecting park protection to the vicissitudes of American voters and political appointees.

In 1996, the policy-making determinant stars were aligned, with the brightest one being the contemporary political climate. Had that particular star not been as bright, the mining issue would likely have seen a very different outcome. By 1998 the scientific link between mine development and its actual impacts upon Yellowstone was firmly established, but it is highly unlikely that Clinton's successor in the White House would have taken the same anti-mining stance. A good indication of how the George W. Bush Administration would have approached the mine can be taken from the actions of Julie MacDonald, deputy assistant secretary for Fish, Wildlife and Parks in the Department of the Interior under Bush: she eventually had to resign due to her manipulations of research findings to advance the Bush Administration's political agenda. In one flagrant example, MacDonald removed key elements of a FWS report about whether the sage grouse should be placed on the endangered list of the Endangered Species Act (the listing would have likely limited oil and gas exploration in the grouses' habitat); the passages she removed supported such a listing. MacDonald did not care what the scientific data stated; rather, it was the political agenda that she shared with President Bush that mattered to her.[109] Thus, had the New World Mine controversy been negotiated under the Bush administration, it is likely that the scientific research relating to the New World Mine would have been similarly ignored, and Yellowstone would have gained a large mine for a neighbor. Ultimately, then, scientific research and data, as powerful as it can be in NPS policy making, can take a back seat to politics.

Politics is the world of compromise and so, not surprisingly, the New World Mine controversy initially seemed to end in compromise (mainly, the twenty-year mineral withdrawal limitation). Like park managers in the Fishing Bridge Village issue, though, park managers and other opponents of the mine project were able to revise the compromise later, to further protect park resources. Happily, withdrawing the mineral lands from permanent leasing after Margaret Reeb died was a far stronger modification of the compromise than simple cleanup of the former Fishing Bridge campground. The permanent mineral-land withdrawal effectively changed the initial compromise to a clear policy victory, for there will not be a New World Mine, or negative mining impacts, upon Yellowstone National Park for the foreseeable future.

Such political impermanence is evident in the remaining three controversies in Yellowstone in the contemporary policy-making era: wolf reintroduction, snowmobiles, and bison management. All of these bear the imprint of politics, as well as that of science, issue framing, implications for public access and local economies, and varying power of coalitions interested in the issue. The following chapter covers all three of these controversies and the relative contributions of each of these policy determinants.

Chapter Four

Wolves, Bison, and Snowmobiles

Facts mattered, but political power mattered more.
—Hank Fischer, on the reintroduction of wolves

The roller coaster that snowmobiling in Yellowstone has
become epitomizes the dangers of political decision making. . . .
—Hillary Prugh, on the recent history of the snowmobile controversy

We are participating in something that is totally unpalatable to
the American people, and it's something we are not convinced
that science justifies . . . . [These bison are] political hostages.
—Mike Finley, referring to the bison test and slaughter program

DURING THE CONTEMPORARY POLICY-MAKING ERA IN YELLOWSTONE, in addition to Fishing Bridge Village, the fire policy review, and the New World Mine, the park's managers were dealing with three other major controversies: whether to return gray wolves to Yellowstone, whether visitors should be allowed to tour Yellowstone by snowmobile, and how to manage brucellosis-infected bison when they leave the park in winter. Each of these

---

issues dated back many years, but grew throughout the 1980s and 1990s into major policy-making issues. All reached their peak, in one way or another, in the 1990s and 2000s. Park managers succeeded in returning the gray wolf to Yellowstone in 1995; they began the first environmental impact statement (EIS) on winter snowmobile use in the late 1990s; and they completed another EIS on bison management at the same time, with a tentative solution reached in 2011. Given the contentious nature of each of these issues (evident in the quotes on the previous page), the late 1990s and early 2000s were intense policy-making times for Yellowstone managers; stretched thin between the different controversies, park managers deserve credit for achieving any success on these different fronts.[1]

As with the issues discussed in the previous chapters, these three involved substantial public discussion, scientific debate, and national political interest. Although they all reached a climax during the contemporary policy-making era, all three controversies continue today, ranking in the top ten of the National Park Service's (NPS) nationally important issues. For these reasons (and because they involve Yellowstone policies), an examination of each is necessary to complete the controlled comparison in this study; they round out the suite of major policy-making controversies that have occurred in Yellowstone since 1981. Most important, each provides additional insight into the roles of the differing policy determinants in NPS policy making in the modern era.

Each of the aforementioned issues has inspired at least one book-length publication, while wolf recovery and management has been featured in several books.[2] With this available scholarship, there is no need to retell the full stories of how the NPS was able to bring wolves back, or how snowmobiles came to be in Yellowstone, or why the NPS has prevented bison from leaving the park in winter. Instead, brief overviews of the controversies will be presented and the six major policy determinants and their role in each controversy will be thoroughly discussed. Four of the determinants will be discussed in pairs: coalitions and issue framing (because interest groups are often pivotal in framing the issue for the public); and the implications of public access and economies (because these two generally go hand-in-hand). The other two, science and politics, will be discussed separately. For each policy determinant, vignettes from the past thirty years, illustrating the major role of that determinant in the controversy, will be presented. As in earlier cases, the three subjects (wolf reintroduction, snowmobiling in winter, and brucellosis-infected bison) will reveal that NPS policy-making controversies are mainly settled by the interplay of the six determinants outlined in this book, with science and politics being the most influential. Of those two, the contemporary political situation will once again carry the most influence.

Wolf Reintroduction

On January 12, 1995, a truck pulling a horse trailer loaded with fourteen gray wolves passed through the Roosevelt Arch in Gardiner, Montana (figure 24). Children from the nearby school, along with wolf-reintroduction proponents, stood on the roadside to witness the historic event: after nearly two decades of paperwork and politicking, the NPS and U.S. Fish and Wildlife Service (FWS) were finally reintroducing the wolf to Yellowstone National Park. From Gardiner, the wolves were taken to several large acclimation pens, where they were held for several months before being released into the wild. Since then, wolves have been successfully reestablished in Yellowstone and the surrounding area.[3]

Historically, gray wolves have always been present in the Yellowstone area. Elk were likely their dominant prey, with moose, deer, sheep, and bison being other prey animals. In one of the NPS's first actions upon taking over Yellowstone's management from the U.S. Army in 1918, the early park rangers eliminated the animal from the park. Wolf numbers had already been reduced by that time, due to poisoning by area ranchers and occasional shootings by Army scouts. NPS managers were replicating the actions of federal and state authorities who were eliminating wolves from throughout the country at the time, because it was believed that the absence of these predators would protect native ungulates like elk and deer. By 1930, wolves were gone from Yellowstone—and within a decade, park managers had begun controlling surplus ungulate populations.[4]

Over the next four decades, public perceptions of wolves gradually shifted. No longer did everyone view the wolf as Little Red Riding Hood's nemesis; instead, they began to see the wolf as a part of the natural landscape and an appropriate creature to protect in some places. Passage of the Endangered Species Act in 1973 cemented this new perception into law, with the wolf being one of the first animals placed on the endangered list. Sensing that the time had come to reconsider predator elimination from places like Yellowstone, park managers gradually began discussing a wolf-reintroduction effort, in

FIGURE 24: Wolves arriving back into Yellowstone, 1995. In January 1995, the National Park Service and U.S. Fish and Wildlife Service reintroduced the wolf to Yellowstone National Park, where the animal had once roamed (until eliminated in the 1920s). Trapped and then translocated from western Canada (where the same subspecies occurs and preys upon the same animals found at Yellowstone), the wolves were flown and then hauled in crates in this horse trailer to their new homes. Held in acclimation pens for a couple months, they were released into the Yellowstone wildlands in March 1995. NPS photo.

the 1970s. The first to push this idea was Dr. John Weaver, the author of a pivotal 1978 study that found a lack of breeding wolves present in Yellowstone. Weaver concluded his study with a recommendation to the NPS to reintroduce the animal to the park.[5]

The actual reintroduction took seventeen more years to accomplish. The movement gathered steam when William Penn Mott assumed the NPS directorship under President Reagan, in 1985. Mott was an ardent torchbearer for reintroduction, repeatedly promoting the idea despite considerable opposition from the congressional delegations of Wyoming, Montana, and Idaho. Mott's efforts began to pay off in 1989, the same year he left the agency, when Congress appropriated $175,000 to study the potential effects of wolf reintroduction on big game animals and grizzly bears in Yellowstone, as well as on livestock and the economy in towns near the park. Entitled *Wolves for Yellowstone?*, the study essentially answered the question posed in the title: yes, return wolves to Yellowstone.[6]

Congress followed up on the studies in late 1992, when it appropriated about $350,000 to the FWS—the agency responsible for the stewardship of threatened and endangered species and with whom the NPS worked very closely on this effort—to draft an EIS examining several different reintroduction options. Completed two years later, the EIS, written by the NPS and FWS (hereafter, "the agencies"), concluded that the wolf should be reintroduced as an "experimental-nonessential" population. This designation would allow wolf reintroduction to proceed, but ranchers would be able to kill wolves they witnessed preying on their livestock outside the park. Were wolves to reestablish themselves naturally—as they were doing at that time in Glacier National Park, just a few days walk for a wolf from Yellowstone— then they would enjoy the full protection of the Endangered Species Act and ranchers would not be able to kill depredating wolves. Seeing that wolves were coming one way or another to the park, some politicians by this time had become resigned to wolf reintroduction under the experimental-nonessential designation. Taking advantage of that sentiment, Interior Secretary Bruce Babbitt approved the reintroduction plan stated in the EIS and then helped resolve last minute legal action from ranching advocates attempting to prevent wolf reintroduction. In January 1995, Babbitt traveled to Yellowstone to celebrate success and to participate in the reintroduction, by helping move the crates with the wolves inside to their new homes.[7]

Since then, wolves have firmly reestablished themselves in the park. Without competition from other wolves, but with an abundant prey base, their population grew quickly, averaging 17 percent annual growth in the first few years. By 2002 wolves met the criteria for removal from the endangered species list: ten packs of wolves had each bred successfully for three years in a row. Since then, wolf populations in the Yellowstone area have averaged over three hundred, with one hundred and fifty to two hundred present in the park itself. They were delisted in 2008 for a few months; however, legal action soon put them back on the endangered list, but Congress—fed up with endless litigation about wolves—took the wolf off the list once again in 2011 (except in Wyoming, which has not been able to issue a wolf management plan acceptable to the FWS). Management of wolves outside of Yellowstone, including allowing the hunting of wolves, is now a state responsibility, except in Wyoming.[8]

Debate, heated at times, continues to this day about wolves and their management.[9] The focal points have changed somewhat since reintroduction, but fundamentally the debate still involves questions about the animal's appropriateness in Yellowstone and its effects on livestock, wildlife, and the local economy. The following discussion will focus on the debate over these issues in reference to the proposed, and ultimately successful, reintroduction of wolves to Yellowstone in 1995.

Coalitions and Issue Framing

A decade before his agency actually brought wolves back, Yellowstone superintendent Bob Barbee knew the NPS would need a strong coalition of wolf proponents to make reintroduction a reality. Sharing that thought in 1984 with Hank Fischer, the field representative of the national conservation organization Defenders of Wildlife, Barbee planted the seeds of what would become a strong, long-lasting coalition. By the time wolves were reintroduced, virtually every conservation group that focused on national parks or wildlife was a part of the reintroduction coalition, with Defenders of Wildlife leading the way. Beyond just engaging in many of the lobbying and public engagement activities typical of conservation groups, the Defenders of Wildlife took an important step by actually putting together a $100,000 fund to compensate ranchers who lost livestock to wolves. Therefore, not only did the conservation community ally itself with the federal agencies sponsoring wolf reintroduction, but some members took a far stronger step: putting their money where their mouth was.[10]

The wolf-reintroduction coalition did not stop with conservation groups. The FWS, tightly allied with the NPS, took the lead on the reintroduction EIS, devoted as much staff time to the issue as the NPS, and gathered some 160,000 public comments on the issue (the great majority of which were in support of wolf reintroduction). Complementing both agencies was the scientific community, which was as supportive of wolf reintroduction as it was in the NPS's effort to continue allowing prescribed natural fires to burn in the park. Allied with three kinds of groups—like-minded federal agencies, conservationists, and scientists—Yellowstone's managers enjoyed robust support for their proposal. Indeed, these are three of the four kinds of external groups NPS typically partners with, indicating the strength of the coalition. Gateway (or local) communities and businesses are the fourth common ally; while some business owners did indeed support wolf reintroduction, their support was not as robust as that from the other three groups, and no community came out officially in favor of reintroduction.[11]

As noted previously, it is often the external partners who develop the most compelling framing in a policy controversy. In this case, scientists provided the most resonant framing. L. David Mech, the country's foremost authority on wolves, summed up the Yellowstone reintroduction issue this way:

> Yellowstone Park is a place that literally begs to have wolves. It's teeming with prey; it used to have wolves, and all the species that were there originally should be restored. Wolves would add an element to the ecosystem that would restore it to a more natural state, that would allow the public to better enjoy the park. The only thing missing in Yellowstone is the wolf, and the park can't really be wild without it. It's not a complete or natural wilderness to have all the species of prey that are there and not have the main predator they evolved with.[12]

Conservationists and the agencies took their cue from Mech and consistently framed the wolf as the pinnacle of "wildness"—the key ingredient needed to make Yellowstone whole and completely wild again. Yellowstone was indeed one of the wildest places remaining in the country outside of Alaska, with every animal species that had historically been present still there—but one. Thus, without the wolf, the place could not be whole or truly wild. Hank Fischer perhaps said it best: "The [Yellowstone] wildlife spectacle is as close as this hemisphere comes to Tanzania's Serengeti, but there's a significant flaw: its most significant predator—the gray wolf—has been missing for most of the twentieth century. Would the African plains be the same without the lion?"[13] Clearly such framing meant that one and only one animal could bring wholeness back to Yellowstone: the gray wolf.

Such imaging took advantage of a groundswell of public attention increasingly being paid to wilderness in general and to wolves in particular. In the 1980s, alarmed at the onslaught of attacks on federal land protection during the Reagan Administration, Americans joined conservation groups in droves. Two films debuted during this period that drew specific attention to wolves: *Never Cry Wolf* (1983) and *Dances with Wolves* (1990). The latter, in particular, was wildly popular and certainly helped predispose many Americans toward favoring wolf reintroduction in Yellowstone.[14]

In a political climate that was not quite ready for wolves to be returned anywhere in the country, compelling framing was crucial in galvanizing popular support for recovery. Ultimately, as we have seen, the wolf framing was indeed successful. As Fischer explained, "On March 21, 1995, Park Service biologists began releasing the wolves from their pens. The metal gates swung open, and Yellowstone Park was on the road to being whole once more."[15] The framing of "wildness" and the wolf returning to the park continued to resonate years later, as evidenced by the title that Yellowstone wolf biologist Douglas Smith chose for his 2005 book: *Decade of the Wolf: Returning the Wild to Yellowstone*. Similarly, by the late 1990s, visitor surveys revealed that seeing wolves and bears had displaced seeing the park's famous thermal features as the number one reason people came to Yellowstone. The pinnacle of wildness was back in the country's grandest wilderness preserve; biologists were celebrating and visitors were enjoying the spectacle.[16]

That image of enduring nature and wildness indicates both the resonance of this framing device and its power. Of all the policy-making controversies discussed in this book, the issue-framing determinant probably played the most pivotal role in wolf reintroduction. Framing the wolf as the key ingredient needed to restore a complete and wild ecosystem in Yellowstone galvanized thousands of people to express their support for reintroduction; cemented the bond between conservationists, scientists, and the agencies; and provided a compelling vision for the same groups to rally around when reintroduction efforts seemed about to fail. Advocates of wolf recovery used this powerful framing vision to address all public concerns regarding wolves, which in turn helped garner the political support they needed to make reintroduction a reality.

Implications for Public Access and Local Economies

With no explicit threat to motorized vehicle use in Yellowstone (whether snowmobiles, RVs, automobiles, or boats), there was little public concern about wolves diminishing access to the park. Only a few residents of the three affected states expressed their concerns that their ability to reach mines, logging areas, and grazing areas on USFS lands around Yellowstone would be curtailed by wolf-related closures. Such concerns were addressed by the experimental-nonessential designation for wolves, which meant that there would be no public lands closed outside of Yellowstone because of the wolf. Furthermore, even within the park, any closures for wolves would be small and temporary, and probably only around active wolf dens in spring. This has indeed been the pattern in Yellowstone, with no known wolf-related closures outside of the park. For these reasons, worries about restricted public access to Yellowstone played little role in the debate about wolf reintroduction.[17]

However, wolf reintroduction was perceived to be a serious threat to local economies, particularly the ranching component. Wolves do occasionally prey upon livestock, and such losses can be significant to individual ranchers. Reintroduction projections from the early 1990s indicated that increased spending from tourists eager to see wolves would far outweigh livestock losses, but such projections meant little to a rancher already struggling to get by. Moreover, they meant little to the politicians who were sympathetic to area ranchers. Consequently, addressing the ranchers' concerns was critical for wolf-reintroduction proponents.[18]

Hank Fischer realized the pivotal role that fears of economic harm, such as livestock loss, could play in the reintroduction issue. He probably sensed that finding a way to address this issue would advance wolf reintroduction as much as would a solid scientific base. Fischer, however, found that the board of directors of Defenders of Wildlife was reluctant to "put its money where its mouth was" relating to a wolf-depredation compensation program. This changed after the lack of such a compensation program was highlighted, in the negative, when a pack of wolves migrating south from Canada killed ten sheep and five cows near Browning, Montana. Because they were among the first wolves to reestablish themselves in Montana, their actions and subsequent loss to the ranchers garnered extensive negative press. Arguing that the Yellowstone wolf-reintroduction efforts were at risk due to this press, Fischer talked his group into assembling $5,000 to reimburse the ranchers for their losses. In this way, he and Defenders of Wildlife broadcast the message that they were willing to shoulder the economic burden of reintroducing wolves (at least for individual ranchers). This action proved to be successful, for the negative press coverage quickly stopped. Soon thereafter, the Defenders of Wildlife board of directors committed to assembling $100,000 for a permanent livestock-compensation fund.[19]

The organization had the fund in place by 1989, and soon thereafter had another opportunity to demonstrate its value. That year wolves killed two cows and thirteen calves near Kalispell, Montana. Defenders of Wildlife quickly reimbursed the affected ranchers $5,500 for the lost livestock. Between 1995 and 2010, the group paid out $542,426 to ranchers in the Yellowstone area. In 2010, the federal government took over the compensation program (with the states administering it), but Defenders of Wildlife continued to provide assistance to some western states. Consistently, the group has demonstrated its commitment to sharing in the economic pain caused by somewhat incompatible land uses.[20]

Establishment of the compensation fund is widely seen as a turning point in the wolf-reintroduction controversy. For example, Ed Bangs, the FWS employee in charge of the reintroduction effort in the 1980s and early 1990s, stated: "The livestock compensation program certainly made wolves much more tolerable to livestock producers . . . and has made wolf recovery more easily attainable."[21] With the program in place and reasonably used, the agencies were able to quell fears of economic harm by pointing to the fund's successful track record. Moreover, the agencies could then direct attention to a more favorable economic message: wolf reintroduction actually promised potential economic gains. Economists estimated that tourists seeking wolf viewing opportunities would increase the region's economy from $5 million to $19 million annually. Regional livestock losses would be trivial in comparison, at only $30,500 or less annually (but losses to individual ranchers could still be significant). In addition, losses in hunting opportunities would likely amount to only $465,000 or less, and wolf management costs were expected to be less than $320,000 annually (and would be paid for mainly by the federal government). Certainly, wolves promised a net economic benefit—and the worst potential economic harm was now mitigated, thanks to the Defenders of Wildlife livestock-compensation fund.[22]

Such estimates proved to be largely accurate. Visitors today spend an average of $20 million to $35 million per year in their efforts to see wolves at Yellowstone. Direct losses of livestock have also been within the original estimates, though management costs have been substantially more, at around $1.5 million per year. All told, as of 2008, a group of economists found that the net economic benefit of wolf reintroduction was over $30 million per year. Economically, then, wolf reintroduction has been a success.[23]

Science

In 1991, L. David Mech succinctly summarized the scientific opinion about wolf reintroduction for Yellowstone: "Finally, no more research is necessary to restore the Yellowstone wolf."[24] Such a bold statement, from this noted authority on wolves, indicates the strength of the scientific research base assisting the NPS and FWS in justifying their reintroduction efforts.

The amount of research into all aspects of wolf ecology had been growing since the mid-1940s, when Adolph Murie (Olaus Murie's brother, who had suggested closing Fishing Bridge) published the first scholarly account of wolf ecology in Denali National Park in Alaska. By the time Congress issued its wolf-research directive in 1989, wolves and their management were solidly understood. However, Congress wanted to understand what the effects of wolf reintroduction would be to Yellowstone specifically (and given the anti-wolf political climate in 1989, may also have been looking for delaying tactics). The resulting report, *Wolves for Yellowstone?*, concluded that wolves had been in Yellowstone historically; wolves would have a minimal effect on the livestock industry in the three-state area; wolves would not harm the threatened grizzly bear population or the ungulate populations (elk, moose, bison, bighorn sheep, mule deer, white-tailed deer, and pronghorn) in the area; and finally, wolves would benefit the gateway (or local) economies. When reminiscing on the report, Hank Fischer summarized its implications stating: "Although the report's conclusions may not have been earth-shattering, the *Wolves for Yellowstone?* studies played an essential role in public education and laid the foundation for a rock-solid EIS."[25] Clearly, the scientific research base supported wolf reintroduction to the park.

Once the EIS and associated reintroduction plan were underway, scientists again weighed in. Their response was nearly unanimous: the reintroduction plan was sound. In fact, sixteen of North America's leading wolf scientists described the preferred alternative—including the experimental-nonessential designation—as a "practical plan that meets the needs of state governments and local residents while facilitating prompt, effective and economical recovery."[26]

In sum, the scientific research base was already robust, uniform in opinion, and supported park managers' intentions. More important, it could be summarized clearly and succinctly, even answering a yes-or-no question readily repeatable and understandable by the press: do wolves belong in Yellowstone—or, as the authors of the research report put it in the report's title, *Wolves for Yellowstone?* The answer was (and is) an unqualified *yes* (figure 25).

Once wolves were reestablished in Yellowstone in 1995, scientists jumped at the new research opportunity, producing close to one hundred new publications (most were peer-reviewed and included several books) in the following ten years. Generally, they found that reintroduction and subsequent

FIGURE 25: Howling wolf on rock, early 2000s. In their efforts to return wolves to Yellowstone, park managers and the U.S. Fish and Wildlife Service were able to draw upon a robust science base that was readily comprehensible and of uniform opinion. NPS photo by Jim Peaco.

management had equaled or exceeded their expectations. Grizzly bears were doing so well (in part because some bears learned that they could steal carcasses from wolves) that they were about to be removed from the endangered species list; all ungulates were still present and abundant (although elk numbers were dropping more than expected, with grizzly bears being partly responsible for that decline); willows that had been heavily grazed by elk were showing signs of recovery (possibly a result of wolves reducing elk numbers); the region's economy was booming (with ranching holding its own as a minor component); and visitors were enjoying exceptional wolf-viewing opportunities. Overall, there was again unanimity in pronouncing success.[27]

Drawing upon the solid scientific opinion, and batting a thousand with the policy determinants thus far, park managers and wolf-reintroduction proponents went to the key politicians in the region to make their case.

Politics

In the 1980s, wolf-reintroduction proponents faced strong and certain opposition from politicians in Montana, Wyoming, and Idaho. For example, in response to a comment from Superintendent Barbee in the mid-1980s that increasing numbers of people were talking about wolf reintroduction to Yellowstone, Senator Malcolm Wallop, a Republican from Wyoming, stated, "I don't want you to utter the 'W' word. Don't even think the 'W' word."[28] Such statements were reinforced by political actions, as Congress issued a number of directives explicitly prohibiting wolf reintroduction in the late 1980s.

Despite the congressional opposition, NPS director Mott continued to prompt a dialogue about wolf reintroduction. In 1987, for example, he suggested that an EIS would be the next logical step toward reintroducing wolves. Predictably, the Wyoming congressional delegation reacted angrily, eventually forcing Mott to promise that no reintroduction would occur unless he had their support. Still, Mott's efforts eventually succeeded (although after he left office), with the congressional appropriation to produce the *Wolves for Yellowstone?* report.[29]

This report, in which the scientific consensus about wolves was gathered, added to the consistent and compelling framing of wolf reintroduction and the new livestock-compensation fund to make it increasingly difficult for politicians to ignore the growing public desire to see wolves returned to Yellowstone National Park. Furthermore, the natural migration of wolves into northern Montana highlighted the fact that despite the political stalemate, wolves would eventually find their way into Yellowstone anyway. According to the wolf management rules at the time, if that happened, the wolves would enjoy the full protection of the Endangered Species Act and ranchers would not be allowed to shoot depredating wolves. Wolves were coming to Yellowstone, like it or not; political grandstanding would do nothing but backfire, resulting in a situation considerably less tolerable than if the government reintroduced wolves under the experimental-nonessential designation.[30]

While most of the region's politicians refused to read the writing on the wall, Senator James McClure, a Republican from Idaho, was different. McClure made his stance on the issue clear at a 1990 public hearing on wolf reintroduction. After listening to opponents present their case against an active wolf-reintroduction effort, McClure ended the meeting by criticizing them for not acknowledging the obvious. Senator Wallop then stated: "I have to say what Jim McClure has done is to point out a reality. The reality is that recovery, one way or another, is going to take place."[31] McClure retired later that year, but not before convincing Congress to appropriate funds for a special congressional committee to examine wolf reintroduction, an action that soon led to the wolf-reintroduction EIS—the last major step in bringing the animals back.[32]

McClure's forward thinking resulted in an EIS proposing to reintroduce wolves under the special designation. By the time the EIS was complete, Bill Clinton was in the White House and Bruce Babbitt in the secretary's chair at the U.S. Department of the Interior (USDI). Babbitt knew that reintroducing wolves to Yellowstone would be a highly visible statement of his administration's approach to national parks. He effectively took the torch for wolf reintroduction from Mott and pushed for it to happen quickly, before the newly elected Republican Congress assumed power in January 1995. When the wolves were returned to Yellowstone, Babbitt personally traveled there to take part in the reintroduction activities (figure 26). Around the same time, opposition from the region's congressional delegations quietly disappeared, McClure having successfully prodded them into realizing that wolf reintroduction was coming and any concerns they may have were effectively addressed by the experimental-nonessential designation.[33]

Ultimately, wolf reintroduction did not occur until the USDI had a secretary amenable to this issue. It was useful to have conclusive scientific data and a supportive public, but, as the quote at the beginning of this chapter suggests, the bottom line was political support. Superintendent Bob Barbee was right in his prediction: for actual wolf reintroduction to occur, there needed to be a favorable political climate. Had Interior Secretary Babbitt waited, or had other events delayed the reintroduction to 2001 or later, wolf reintroduction would surely have been put on hold by the following interior secretary, Gale Norton. Early in her tenure at Interior, Norton halted the department's plans to reintroduce grizzly bears into northern Idaho, despite the fact that several divergent interests had collaborated on the bear-reintroduction proposal. Norton's take on wolf reintroduction would almost certainly have been the same.[34]

Yellowstone's managers can look back today and realize they successfully aligned all the crucial policy determinants for wolf reintroduction. Just as with the New World Mine and the fire policy review, every single one of the policy determinants went in their favor—thanks to the park managers' due diligence and partnership with the environmental community, the scientific community, and the FWS in the years leading up to 1995. Still, the final vote of approval for wolf reintroduction, notwithstanding the green light from all other policy determinants, still came down to politics.

FIGURE 26: Secretary of the Interior Bruce Babbitt helping to carry a wolf in its crate to an acclimation pen, 1995. Babbitt (far right) promoted wolf restoration to Yellowstone and traveled to the park to take part in the reintroduction activities. Here he assists, from his right: Superintendent Mike Finley, U.S. Fish and Wildlife Service director Mollie Beatty, and Yellowstone park employees Jim Evanoff and Mike Phillips. NPS photo.

Summary of Wolf Reintroduction

Rarely have NPS park managers had the luxury of time like they did during the wolf-reintroduction issue. They had time to put together a supportive coalition composed of interest groups, another agency (FWS), and wolf scientists, all of whom crafted together a compelling way to frame the issue. They had time to gather the relevant scientific research and to fill the gaps in that research. They had the time and the assistance to defuse economic worries and concerns about public access. With an animal as polarizing as the wolf, they *had* to do all these things, so that they could in turn align the deciding factor in their favor—political support (or at least a lack of opposition). That too took time, but by 1995 their home run was obvious. Future park managers would envy the amount of time Yellowstone managers had to get the wolf-reintroduction stars aligned in their favor.[35]

But the actual means of wolf reintroduction—the experimental-nonessential designation—was still a compromise, and one that some members of the environmental community bitterly fought.[36] For park managers and the FWS, though, it was an easy compromise to make, and one that made little difference in Yellowstone, where wolves are abundant and widely sought out by wildlife-watching visitors.

With wolves back in the park, Superintendent Finley had time to address another festering issue: wintertime snowmobile use in the park. He would not enjoy the luxury of time in this effort, and as a result he and his successors experienced a more mixed policy-making track record.

Snowmobiles

In 1963, the first visitors on snowmobiles entered Yellowstone, triggering almost five decades of debate about whether these machines are appropriate in the park. Park managers originally admitted them—along with snow-coaches, which are multi-passenger vans or small buses converted to travel over unplowed snow-covered roads with tracks and skis instead of wheels—to enable the public to experience the park's winter wonders without having to plow the roads. The managers feared that plowed roads would turn Yellowstone's parkways into busy thoroughfares; would resemble snow tunnels; and would be difficult for park wildlife to traverse (as plows would create deep trenches). Consequently, when snowmobiles became widely available in the late 1960s, managers decided to encourage oversnow visitor use rather than provide access via plowed roads. To accommodate snowmobiles and snowcoaches, park managers began packing the snow in place on the roads and grooming them to provide smooth touring conditions, and opened a lodge at Old Faithful for overnight stays. Spurred on by these changes, visitation by snowmobiles and snowcoaches increased steadily throughout the 1970s.[37]

In the 1980s and 1990s, winter use continued to climb; by the late 1990s the park received about 795 snowmobiles and fifteen snowcoaches per day (figure 27). This large number of snowmobiles brought a collection of problems to the park (the low number of snowcoaches were not considered to be a problem at the time). Most noticeable were air and noise pollution, and the impacts of snowmobilers' behavior on wildlife. Snowmobiles used in the park prior to 2003 were powered by two-cycle engines, which mixed oil with gasoline for combustion. The process was inherently polluting, resulting in high levels of particulate and carbon monoxide emissions, along with some hydrocarbon releases (including chemicals such as benzene and formaldehyde). On calm, windless days, especially at the park's west entrance, carbon monoxide would accumulate to levels dangerously close to violating the Clean Air Act (CAA) for national parks. At the same time, particulate emissions resulted in an overall bluish haze at ground level. Park employees at the west entrance complained of headaches, nausea, and fatigue; they eventually resorted to wearing gas masks to protect themselves against the snowmobile fumes (figure 28).[38]

Snowmobile noise was equally noticeable. Most snowmobiles at the time emitted between 75 and 80 decibels of noise at or near full throttle (roughly equivalent to the noise of a freight train). The large numbers of snowmobiles

FIGURE 27: Snowmobiles parked behind Old Faithful Inn, circa 1995. An average of 795 snowmobiles per day entered Yellowstone in the 1990s, with many snowmobilers visiting Old Faithful during their park tour. This large number of snowmobiles brought a host of problems to the park, including noise, air pollution, and wildlife harassment. Author photo.

FIGURE 28: National Park Service employee with gas mask at Yellowstone's West Entrance, 2002. Park rangers stationed at the West Entrance began wearing gas masks to protect themselves from noxious snowmobile fumes. This was the same area of Yellowstone that almost violated the Clean Air Act due to high ambient carbon monoxide levels, during this same time period. NPS photo by Jim Peaco.

emitting such noise, combined with the tendency of cold air to propagate noise, produced a consistent, dull roar at Old Faithful and along the park's busier roadways. Snowmobile noise could also be heard miles from the roadways at times; backcountry skiers, for example, complained of hearing such noise as far as five or even ten linear miles from the nearest road. For many visitors, the hushed winter landscape they expected to find in Yellowstone was difficult or impossible to find.[39]

Visitors also observed that some wildlife, particularly bison, was being harassed by snowmobilers (figure 29). The same hard-packed roads facilitating snowmobile travel also made it easy for bison to travel from one meadow to another in search for food. Often, snowmobilers and bison came into conflict with each other, with many unguided and inexperienced snowmobilers not knowing how to pass the bison without causing them to run and thereby expend precious calories needed for winter survival. Visitors and park managers commonly observed some bison being batted about like hockey pucks between groups of snowmobilers traveling in opposite directions, while other bison were driven off roads. To some, winter snowmobile use in the park, which seemed to be occurring at the expense of wildlife preservation, clean air, and winter silence, was in violation of the NPS's mission.[40]

By the late 1990s, concerns about snowmobile impacts on air quality, winter silence, and wildlife—or more broadly, whether snowmobiles are appropriate at all in Yellowstone—had grown so much that the NPS found

FIGURE 29: Bison walking on snowmobile route, early 2000s. Around 1980, bison began using the snowmobile routes to travel from one meadow to another, finding the hard-packed routes easier than breaking their own trails in deep snow. Snowmobilers often found the animals interesting but very slow, with the result that some bison were chased or forced to leave the road as snowmobilers attempted to pass them. Such conflicts were a primary reason that park managers required snowmobilers to travel with guides who were trained in how to sensitively pass the animals, starting in 2004. This change virtually eliminated the free-for-all character of snowmobile visitation in Yellowstone during previous winters. Author photo.

itself the defendant in a lawsuit over winter use in the park. Resolving that suit by agreeing to write an EIS addressing the issue, the agency found an insufficient research base regarding the impacts of snowmobiles on air, noise, and wildlife. NPS did, however, find high levels of political interest in the issue. Under these circumstances, the agency produced a second EIS in 2003 (which featured a conclusion that conflicted with that of the previous EIS, finished in late 2000). Both of the environmental impact statements were rushed by court-imposed deadlines, then litigated and remanded back to the NPS by federal judges (along with a third EIS in 2007).[41] The snowmobile situation remains unresolved to this day.

Through some adroit policy moves, however, Yellowstone managers were able to substantially improve the winter situation in 2004. Taking advantage of a political détente, they mandated that all snowmobiles entering the park use best available technology, which virtually eliminated the air pollution problems and somewhat reduced the noise issues. All snowmobilers also had to use professional guides trained in park resources and wildlife-sensitive touring, a requirement that virtually eliminated the wildlife harassment. Finally, over the next four years, park managers implemented daily snowmobile limits, dropping the number allowed per day from 720 to 318. As a result of these changes, winter visitors to Yellowstone today find an orderly touring system, cleaner air, abundant wildlife, and some periods of quiet.[42]

In 2012, park managers began yet another EIS relating to snowmobile use, the fifth one on this issue. Despite having a substantial research base to draw upon, holes in the knowledge base remain, and polarized stakeholders accept only the research that supports the positions they have held on the issue for some time. Environmental groups, for example, continue to advocate an elimination of snowmobiles and conversion to a mass-transit system of snowcoaches, despite increasing research and monitoring information that indicates snowcoach environmental impacts are as significant on a per-traveler-basis as those of snowmobiles. In advocating these vehicles, environmentalists have helped boost snowcoach-tour averages to between thirty-two and forty-one per day (depending on the time of winter), resulting in elevated noise and wildlife issues similar to what rampant snowmobile use had produced a decade earlier. (Snowmobile advocates also remain interested in the issue, with concomitant political interest.) Other potential solutions, such as plowing more roads, have not been seriously discussed, even though experience over the last forty years has shown that most of the earlier concerns with road plowing lacked substance.[43]

Overall, the policy question concerning snowmobiles revolves around the appropriateness of their use in Yellowstone, with air quality, wildlife, and noise impacts being the focal points of the debate. While there is some discussion about snowcoaches and their impacts, the majority of public debate continues to revolve around snowmobiles specifically. The six policy-making determinants, especially scientific data and politics, have played (and will continue to play) key roles in determining the snowmobile policy-making outcome.

Coalitions and Issue Framing

At least two different kinds of coalitions have formed over the last fifteen years of the snowmobile controversy. Through the end of 2000, Yellowstone's park managers enjoyed a strong coalition with the environmental community; both deplored the situation, with snowmobiles so dominating the park in winter and compromising park resources. Environmentalists drummed up support for a ban on snowmobiles, even getting 300,000 people to submit letters or comment cards supporting a conversion to snowcoach travel. For its part, the NPS ran the political traplines to reduce snowmobile impacts in the park, culminating in the decision in late 2000 to ban snowmobiles altogether.[44]

With the inauguration of President George W. Bush and his Interior Secretary Gale Norton, however, NPS's coalition with environmentalists was forced underground and a stronger coalition took its place. Exemplified by a personal friendship between Norton and Christine Jourdain, president of the American Council of Snowmobile Associations, a coalition between key politicians and the snowmobile industry became more visible and powerful. That coalition would become evident to all in 2005, when Norton visited Yellowstone in the wintertime with Jourdain. Norton made no secret of her disdain for snowcoaches and her passion for snowmobiles, confirming to many that the NPS's reversal of its earlier decision to ban snowmobiles reflected Norton's influence (the politics section later in the chapter will discuss this matter in greater detail). The industry-politician coalition was also evident in Wyoming, where elected officials regularly defended snowmobile access to Yellowstone from 2000 onward, partnering with the snowmobile industry in lawsuits contesting restrictions on snowmobile use proposed by the NPS for Yellowstone. (The state eventually took over the litigation effort.) The coalition between the snowmobile industry and Wyoming officials remains.[45]

Even though the end of the Bush Administration made it possible for park managers to rekindle their coalition with the environmental community, they have chosen not to, mainly because they have come to understand that snowcoaches are no longer the unmitigated blessing that the environmental community professed (and still professes) them to be. In fact, by 2008 an improved research and monitoring information base showed that snowcoaches accounted for the majority of the park's ongoing noise problem; consumed an amount of gasoline and produced air pollution equivalent to that of snowmobiles when computed on a per passenger basis; and were as expensive to use for touring as snowmobiles. In general, environmentalists have refused to acknowledge the significance of these problems, so the coalition between them and the NPS has not been rekindled.[46]

In terms of framing the issue, both environmentalists and the snowmobile industry-political coalition have chosen a compelling framing, with the framing chosen by the latter proving to be stronger. The industry-political coalition has framed the issue as the NPS threatening public access to the park and the economies of gateway (or local) communities through proposed bans on snowmobiles. Because snowmobile access can provide visitors with the freedom to tour Yellowstone independently, this framing is broadened at times to a vision of the NPS threatening individual freedom. As illustrated throughout this book, when an issue is framed as a matter of threats to park access or local economies, the NPS has great difficulty succeeding with its proposed policy move. Worse, a policy move that appears to restrict access also appears to threaten the enduring American value of freedom. For these reasons, the industry-political coalition way of framing the issue put the NPS on the defensive.[47]

Nonetheless, most of the public continues to believe that snowmobiles should be banned from Yellowstone in favor of snowcoaches (and very few promote the plowing of roads). This support is due in large part to the issue framing done by the environmental community. In the late 1990s, environmentalists put forth an image of snowmobiles as "machines of the devil" invading a precious sanctuary. The fact that snowmobilers somewhat resembled Darth Vader, with black snowmobile suits, shiny helmets, and a plume of smoke rising from behind them, aided the environmentalists' cause. So did rangers at the park's West Entrance, who wore gas masks to protect themselves from the fumes of the machines ridden by the Darth Vader look-alikes. By 2008 environmentalists had even begun to conflate snowcoaches themselves with Yellowstone's sacredness, as evidenced by the home page image on the Greater Yellowstone Coalition's (GYC) website that year: a photograph of a snowcoach against a pristine Yellowstone winter landscape.[48] The implicit message of the uncaptioned image was that snowcoaches and Yellowstone were compatible, perhaps even equivalent: pristine, beautiful, and sacred. Such framing takes advantage of another strong American value: that wilderness is sacred. In contrast, snowmobiles, as presented by environmentalists, were the unsightly machine in the pristine winter garden—an image that continues to resonate, making it difficult for park managers to defend snowmobile access and attesting to the persistence of well-crafted images. That the snowmobiles in use in Yellowstone today have lower air and lower noise impacts does little to diminish the effectiveness of the environmentalists' snowmobile and snowcoach framing.[49]

Despite the environmentalists' efforts, snowmobiles remain in Yellowstone. Their continued presence attests to the strength of the snowmobile industry-political coalition and its framing of the issue as relating to access, economics, and freedom threatened—a framing that has proven to be the most influential in the end. Moreover, the NPS has been left without an ally, unable to partner with environmentalists or with the industry-political coalition.

Implications for Public Access and Local Economies

As suggested above, there has been a widely perceived threat to both public access and local economies from the NPS proposal to ban or restrict snowmobile use in Yellowstone. Not surprisingly, then, park managers have had an uphill battle trying to curtail snowmobile use in the park.

In the 1990s, the great majority of Yellowstone's oversnow travel occurred by snowmobile, with only about 10 percent of winter visitors traveling by snowcoach.[50] With that majority being so large, the NPS's proposal in 2000 to shift all park winter travel to snowcoaches would have been a major change. Snowcoach travel is group travel, has set itineraries, offers little of the touring freedom of snowmobiles, and requires purchasing tickets (figure 30). Furthermore, almost no one owns a personal snowcoach, while many local residents and Yellowstone visitors owned the snowmobiles with which they toured Yellowstone. The proposal to switch to snowcoaches, then, presented several important changes to public access that alone would have met resistance.

While some snowmobilers did indeed own their own machines, many more had to rent them from businesses in nearby communities, especially in West Yellowstone, Montana. The typical snowmobile visitor to Yellowstone

FIGURE 30: Snowcoaches in Yellowstone, 2008. Snowcoaches are multi-passenger vehicles able to travel over snow-packed roads. The ones shown here are conventional wheeled vehicles that have been retrofitted with tracks and skis for oversnow use. Some visitors to Yellowstone prefer to travel in snowcoaches rather than on snowmobiles. The per capita air emissions and fuel consumption of snowcoaches are about equal to those of snowmobiles (using fleet averages for both kinds of machines). However, certain snowcoaches (mainly ones with rubber tracks, like the white one shown here, but also some older vintage models) are now the loudest vehicles used in Yellowstone. Author photo.

would also stay overnight in the small town, purchasing meals and gifts and perhaps snowmobiling on surrounding national forest land for another day or two. On such a visit, the average snowmobiler typically spent hundreds of dollars in West Yellowstone. Such spending collectively constituted as much as 75 percent of the town's winter economy. As noted in the early 1980s, by Dean Nelson, president of the West Yellowstone First Security Bank, West Yellowstone's winter economy "*is* the snowmobile."[51] In the following two decades, little changed relating to snowmobile use in the area or its contribution to the local economy. Snowcoach visitors may have individually spent similar amounts in West Yellowstone, but they were vastly outnumbered by snowmobiling visitors, so their contribution to the local economy was relatively minor. Also, the profit margin on snowcoach tickets, which could be purchased from merchants in West Yellowstone, was less than it was on snowmobile rentals. For all these reasons, the proposal to discontinue snowmobile use in Yellowstone obviously presented a threat to West Yellowstone's economy.[52]

As snowmobile use gradually declined in Yellowstone, during the 2000s, the threat of economic harm became a reality in West Yellowstone, although not to the extent that some had feared. Some merchants did indeed close up for the winter or lay off employees, but others hired drivers for their new snowcoaches.[53] Despite the new snowcoach business, however, the perception remains that the curtailment or elimination of snowmobiles in Yellowstone will continue to bring economic harm to West Yellowstone.

Similarly, the perception remains that the public is losing access to Yellowstone in the winter, despite the increased availability of snowcoach touring. For those who formerly snowmobiled independently throughout Yellowstone and do not wish to tour via guided snowmobile or snowcoach, the perception is based in reality. For those who accept such guided tours, the access is still there, having changed for the better in some ways—many visitors enjoy and learn from the guide's commentary—and for the worse in other ways, as guided tours do lack the touring freedom of independent snowmobiling. And for those who could not afford snowmobile rentals in the 1990s, and cannot afford snowcoach tickets today (a typical tour to Old Faithful Geyser costs about one hundred dollars per person), the perceptions of changes in access are meaningless, as they never had real access to begin with—a point often overlooked by all participants in the snowmobile debate.[54]

These perceptions—public access to Yellowstone will be harmed by the curtailment or elimination of snowmobiling, which will also cause economic decline in the region—are slow to die and continue to haunt park managers' attempts to resolve the remaining winter visitation problems. Park managers do their best to broadcast a different message—that visitors can still enjoy Yellowstone in winter and that economies of nearby towns are performing at levels similar to those of the late 1990s. But perceptions are slow to change, especially those linked to things as strong as American values and our faith in the goodness of economic expansion.[55]

Science

When the snowmobile controversy first erupted in the late 1990s, Yellowstone managers lacked a solid research base in any of the debate's three focal areas: wildlife, air quality, or soundscapes. As a result, they commissioned an increasing amount of research and regular resource monitoring in all three areas. As in any research effort, some knowledge gaps were filled while others were revealed, triggering debate among scientists—and dispute, in this case—about those knowledge gaps. Today some debate on the scientific research continues, with the primary stakeholders adhering to their positions based more on the values at stake than on the increasing knowledge base.[56]

Understanding snowmobile impacts on Yellowstone National Park wildlife was probably the most vexing of the three focal areas. As noted above, bison were using the oversnow vehicle routes as travel corridors, where they came into conflict with snowmobilers. The animals were likely saving energy by using these routes, as compared to breaking trail through belly-deep snow. But how much of that saved energy did they lose when harassed by snowmobilers? The answer was—and still is—difficult to discern. Wildlife monitoring has demonstrated that bison habituate to the presence of snowmobiles as winter progresses, suggesting that they are able to tolerate snowmobile presence without substantial loss of energy. Their continually growing population, throughout the time period of snowmobile use, supports that conclusion. Elk, on the other hand, seemed more bothered by snowmobile use, avoiding the snowmobile routes more and more as winter progresses. However, the elk population also remained stable (at least until the reintroduction of wolves), a conclusion seeming at odds with (but ultimately more significant than) the observation of their avoidance. Physically measuring actual energy gains and losses in an individual animal is virtually impossible, so biologists were left with these more indirect observations for assessing the energetic impacts of snowmobile use on park wildlife. Based on such measures, scientists gradually reached a consensus that winter use in Yellowstone caused some stress in animals at the individual level, but that such effects were not enough to harm the breeding potential of the animal population as a whole.[57]

The 2004 requirement that all snowmobilers utilize professional guides, who enforce sensitive-driving patterns, has meant that virtually all wildlife harassment from snowmobilers has disappeared. However, more research needs to be done on the effect that snowcoaches, with their larger profile and increasing numbers, have on park wildlife, and the related concerns about bison range expansion (discussed in the bison controversy section). Overall, the increasing amount of research and related scientific consensus have brought some winter-travel policy successes for Yellowstone's park managers, especially in recent years.[58]

Air-quality research results have followed a similar trajectory. Initially, almost no information was available that reliably detailed snowmobile emissions or their effects on Yellowstone. Eventually, park managers began monitoring air quality at the park's West Entrance and at Old Faithful. They also commissioned substantial amounts of new research on snowmobile emissions. That research demonstrated unequivocally that the two-cycle snowmobiles, in use in the 1990s and early 2000s in the park, were extremely dirty, producing large amounts of noxious hydrocarbons, carbon monoxide, and other particulates. Park managers used this research to justify the requirement that all visitors use snowmobiles with best-available-technology beginning in 2004, and have since seen the air quality in the park improve dramatically. (Minor concerns do remain about the less important benzene and formaldehyde emissions from snowmobiles and snowcoaches in the park.) Yellowstone's clean air today has vindicated park managers' efforts to mandate the use of cleaner oversnow vehicles.[59]

Soundscape research and monitoring, which also went from nil in the 1990s to considerable research and monitoring results in the 2000s, had more mixed results. Snowmobiles in use today in the park are quieter than those used in the 1990s, but are still relatively noisy at or near full throttle. Consequently, conditions have improved somewhat, but Old Faithful and the busier roadways are still noisy at certain times of day. Part of the problem relates to the fact that best-available-technology snowmobiles produce a lower frequency noise that travels farther in the cold, dense air found in the park than the higher frequency noise emitted by snowmobiles previously used in Yellowstone. The limited backcountry soundscape-monitoring data available indicates that a fair amount of snowmobile noise may still be heard in areas distant from the roadways.[60]

In addition, as snowcoach numbers have increased, so has their noise. By far the noisiest vehicles used in Yellowstone in the winter now are snowcoaches (particularly those with rubber tracks and some of the older Bombardiers), some of which produce over 80 decibels of noise at or near full throttle—that is louder than a freight train. Quieter snowcoaches will soon be required in the park, so noise conditions may improve, but to an uncertain extent. Scientific research, then, indicates that both snowmobiles and snowcoaches are still loud and, unfortunately, this fact is helping prolong the debate concerning winter use of Yellowstone. In fact, it was a question about snowmobile noise that partly resulted in the snowmobile EIS of 2008 being remanded to the NPS by a federal judge in Washington, D.C., in 2009.[61]

In all three subject areas (wildlife, air quality, and soundscapes), park managers were initially faced with a distinct dearth of research and monitoring information. Only more recently, with the advent of more cohesive research results, have they been able to make headway on addressing the air quality, wildlife, and soundscape research needs and related concerns, as well as produce substantive change in the park's winter use.

Politics

As the aforementioned examples have shown, elected and appointed politicians have played an enormous role in winter-use policy making at Yellowstone. In particular, they have heavily influenced NPS park managers when completing the environmental impact statements in 2000, 2003, and 2008. The following discussion will provide three more examples of political influence upon winter-use policy making in Yellowstone, one drawn from each of these environmental impact statements.

In 1999, park managers completed a draft for the first EIS, in which the NPS proposed plowing the road from the town of West Yellowstone to Old Faithful for winter visitors, while allowing snowmobile and snowcoach use to continue on the rest of the oversnow road system. The final EIS of 2000, however, concluded that all winter travel would convert to snowcoaches by 2003, and no roads would be plowed and no snowmobiles allowed. Pushing the NPS toward that conclusion was Don Barry, assistant interior secretary for Fish, Wildlife and Parks. Early in 2000, Barry sent a memorandum to Yellowstone managers directing them to revise the EIS so that the preferred alternative would be a snowmobile ban and conversion to snowcoach-only travel throughout the park. Whether park managers shared Barry's thinking or were merely complying with his wishes may never be known, but because he was their boss (and a Clinton appointee), they had to comply. Worried about the disposition of the incoming Bush administration, they moved heaven and earth after the 2000 election returns were in to have the snowmobile ban in place before President Bush took office. They succeeded: the decision banning snowmobiles from Yellowstone was one of the very last policy-making endeavors of the Clinton Administration to be finalized. However, it would not remain in place for long (and was never implemented).[62]

Just days after the decision became final the incoming Bush Administration put it on hold. By using a lawsuit that had been filed against the NPS by snowmobile advocates and the State of Wyoming, the Bush Administration found a way to reverse the snowmobile ban. Without conferring with Yellowstone superintendent Mike Finley, the Bush Administration settled with the plaintiffs by agreeing to complete a supplemental EIS by 2003. During that time, it became clear to park managers that new Interior Secretary Gale Norton was (in their words, not hers) "personally interested in this issue" and wanted "to be able to come away saying some snowmobiles are allowed."[63] Regardless of what happened behind the scenes, the final supplemental EIS released in 2003 provided for snowmobile use to continue in the park, with mandatory guiding, best available technology, and restrictions on the number allowed (950 per day). Further, when Norton visited Yellowstone two years later, she left no doubt in anyone's mind where she stood on the issue of snowmobiles, confirming to all that the supplemental EIS had indeed reflected her disposition on the matter.[64]

Both of the environmental impact statements (2000 and 2003) were thrown out by different federal courts: the conservative Wyoming federal district court tossed out the anti-snowmobile decision from 2000 and the more liberal District of Columbia federal district court tossed out the pro-snowmobile decision from 2003. Such judicial actions are a form of political influence, but not as overt as the interior secretary's influence just discussed, or the political pressure park authorities would soon feel from the vice president.[65]

In 2007, Dick Cheney and his Wyoming constituents became worried about an NPS proposal in the third EIS (completed in 2008) to close Yellowstone's East Entrance in winter to eliminate avalanche danger to visitors and employees. This route, over Sylvan Pass, had been open to snowmobilers for years, but was a constant source of concern to park managers. Their employees had to travel beneath ten uncontrolled avalanche paths to reach a howitzer from which they would attempt to release the slides on those paths and ten others. Any slides released would then be cleared from the snowmobile roadway, which park managers would then open to the public. By 2007 visitor use over Sylvan Pass had dropped substantially, falling to as low as about five hundred visitors for the entire winter. (In addition, it was never used by more than 5 percent of all winter visitors.) Park managers questioned the wisdom of spending as much as $200,000 annually to keep the pass open for so few visitors, so in 2007 they proposed to close it in the wintertime.[66]

Upset over the possible loss of motorized winter access to Yellowstone over Sylvan Pass, Cody residents and Wyoming congressional representatives reacted strongly. Opposition sprang up from citizens groups in the Cody area, as well as from all levels of Wyoming government (city, county, and state).[67] It did not take long before Vice President Cheney heard from his former neighbors. As Cheney later stated:

> We did work with the Park Service. My office was contacted by folks from Cody. I talked to Colin Simpson [Cody state senator and son of Alan Simpson]. I'm familiar generally with the importance of that east entrance to the folks in Cody, the business community there. I recommended that my staff work on trying to keep that entrance open. As vice president, I don't run anything. I'm not in charge of the Park Service, but I can make suggestions, and my staff is actively involved in a lot of those issues on my behalf.[68]

Cheney understated his influence, for just a few months later Yellowstone's managers changed their plans and decided to continue their avalanche-control program with only minor changes. They would close Sylvan Pass about ten days earlier in spring than the rest of the park roads, to save a small amount of funding, but the safety issues were not addressed in any significant manner. Park employees continue to travel under the uncontrolled avalanche zones to reach the howitzer.[69]

As the winter-use policy discussion illustrates, three environmental impact statements produced three instances of high-level political pressure on Yellowstone managers, pressure that forced them to change course each time. Most importantly, in each case, the policy-making outcome matched the White House political agenda of the time: under the Democratic administration of Clinton, snowmobiles were to be banned in favor of snowcoaches, because the latter were thought to be better for the environment; under the Republican administration of Bush, snowmobiling would continue in Yellowstone, because it would provide individual public access and sustain local economies; and also under the Bush Administration, winter travel would remain possible over Sylvan Pass, because it would preserve access to the park for visitors from the Cody area. Such outcomes certainly attest to the powerful influence of politics on NPS policy making in Yellowstone in the modern era.

Summary of Snowmobiles

Through 2000, the NPS did have a good coalition and issue framing on its side, along with high-level political support from Don Barry concerning a snowmobile ban in Yellowstone. Although there was a widely perceived threat to access and to local economies, and the scientific research was lacking, the agency succeeded, if only for a few days, in a policy victory. That victory was clearly fragile, for it was quickly overturned when political winds changed. NPS's coalition went underground, but still marshaled an impressive amount of public support for the snowcoach-only option. However, ultimately, that support did not matter, for the decision in 2003 allowing continued snowmobile use was largely determined by Interior Secretary Gale Norton, who drew upon public concerns about threatened economies and restrictions to park access. Norton's and Barry's influence give testimony to the outcomes possible when political influence is strong and decision making is not based on good scientific research: policy decisions that the agency did not necessarily want.

Park managers took the lessons about scientific studies to heart, inaugurating regular resource monitoring on all three focal points of the snowmobile issue, as well as a number of in-depth studies into more nuanced aspects of them. Those studies have built a stronger science base, one that has helped managers address many of the problems relating to winter use of Yellowstone.[70] Managers also astutely took advantage of the political détente in 2004 by significantly improving the winter situation through requirements for cleaner and quieter snowmobiles and guided snowmobile tours. However, park managers still do not have a strong coalition with any group outside their agency (as regards this issue), nor do they enjoy the compelling issue framing that often comes with such a coalition. Public concerns about access to the park and local economies continue to fester, if at a reduced level. These issues continue to draw political attention, and major stakeholders continue to draw upon their own values when interpreting the scientific research results. The outlook today is more positive than it was in the past, with an expanding research base and the 2004 policy successes, but the lack of alignment of the remaining policy determinants is cause for concern.

Bison Management

Yellowstone bison carry brucellosis, a debilitating disease that causes aborted fetuses (especially a bison's first), retained placentas, reduced milk production, lameness, infertility, and swollen joints. Bison originally contracted the disease around a century ago from cattle held in the park to provide dairy products for summer visitors. The epidemiology of the disease in bison is complex— some animals are able to heal and be clear of the disease while others are not. In the latter cases, the bacteria will localize in the animal's lymph system, where they can lie dormant for months or years; pregnancies then trigger the onset of the disease, sometimes repeatedly. Calves born from an infected female may or may not inherit the disease. Epidemiologists do not know why some animals eliminate the bacteria from their body successfully, why others suffer repeated infections, or why some seem to have a natural resistance to it. Research studies have revealed that the disease is not native to bison, and some bison may carry and possibly transmit the disease for much of their lives.[71]

The disease is not desirable in cattle for many of the same reasons; in humans, the disease is called undulant fever, which is controllable but not curable. Seeking to eliminate these negative consequences of brucellosis, the federal government launched a nationwide brucellosis eradication campaign in 1934. The Animal and Plant Health Inspection Service (APHIS), the USDA agency responsible for this campaign, succeeded in ridding all American cattle of the disease in early 2008 (though elk transmitted the disease to a cattle herd in Montana just a few months later), and cases of undulant fever have almost disappeared as well. Since the late 1980s bison and elk in the Yellowstone area have served as the country's largest continuing reservoir of brucellosis. Mainly for this reason, APHIS has focused its eradication efforts in the last several decades on bison in Yellowstone. The possibility of disease transmission from elk, however, has been largely ignored, probably because elk are an important part of the region's hunting economy.[72]

In Yellowstone, bison populations have grown continuously since the 1910s. Until the natural regulation policy became institutionalized in the 1960s and 1970s, park managers controlled bison numbers much as ranchers would a herd of cattle (i.e., by selling or sending excess animals to slaughter), allowing from four hundred to about twelve hundred animals, depending on the time and circumstance. Since 1966, park managers have allowed natural forces to limit bison numbers. As a result, the bison population grew quickly throughout the 1970s and into the 1980s; on average, from 1969 to 1981, there was 16 percent annual growth in the bison population in the park's northern range. By the 1980s they numbered over two thousand.[73] With their numbers growing so rapidly, it was only a matter of time before the park would not have enough forage for the animals in winter (in many places in the park, heavy winter snows bury the grass too deeply for most bison to reach). Beginning in the late 1970s, bison began following natural migration paths down toward lower elevations outside the park, in search of more easily obtainable forage. Had they been allowed to continue in the direction they were migrating, they would have left the park near the small towns of Gardiner and West Yellowstone, Montana, both of which had nearby cattle ranches.[74]

Initially, only a few bison attempted to cross park boundaries, so Yellowstone managers agreed to contain the bison inside the park, a policy that worked for a few years. Inside Yellowstone National Park, infected bison posed no threat of transmitting the disease to cattle, which can only contract it through physical contact with an infected animal, afterbirth, or other aborted substances. By the winter of 1988–1989 (the harshest winter in about a decade), this policy no longer worked, as bison attempted to leave the park by the hundreds. Since the early 1980s, the State of Montana had been allowing hunters to harvest bison after they crossed park boundaries, so the state merely escalated the hunt to deal with the larger numbers of exiting bison. Staged in a very public area without an element of fair chase, the bison hunt drew widespread protest. By spring 1989, 569 bison had been killed by hunters in Montana, a large number for the time. Not long thereafter, the state suspended its bison hunt as a result of the national outcry.[75]

Responding to the outmigration, subsequent outcry, and related directives from the Secretary of the Interior, park managers began an EIS on bison and brucellosis management in Yellowstone, in cooperation with the USFS and APHIS. They also constructed a facility on park lands near Gardiner to capture departing bison, pursuant to an interim agreement with the State of Montana for managing bison attempting to leave the park (the state had built a similar facility near West Yellowstone) (figure 31). Captured bison were tested for brucellosis; those testing positive were sent to the local slaughterhouses, which distributed the meat to Native American tribes in Montana. (Once it is fully cooked, the meat poses no disease transmission potential.) Bison testing negative for the disease were either held in the facilities until the spring green-up lured the animals back into the park, or were sent to slaughter if the holding facility was full. Before the agencies could complete the EIS, another difficult winter arrived, in 1996–1997, one of the three harshest of the twentieth century.

Bison tried to leave the park in droves, but by winter's end, in April 1997, 1,084 bison had been sent to slaughter (a new record), with another four hundred perishing of natural causes.[76]

FIGURE 31: Bison in Gardiner capture facility, early 2000s. Bison migrating out of the park are herded into this facility, where they are tested for brucellosis. Those testing positive are sent to slaughter houses, with those testing negative held until the spring melt lures them back into Yellowstone (unless the capture facility is full, in which case they are sent to slaughter as well). In 2011, a new agreement among the state and federal land managers in the area began allowing some bison to roam throughout the Gardiner area in winter (that agreement was being tried in court as of 2012). NPS photo.

In 2000, the agencies (NPS, USFS, and APHIS) finally completed the EIS under court mediation. The preferred alternative called for the removal of infected bison to slaughterhouses to continue, as long as the bison population stayed above three thousand, and for bison to be inoculated against the disease once an effective vaccine became available. To examine the effects of an inoculation program, Yellowstone managers wrote and released a different EIS in 2010. That plan proposed to reduce brucellosis prevalence through a remote vaccine delivery program, in which "biobullets" of vaccine would be shot into the animals from afar using compressed-air-powered rifles. As of October 2012, that inoculation program has not begun. Complete eradication of brucellosis in bison remains an elusive, nearly impossible task, in part because the current brucellosis vaccine is generally only 80 percent effective in bison. Consequently, the NPS is still seeking ways to reduce the prevalence of the disease in bison.[77]

While the NPS was in the midst of drafting the second EIS, a third large bison-killing event occurred. In the winter of 2007–2008, about twelve hundred bison were sent to slaughter, the largest killing to date. (The total bison population in the 2000s has fluctuated between thirty-three hundred and five thousand.) Pushed by the brucellosis crisis, and recognizing that some bison would always leave the park (especially in harsh winters), park managers and officials from the State of Montana began to discuss more seriously the possibility of allowing some bison to range freely outside of Yellowstone, in the Gardiner area. Such a solution had been first outlined in the 2000 EIS. Discussions on this proposal proceeded fitfully, even after two Native American tribes and a tribal collective became formal participants in the bison management plan (in 2009), bringing more attention to the perspective that bison should be treated humanely. Mother Nature, however, soon provided another motivating crisis, in the winter of 2010–2011, when some of the heaviest and most persistent snow in a decade fell on park grounds, driving bison toward the Gardiner boundary in very large numbers. After moving towards the boundary, they soon filled the capture facility; observers worried that another large bison slaughter was imminent. Fearing the negative press that such an event would bring, and evidently making a statement that shipment of brucellosis-infected bison into Montana could spread the disease further, Montana governor Brian Schweitzer issued an executive order that prohibited bison from being shipped to slaughter in his state. The order worked for a short time, but large numbers of bison continued to move toward the boundary.

Something would have to give, for the bison had nowhere to go and the capture facility was completely full.[78]

By this time—late in the winter of 2010–2011—two other events were coming to bear on the situation. First was a decision by APHIS, in December 2010, to relax its brucellosis rules so that only the actual cows found to be infected with the disease had to be destroyed, not the entire herd of which they were a part. The agency also removed the penalty for finding brucellosis in a cattle herd; until then, if two herds in one state contracted the disease within any two-year period, the entire state lost its brucellosis-free status and had to quarantine every cow leaving the state. Under the new rules, states with brucellosis present in wildlife would only lose their brucellosis-free status if they failed to develop and implement a brucellosis management plan for such wildlife. While APHIS's actions seemed to make some kind of resolution more possible, because bison outside the park were no longer much of a threat to the state's brucellosis-free status, bills being debated by the Montana legislature at this time were not so sanguine. Concerned by the situation in Yellowstone, the conservative legislature was debating no fewer than eight bills or resolutions pertaining to bison management, the majority of which would strengthen the state's opposition to bison leaving Yellowstone.[79]

Meanwhile, winter's grip was not relenting and something had to be done about the bison. Hundreds were moving toward Gardiner, where they would find "no room in the inn" (the park's capture and holding facility). Park authorities could not possibly contain all of them in Yellowstone by hazing, so it was a near guarantee that some bison would cross the park boundaries (many, in fact, were already outside of the park and the holding facility). Realizing the impossibility of the situation, Governor Schweitzer worked with Yellowstone authorities, the USFS, and the tribes to come up with an agreement allowing some bison to range freely in a "buffer zone" of about 75,000 acres, extending 13 miles north of Gardiner, Montana (the Gardiner Basin). Many bison would still be captured and tested for brucellosis at the Gardiner capture facility, but some would be allowed more freedom of movement in the buffer zone (but any that moved out of the Gardiner Basin would be shot). Also, as part of the negotiations, most cattle in the Basin were removed; as of 2012, only fifty cattle remained. All the parties involved implemented this agreement in April 2011.[80]

While the agreement was notable, to some observers it only legalized what nature was already making happen: by April of 2011 over one thousand bison were already ranging freely outside the park (with another six hundred in the park's holding facility). To other observers, however, the agreement seemed revolutionary. For example, Tom France, regional director of the National Wildlife Federation, characterized the decision concerning bison as "a problem solved." He went on to state that for this issue it was akin to "the Berlin Wall coming down."[81] Still others were not so pleased, particularly some Gardiner area residents who now had to share their land with wild bison that had the potential of being dangerous. Stockgrowers in the area, citing concerns about brucellosis transmission in cattle, quickly took their concerns to court, suing the state to overturn the decision. As of October 2012, no decision has yet been rendered on the case, leaving the bison agreement of April 2011 in limbo.[82]

The ongoing lawsuit is evidence that controversy regarding bison management in the Yellowstone area continues. Currently, public discussion seems to be focusing on whether bison should be allowed to range outside of Yellowstone and how far. Until recently, stakeholders also debated the extent to which roads groomed for oversnow vehicle travel facilitated bison movement out of the park. As noted, the bison issue, which has festered for more than two decades, may be finally moving toward a successful resolution. This policy success appears to be due to changes in four determinants: coalitions, economics, science, and politics.

Coalitions and Issue Framing

Throughout the bison debate, Yellowstone managers have strongly—and admirably—defended the free-roaming nature of bison. In fact, Yellowstone's bison are the only herd in the country that has remained continuously free roaming. While the fact that they are not allowed to roam outside park borders seems to diminish that free-roaming potential to some, the park's 2.2 million acres does offer an area large enough for most of the bison to roam freely, most of the time. In addition, the park's bison are the only genetically pure bison in America; all others possess at least some cattle genes (for the two species can interbreed) (figure 32).[83]

For many, the idea of a bison herd with these special attributes being unnecessarily sent to slaughter has been the most resonant framing concerning park bison management. It has lasted throughout the debate, inspiring many observers to continue their efforts to find a workable solution. However, there have been other, sometimes competing, attempts to frame the issue. For example, members of the Buffalo Field Campaign (BFC), a regional bison

FIGURE 32: Bison in Upper Geyser Basin, 2009. The bison at Yellowstone remain the only bison in the country that are allowed to continuously roam free. Here, a bison rests near thermal features at Old Faithful. The warm ground and forage (with snow melted by thermal activity) in the area allows bison to live in an environment that would otherwise be too harsh in winter. Author photo.

advocacy group, have tried to frame the issue as a needless killing and harassment of bison "babies" and "beloved buffalo." This vision of buffalo imparts an anthropomorphism that does not resonate with many people, perhaps because bison are not as commonly anthropomorphized as are other animals, such as cows. Native Americans describe bison as sacred (as does the BFC), as a source of sustenance, and as a source of healing. These are accurate representations of their cultural perspectives toward the animal, but most Americans do not embrace this vision of bison. Likewise, the representation put forth by the State of Montana and APHIS—of brucellosis-infected bison as a threat to human health and security—does not resonate with most Americans, because only a few people (mainly hunters harvesting infected game) have contracted the disease. Brucellosis is simply not a big threat to

Americans, the majority of whom live in urban areas where other diseases like influenza are more common.[84] In summary, the description of Yellowstone bison as America's last free-ranging and genetically pure bison—the last *real* bison—being killed unnecessarily was the compelling issue framing for many. It was easy for many to pity these icons of the frontier, being brutally handled by an ugly contemporary reality.

Thankfully, park managers have been consistent in preserving wild bison in Yellowstone. Due to this stance, though, they have been unable to form a coalition with APHIS representatives or the State of Montana. Before 2011, if left to their own devices, APHIS and the State of Montana would have likely rounded up every last bison from inside the park, tested the animals for brucellosis, and killed all those that tested positive. Such an effort would likely have resulted in a substantial decline in the bison population, and might not have even been successful, given that some elk also have the disease and have transmitted it to cattle several times in the last five years. Such a proposal for brucellosis control in bison was (and still is) completely unpalatable to park managers, so any alliance between them and APHIS or the State of Montana was therefore forced and fraught with conflict. The conflict was evident in the fact that it took the NPS, APHIS, and State of Montana ten years—even with court mediation—to produce the first EIS on bison management; more than once, discussions between them broke down. Moreover, the fact that the EIS presented a preferred alternative that differed so little from ongoing practices suggested little common agreement among the agencies; no strong coalition among them was present.[85] (The section below on bison politics provides more examples of agency distrust during this period.)

And yet, NPS has been a partner, if a reluctant one, in controlling the movement of bison outside park boundaries. The agency built and operates the Gardiner capture facility, sending some bison to slaughter in winters with heavy snowfall (figure 33). If the NPS finalizes the 2010 draft EIS on brucellosis inoculation in bison, it will launch a relatively invasive brucellosis-reduction procedure in the park's bison (as of 2012, the final EIS has not been released). Such actions are the primary reasons that park managers have been unable to build strong coalitions with environmentalists or Native Americans. Despite the agency's rhetoric in support of free-roaming bison, NPS's actions in sending bison to slaughter have been a hurdle too great for most conservationists or Native Americans to look past.[86]

Instead of achieving support for its bison control program, the NPS has

FIGURE 33: Rangers herding bison into the Gardiner corral, late 1990s. One of the less desirable duties for some Yellowstone park rangers is herding, testing, and sending to slaughter brucellosis-infected bison. NPS photo.

actually been the target of active opposition—direct protests or nonviolent opposition—from the conservation camp and concerned Native Americans. On the side of conservationists, the BFC closely monitors bison removal operations, mainly in the West Yellowstone area—where the State of Montana sometimes used snowmobiles or helicopters to aggressively drive bison into corrals—and also in the Gardiner area. BFC members staged protests in both areas. In one instance, they chained themselves to 50-gallon drums filled with concrete and blocked the road leading to the West Yellowstone capture facility. Another time they displayed a large banner highlighting NPS's slaughter actions at a public NPS celebration in Gardiner, in 2003. Native American actions against the NPS were of a more ceremonial nature; for example, a member of the Lakota Sioux tribe pierced his own skin in two places to attach strings connected to a bison skull that he then dragged behind him in a dance celebrating the bison's significance to his tribe. Such actions illustrated the tension between park managers and those with whom they could most likely build an alliance.[87]

Today, while the solution concerning bison leaving Yellowstone is still being tried in court and awaits full implementation, it appears as though the NPS, the tribes, the State of Montana, and APHIS may be working together in a more cooperative way to address the ongoing problem. Only time will tell whether the solution will pass court muster, or whether this budding coalition will survive and strengthen.

Because they have been seen as both villains and heroes in the bison issue, Yellowstone managers have been unable to form a positive and successful coalition with any single outside agency or interest group, until possibly recently. A consistent motivation for park managers and other bison defenders was the vision of Yellowstone bison as authentic reminders of "primitive" America, in need of protection from harsh modern forces. Once again, in the bison management controversy, the importance of framing and coalitions is evident. This framing provided consistent, low-level motivation for park managers and other proponents of humane bison treatment. Park managers, lacking a coalition, realized little resolution of the controversy until recently, when a budding coalition finally formed. As noted, though, the coalition and the new solution still await the testing of implementation.

Implications for Public Access and Local Economies

Implications relating to public access are a policy determinant that park managers have had going for them all along in the bison debate. There are no public access implications, positive or negative, in bison management policies, actual or proposed. Similarly, there are no perceptions among the public that its access will be curtailed by such policies. Consequently, park managers have not had to contend with members of the public—or their elected representatives—concerning this issue.

The same may now be true regarding public perceptions of economic harm arising from bison management policies. Until APHIS changed its policy in late 2010, ranchers around Yellowstone faced the real threat of having to quarantine or destroy their entire cattle herds if brucellosis was found in them—even in just one animal. Not only would individual ranchers experience such economic losses, all ranchers statewide could face sanctions if the state lost its brucellosis-free status. With so much to lose, it was easy to understand why ranchers and the State of Montana feared economic losses resulting from potential brucellosis transmission to cattle.

Those potential losses were magnified by the perceived importance of the ranching industry to western states such as Montana. Although ranching comprises less than 8 percent of Montana's economy, it is commonly perceived to be a much higher percentage, perhaps because ranching is part of the American myth of rugged individuals living in the West.[88]

For these real and perceived reasons, NPS authorities in Yellowstone faced the belief that local and state economies would suffer if they allowed bison to leave park boundaries. That perception is slow to change, even though APHIS has changed its rules and substantially reduced any threat to Montana's economy. For example, stockgrowers near Gardiner are contesting the recent decision to allow bison to roam more freely there. These ranchers would have to slaughter specific cows caught with the disease, a lesser—but still motivating—threat causing them to oppose the bison policy. In actuality, only a small threat remains; the testing and slaughter program largely mitigates it. Overall, the economic-perception determinant seems to be in the process of changing from something that worked against NPS desires to now being neutral, and possibly working in the agency's favor. Certainly, this change was another reason park authorities and the State of Montana were able to negotiate the tentative bison management agreement in 2011.

Until recently, therefore, Yellowstone's managers were holding a mixed bag of public perceptions regarding the implications of their bison management on public access and local economies. It no longer appears that perceptions of economic harm are working so strongly against park managers in their efforts to humanely manage bison leaving the park.

Science

The scientific-research results regarding bison leaving the park seem to have also changed recently, from being incomplete and confusing to being more complete and understandable, providing increasingly clear direction for park managers. This change appears to have helped make the tentative 2011 bison management solution possible.

The first scientist to offer a hypothesis as to why bison began leaving the park boundaries in the 1980s was Yellowstone's own bison biologist, Mary Meagher. A Yellowstone career employee, Meagher wrote her doctoral dissertation, in 1973, on Yellowstone bison and became a prominent authority on the animal and its habits.[89] Regarding the bison's new migration patterns in Yellowstone, Meagher knew that population growth was an obvious factor, and so was the fact that the lower country around Gardiner had less snow and therefore offered more easily obtainable forage. But how did the bison happen to first travel there, in the 1970s, when the animals likely had no knowledge of the Gardiner snow-free forage?

Meagher suspected that the roads park authorities groomed for over-snow vehicle travel may have played a role. Bison are migratory in nature and, like any animal, seek to minimize energy loss in winter. In a 1993 unpublished paper, Meagher argued that once bison population controls were lifted in the late 1960s, their populations began growing. About the same time, Yellowstone managers began packing and grooming the oversnow vehicle routes, which connected several important bison winter ranges with lower elevation ranges near Gardiner. As bison numbers grew, those in the harshest winter ranges began looking for less densely occupied and more usable range. Learning to use the hard-packed, oversnow vehicle routes (easier to walk on than untracked snow) that led to better pastures, bison began moving about more and more. Eventually, they discovered the better winter range near Gardiner, where bison had once ranged before their wholesale elimination from America in the 1800s.[90] By the late 1980s bison were regularly departing the park and in such large numbers that the bison management policy controversy began.

With their own scientist pointing the finger of blame for the outmigration at them, Yellowstone authorities began to wonder if the groomed roads were indeed the cause of this problem. If the cause were this simple, park managers wondered if blocking those routes or closing them would fix the problem and confine the bison inside Yellowstone. Seeking an answer, park managers tried to block bison from leaving the park by installing fencing across some of their favorite routes and hazing them (herding them in a direction they do not wish to go, usually by rangers on horseback) back inside park boundaries. However, the bison just walked around these obstacles or turned around after being hazed, leaving managers to ponder closing the oversnow vehicle roads, a less feasible option because winter visitors would then have no way to get to Old Faithful. Realizing they needed more sophisticated research analysis, managers commissioned several studies into whether groomed roads were indeed the culprit. Several different scientists agreed that Meagher was right about a growing population needing more room to range, but probably wrong about the pivotal role played by the snowmobile and snowcoach routes. Most of those routes paralleled existing bison migratory routes, such as river valleys with abundant hot spring activity that presented areas of open ground easy to walk on in winter. Thus, the scientists concluded that the bison, with their numbers growing, began a range expansion that occurred naturally. The groomed routes only helped the range expansion happen more quickly.[91]

Based on the new research, an increasing consensus occurred among wildlife scientists who believed that the oversnow vehicle routes did not lead bison out of the park.[92] This understanding aided Yellowstone's park managers in their effort to allow bison to roam outside the park, for the bottom line—scientific "sound bite" number one—is that no matter what happens inside Yellowstone, bison *will* leave the park when their densities get high enough and the winters harsh enough.

The second scientific sound bite is that the chance of bison transmitting the brucellosis disease to cattle is extremely small. As noted previously, the disease is transmitted from animal to animal by contact with live tissue; in the wild, this mainly takes place when an animal licks or ingests afterbirth or aborted materials. However, the *Brucella abortus* bacterium does not survive well in the open air; most die after just a few days of exposure. The bacteria may also be transmitted via mother's milk. For these reasons, males cannot transmit the disease and any transmission from bison to domestic cattle is unlikely, even in the absence of bison control. The reduction in cattle numbers in the Gardiner Basin has made such transmission even less likely.[93]

Putting the two scientific sound bites together creates a compelling case for allowing bison (at least those testing negative for brucellosis) to range in the Gardiner Basin. Land managers were always going to have the outmigration problem, the chances of disease transmission were infinitesimally small, and the economic consequences were manageable (given the APHIS rule change). This new scientific consensus helped lay the foundation for the tentative bison management agreement of 2011 and became yet another policy determinant that assisted park managers in their efforts.

Politics

With so many determinants appearing to shift in favor of allowing some bison to roam outside Yellowstone National Park (or, at least the determinants shifted into neutral positions), it is no surprise that political influence took the same path. Well into the first decade of the twentieth-first century, Montana politicians engaged in a strong defense of local and regional economies.

For example, Senator Conrad Burns, a Republican from Montana, introduced a bill into Congress in 1995 that would have implemented APHIS's original solution to the brucellosis problem: capture and test every last bison in Yellowstone, destroy those that tested positive for the disease, and quarantine the remainder for several years. Burns's bill went one step further, requiring park managers to maintain the disease-free herd at five hundred less bison than the optimum size determined by a team of independent range scientists. The bill went nowhere, but demonstrated Burns's view toward park authorities: keep your bison and their disease from affecting Montana's cattle. Burns made no secret of his disdain for park managers and their desire to keep park bison wild, referring to Superintendent Finley as "this jughead we've got running Yellowstone Park."[94] Beyond his rhetoric, Burns effectively served as a front for the ranching industry, pressuring park authorities into preventing bison from leaving the park.

Burns's efforts were complemented by actions of some State of Montana officials. In 1994, for example, Montana governor Marc Racicot transferred oversight of bison from the state's department of Fish, Wildlife, and Parks to its Department of Livestock, a change that resulted in a much more critical perspective on the bison issue. Illustrating that new perspective was Montana state veterinarian, Clarence Siroky, who apparently colluded behind closed doors with APHIS, asking them to threaten to remove Montana's brucellosis-free status as justification for a new hard-line stance by the state against bison leaving Yellowstone. Montana then sued the USDA and USDI in 1995, alleging that the policy of these federal agencies allowing bison to leave Yellowstone threatened its brucellosis-free status. Eventually, the State of Montana settled its suit with the federal agencies when they agreed to an interim bison management plan, while they completed the first EIS on a longer term plan (the 2000 EIS). Before that EIS could be finalized, however, the bickering agencies had to resort to court mediation. As noted previously, the outcome of that EIS was business as usual: the NPS would partner with the State of Montana in keeping bison inside Yellowstone. Superintendent Finley agreed to the EIS compromise, expressing that he did so because he had little choice, given the political pressure being applied. But, he succinctly stated, "If I were making the decision unilaterally, I would do it differently—I would have bison ranging freely outside Yellowstone on national forest lands."[95]

Burns was defeated in his reelection bid in 2006. His departure seemed to lay the groundwork for the less hostile approach toward the NPS taken by

Montana governor Brian Schweitzer, elected two years earlier. As discussed above, it was Schweitzer who approved the tentative bison management agreement—that allowed bison to range throughout the Gardiner Basin—with park authorities, the USFS, and Native American tribes. Schweitzer's motives were no grander than attempting to find a workable, more durable solution to a problem that was particularly intractable in 2011—but even that motive was a gentler approach than that taken by his predecessors. For the first time in several decades, a prominent Montana official recognized the reality of bison leaving the park and the need for dealing with this issue humanely. For park managers, it was a breath of fresh air.[96]

Overall, political influence in this issue has been consistent and influential: park managers adopted control procedures for many years that they would never have chosen to do otherwise, to an animal so symbolic of their agency that it appears on both the NPS patch and ranger badge (as well as on the USDI logo). Equally significant, they did not succeed in allowing *any* bison outside the park until a less oppositional Montana governor was willing to consider a solution that would help provide more tolerance for the noble creatures outside Yellowstone. Politics became the fourth determinant to move toward support of the NPS policy allowing bison to roam outside the park in the winter. However, given the ongoing litigation, it remains to be seen whether the support for the solution will stand.

Summary of Bison Management

The brucellosis-infected bison issue seems to be in flux and will hopefully transition from a lengthy period of stagnation to a more durable and humane solution. This will likely happen if the solution survives the litigation and if the test and slaughter program can eventually be curtailed or eliminated. As with the wolf study, the bison management issue illustrates the possibilities for solution when determinants change from working against park managers' preferences to supporting park managers' intentions (or at least appearing to be neutral). Between 2009 and 2011, park managers found that formerly hostile policy opponents had become willing to consider a new solution. APHIS's rule change meant that the perceived threat of bison to the state economy had dropped considerably. Scientists gradually came to a consensus that bison would leave the park in winter, no matter what the NPS did with its roads, and that they posed little if any risk to the few cattle remaining in the area. And finally, political influence changed from almost hostile opposition toward bison leaving Yellowstone to a willingness (if grudging) to consider disease-free bison roaming in a limited area. Not facing any public concern about a loss of motorized access due to bison management changes, park managers found themselves with more determinants aiding their cause, such as issue framing, scientific data, and perhaps coalitions, and others appearing more neutral, including economics and politics. Only time will tell if the park managers' bison solution will need any further revision.

Reflections

In all three of the issues discussed—gray wolf reintroduction, snowmobile access, and bison management—the same six policy-making determinants were at work. The following is an examination of the role played by each of these different determinants in these three issues.

The NPS's ability to form a coalition with like-minded interest groups, scientists, and various federal and local government agencies has had a strong bearing on the outcome of policy-making decisions. For example, with such strong coalitions in place, the NPS was able to return wolves to Yellowstone. However, in the case of snowmobiles and bison, the NPS did not have such coalitions, and as a result floundered in its ability to resolve these issues (at least until recently in the latter).

Issue framing has also been important to NPS managers. Framing wolves as the missing key to a complete ecosystem greatly aided park managers in that issue; and framing bison as the last vestige of a primitive America helped give park managers the persistence needed to resolve that issue. In the instance of snowmobiles, however, the industry-political framing of a snowmobile ban as detrimental to regional economies and park access has only encouraged that issue to fester. Compelling framing depends on a visionary idea and leaders with the strength and abilities to promote that vision. With wolves, the vision was clear—return an important species that was missing from Yellowstone ecosystem—and there were a number of leaders willing to advance that vision, from NPS director William Penn Mott to superintendents Barbee and Finley to Interior Secretary Bruce Babbitt. With snowmobiles, the key players and their vision changed dramatically over time, ending an early coalition and leading to competing ways of framing the issue. Inextricably linked, strong leaders and their progressive visions often lead to strong coalitions and compelling framing.

The public's worries about restricted public access to Yellowstone and effects on regional economies have had a similar influence on NPS policy-making outcomes. For instance, the public concerns about diminished access to Yellowstone if snowmobiles were banned have fanned the flames of that controversy for years. In the wolf-reintroduction issue, the NPS and FWS were able to quell fears of curtailed access to national forest lands, helping to pave the way for wolves to return. With bison, there have been few access concerns, but fears about the regional economy being threatened by brucellosis transmission kept this controversy going, until APHIS's new rules diminished the threat of disease transmission and made a new solution possible. Economic fears also fueled the debate about banning snowmobiles and returning wolves. An interest group helped douse such fears regarding wolves, but snowcoaches and their boosters have not had the same effect with the snowmobile controversy.

The existence of a strong research base and the uniform opinions of scientists (or the lack thereof) played crucial roles in all three controversies. For example, the NPS and FWS found the strong research base regarding wolf effects on Yellowstone animals and the unanimity of scientists' opinions on the same subject to be immensely helpful in returning wolves to Yellowstone. Having the time necessary to accrue such a research base was quite helpful. In the case of the snowmobiles, tight court deadlines made for rushed, incomplete scientific studies and persistent knowledge gaps. This insufficient research base and the conflicting opinions regarding the effects of snowmobiles on wildlife stoked the flames of that controversy for years. Only recently have park managers begun to accrue an adequate science base, making resolution of the issue more possible than it has been in the past, though the other policy determinants may keep that controversy alive. Similarly, with the bison issue, an emerging scientific consensus and two key scientific sound bites mean that park managers may soon achieve success in letting some bison roam outside the park.

Ultimately, the aforementioned policy determinants helped influence the trajectory of all three issues, with politicians playing important deciding roles in each. Interior Secretary Bruce Babbitt literally helped carry wolves back into Yellowstone, and his deputy ordered the NPS to ban snowmobiles. Interior Secretary Grace Norton overturned the latter decision, directing park managers to retain the machines. Montana senators and APHIS officials, partnering with Montana state officials, prevented park managers from allowing bison to roam more freely outside of park boundaries, until recently, when Governor Schweitzer took a less adversarial approach to the issue (perhaps because he had little choice) to the benefit of the animals and of park managers. In every case, politicians were reacting to public framing of the issue, to public concerns about access and economies, to the scientific research, and sometimes to the NPS's opinion or advice, along with that of its allies. Park managers played (and continue to play) the most pivotal role in preparing these ingredients for final policy outcomes, succeeding with wolf reintroduction and moving both the snowmobile and bison management controversies toward ultimate resolution.

All told, one can clearly see a correlation between policy outcome and the number of determinants aiding the NPS in each of the controversies. The more determinants in favor of the NPS and its policies, the more likely it will achieve a policy-making outcome favorable to the preservation of Yellowstone National Park.

CONCLUSION

Science and Politics

No amount of good science will stop a politician.
—John Sacklin, management assistant (retired) to
the superintendent, Yellowstone National Park

SIX POLICY-MAKING CONTROVERSIES AND SIX POLICY-MAKING DE-
terminants: a coincidence in number, but not a coincidence in outcome.
As the discussion in this book has revealed, national park policy-making
outcomes are largely determined by National Park Service (NPS) leaders'
ability to form a coalition with supportive, external interests; the compelling way the NPS frames the issue for the public; the implications of the
policy proposal on motorized public access to the park (at least in the mind
of the public); the implications of the policy proposal on gateway (or local)
economies (again, in the mind of the public); the robustness, uniformity,
and clearness of the relevant scientific research and results; and the influence of elected and appointed federal (and, less often, state) politicians. Of
the six determinants, politics and scientific research seem to be the most
influential, with the former usually determining the bottom line, as the
quote above suggests.[1]

In examining each of the determinants in greater detail, it became clear
that park managers' ability to form a supportive coalition with external
groups—scientists, conservation groups, or other agencies—was moderately
influential upon the controversy's outcome. Both in the Fishing Bridge Village and bison issues, park managers actually faced opposition from those

who would otherwise be their ally and found their policy-making efforts frustrated. Contrary to the NPS's desires, most of Fishing Bridge Village remains open (with some of it still not restored to natural conditions) and only recently have park managers been able to negotiate a tentative agreement allowing some bison to roam outside park boundaries in winter. In other instances, however, coalitions turned out to be pivotal, such as in the New World Mine and wolf-reintroduction issues. It is not too strong a statement to say that park managers would not have succeeded in realizing their preferred solutions in these two instances without the assistance of conservation groups and other federal agencies. In the case of the mine, it was a partnership with the Greater Yellowstone Coalition (GYC); with wolves, it was a partnership with both the environmental community and the U.S. Fish and Wildlife Service (FWS).[2] Today wolves are thriving in and around Yellowstone, while the degraded lands of the former New World Mining District are being restored.

Similarly, how compellingly an issue was framed had a distinct influence on the policy-making outcome of each of the Yellowstone National Park controversies. Both naturally ignited fires and wolf-reintroduction issues were portrayed—by scientists, conservationists, and park managers—as integral components of Yellowstone's "wildness," without which the park would be incomplete. The only possible solution in both of these endeavors was to return wildfires and wolves to Yellowstone—and they were. Likewise, in the case of the New World Mine, in part because Noranda was "framed" as the bullying bad guy, the mine was not built. Concerning bison management, the NPS and its supporters consistently framed the bison as the last wild vestiges of America, an image that inspired park managers and their supporters (if at a low level) to push for resolution. In contrast, the poor framing in the Fishing Bridge Village controversy frustrated park managers and their intentions. Even worse was the framing in the snowmobile issue, when the industry's portrayal of snowmobiles as integral to the region's economy (an idea supported by the State of Wyoming) worked against NPS's proposal to ban the machines from Yellowstone. Overall, it appears that an issue's framing can be a moderate influence on policy-making outcomes.

The public perception of NPS proposals on motorized park access has also been a distinct influence on policy-making outcomes. In both the Fishing Bridge Village and snowmobile issues, public fears of diminished motorized access were pivotal in achieving political interest, opposition, and ultimately the outcome: visitors with RVs may still camp at Fishing Bridge and snowmobilers may still travel through Yellowstone. Had park managers proposed increasing motorized access in a policy-making controversy, they probably would have seen external support from at least some members of the public and their elected representatives. In none of the situations presented in this book, however, was that present. Overall, the access determinant is a moderate influence on NPS policy making.

The effect of a policy proposal on the regional economy appears to have been a moderate influence on park managers' policy making, more often operating against the managers' intentions rather than supporting them. In the Fishing Bridge Village, snowmobile, and bison controversies, public fears about local economies being threatened by park proposals initially worked against park managers. The outcomes were somewhat ineffectual: partial closure of Fishing Bridge Village, continued snowmobile access (and noise) in the park, and ongoing debate concerning the bison issue, at least until recently. Conversely, when the public perceived that a policy-making proposal would benefit their economy (or at least not harm it), park managers usually found their efforts more successful. For example, wolf reintroduction benefitted from the news that more tourists would be drawn to the area to see the newly returned carnivores. Concerning the bison issue, when the Animal and Plant Health Inspection Service (APHIS) softened the brucellosis quarantine rules, park managers were able to effectively broadcast the message that Montana's economy would not be hurt by bison leaving the park (though some individual ranchers could still be harmed). Overall, it appears that public thinking about the economic effects of an agency policy proposal can have a moderate to strong influence on the policy-making outcome.

Scientific research was one of two determinants that seemed very influential in NPS managers' policy-making success. In every policy study, it played at least a moderate role in the policy-making outcome; in most, a strong role. For the research base to be a policy-making aid for park managers, it must already be robust, there must be consensus among scientists about the issue in question, and the research must be easily understood. Illustrating the first requirement is the snowmobile issue: when the issue first flared up, in-depth research on snowmobiles' effects on air quality, soundscapes, and wildlife was not available. Likewise, the lack of scientific information in the Fishing Bridge Village issue caused a similar problem: computer modeling was just being developed and was not able to conclusively demonstrate that closure of the area would benefit the grizzly bear's survival in the park. The lack of adequate research did nothing to help park managers resolve these two controversies.

The bison controversy illustrates the second scientific requirement: that there must be scientific agreement about the issue in question. When the bison issue ignited, there was disagreement as to whether groomed oversnow vehicle roads led bison out of the park and to their deaths. Only recently were scientists able to reach a consensus that groomed roads have had little effect on bison movement; rather, bison are leaving the park in a mostly natural migration. The delayed agreement on this issue stoked the flames of the bison controversy for many years; only when this new consensus emerged did a resolution to the problem begin to present itself.

Finally, the Fishing Bridge Village and snowmobile controversies show that, to aid park managers, scientific studies must be easily understood by the public. The connection between grizzly bears, human foods, and bear deaths was easy enough to understand, but the connection between closing Fishing Bridge and preventing grizzly bear extinction was not. The scientific research regarding this connection was muddled at best, and the public could see that. As a result, park managers were unable to close Fishing Bridge entirely. Similarly, research about snowmobile effects on wildlife is not readily understood. It has been shown that elk avoid snowmobile routes while bison do not, yet populations of both species in the park are doing fine. What does that tell managers about snowmobile effects on these animals? It is hard to know, so park managers are left without strong guidance from this component of scientific research.

In contrast, the fire policy review, wolf reintroduction, and the New World Mine controversies all benefited from a preexisting, robust, and easily understood scientific research base, with little disagreement among scientists as to the implications of such research for park policy making. Noted wolf researchers actually stated that no more research was needed for wolf reintroduction; they widely agreed that wolves were a natural for Yellowstone. Concerning the fire policy, park managers had an in-depth research base on fire ecology, almost unanimous scientific opinion that managers should continue to allow naturally ignited fires to burn, and ease in translating the research into comprehensible talking points. In both these controversies, science and research played a pivotal role—if not *the* pivotal role—in the policy-making outcome. In the New World Mine issue, scientific research was pivotal in the successful lawsuit against Noranda Minerals Corporation; it did, however, take a substantial amount of time to conclusively link the commonly known scientific data about mining's effects on water quality to the actual effects on Yellowstone's waters.

Politics (and its key personalities) is the last but not the least of the policy-making determinants—one that is equally, or in some cases more, influential than the science determinant. Only in the fire controversy were elected or appointed federal politicians not pivotal in the controversy's outcome. Senator Alan Simpson essentially forced a compromise on park managers wrestling with Fishing Bridge Village closure; President Clinton arranged the New World Mine buyout; various Department of the Interior secretaries ordered differing solutions to the snowmobile controversy; Montana governors have taken different and yet influential positions regarding bison ranging outside the park; and wolf reintroduction was finally made possible by Interior Secretary Bruce Babbitt. Even the fire policy review bears the marks of politics, for the NPS cannot allow all fires to burn. Politics, then, loom large indeed in NPS policy making.

In most of the NPS policy-making controversies in this controlled comparison, stakeholders generally achieved political interest by expressing concern about reduced public access to Yellowstone or economic decline in the region. Whether it was potential restrictions on RV or snowmobile access, worries about the transmission of brucellosis and its effects on the ranching economy, or snowmobile restrictions harming local tourism economies, constituents were able to get the attention of their elected officials, who reacted in defense of access and economies. Political interest in defense of an economy can also work toward park managers' ends when they are defending the economy, as happened in the New World Mine situation. The potential economic harm posed by the reintroduction of wolves helped generate political attention for that issue, but the broader economic gains offered by wolf reintroduction eventually helped park managers succeed in their efforts.

In comparing the six controversies at Yellowstone in the modern era, three are examples of NPS successes: wolves have roamed the park for the better part of two decades now; naturally ignited fires burn in the park on a regular basis (with some limitations); and the New World Mine is absent from the landscape. In the other three issues, park managers have been less successful, though their efforts have not been a complete failure. The closure of Fishing Bridge Village, snowmobile access to the park, and bison management can all be characterized as struggles for the NPS. The Fishing Bridge campground is gone, but the RV park remains and the cabin area has not yet been restored to natural conditions. Snowmobile impacts on wildlife and air quality are reduced compared to earlier levels, but substantial noise can still be heard in Yellowstone from both snowmobiles and snowcoaches.

The recent decision to allow bison to roam outside the park near Gardiner appears to be a step toward success, but capture and slaughter operations continue and the solution is untested.

These policy outcomes are largely the result of the six policy determinants discussed in this book and their positive or negative influence on park managers' efforts to craft policy. For a clear and succinct chart illustrating the effects and relative importance of the six policy determinants discussed in this book, see table C.1. The table distills the six determinants and six controversies into two components: whether park managers found a determinant helpful or harmful in their policy-making effort, and the relative strength of that determinant in influencing the policy-making outcome. The three policy successes and the three policy struggles are grouped together to illustrate several important insights.

TABLE C.1: A conceptual chart illustrating the importance of the six policy determinants in the outcome of the six policy-making controversies.

	FISHING BRIDGE	BISON (before/after 2010)	SNOWMOBILES (to 2000/ 2001–2008/ 2008–present)	FIRE POLICY REVIEW	NEW WORLD MINE	WOLF REINTRODUCTION
Coalitions	--	--/o	++/---/-	++	+++	+++
Framing	-	+/+	+ and -- (throughout)	++	++	+++
Access	---	o/o	---/--/-	o	+	o
Economies	--	--/+	---/--/-	+	++	-- , then +
Science	---	--/++	--/--/+	+++	++	+++
Politics	---	---/+	+++/---/--	+	+++	---, then +++

Controversies are arrayed across the top, grouping the struggles on the left and the successes on the right. Determinants are arrayed in the left column. In each cell, a "+" or "–" indicates whether the given policy determinant worked for or against park managers in that controversy. The number of "-" or "+" signs indicate the relative strength of that determinant in that policy controversy: one sign indicates slight influence, two a moderate influence, and three a strong influence, with "o" indicating very little influence. Issues that saw a substantial change in determinants are shown accordingly, as are issues that saw determinants work both positively and negatively. All rankings are qualitative, reflecting a general assessment of the level of influence a given determinant had in influencing the outcome of a given policy-making controversy.

The table graphically illustrates the findings of this study. Perhaps the most striking insight is the contrast in determinant alignment between the policy-making struggles and the successes. In the three struggles, park managers had most or all of the determinants arrayed against them (except for the bison issue, which became more favorable in 2010), while in the successes most or all of the determinants worked in their favor. To put it simply, to be successful in a policy-making endeavor, park managers must align *all* the determinants in their favor, or at least five out of the six. This result echoes the findings of political scientist William R. Lowry, who finds that park managers must bat a thousand, at least in controversial policy-making endeavors in the modern era, to succeed. If they do not, he explains, they are more likely to be forced to compromise and experience a festering issue that will not be resolved quickly.[3]

Looking for the most influential determinants across all the policy-making controversies, we see that science and politics are the two most influential. For example (and as noted above), in both the wolf-reintroduction and fire policy controversies, the strong research base greatly aided park managers' efforts to implement policies that were not popular, at least with some members of the public and their elected representatives. The New World Mine is the clearest example of strong political influence on park managers' policy making, while the wolf-reintroduction and snowmobile studies are as well.

The table suggests that politics and science are equally influential in NPS policy making relating to Yellowstone. However, most of the examples discussed in detail in this book suggest that politics and its key players are actually the most influential determinant; indeed, political interest and influence was present in every controversy, even those with a robust science base. Wolf reintroduction, for example, had to wait for success until Bruce Babbitt was in the secretary's chair at the Department of the Interior. The fire policy required the park superintendent to certify daily that any naturally ignited fires burning would not escape control, a requirement bearing the marks of Simpson's influence. The New World Mine proposal was essentially defeated by the Clinton Administration. In the bison controversy, park managers could not allow bison to roam outside the park until Montana had a new governor receptive to the idea (and pushed by natural events to consider it). Snowmobiles still roar through the park, largely due to the politics of the early twenty-first century. Finally, much of Fishing Bridge remains open due to the compromise Alan Simpson was so influential in effecting. As the quote at the beginning of this conclusion suggests, politics can trump even a robust research base.[4]

In short, the experiences relating to Yellowstone National Park over the last thirty years indicate that ultimate policy-making outcomes often reflect political agendas, particularly when the scientific data is weak and the determinants are not fully aligned in favor of park managers' policy proposals.

Even when politicians make a decision that favors natural resource protection (as in wolves, the fire policy review, and the New World Mine), the mere fact that they are still making the final decisions suggests that national park management is subject to the winds of politics. Sometimes those winds favor natural and cultural resource protection, but other times, they do not. While park managers were able to influence or sway the opinions of the interested politicians in most cases, the recent policy-making past in Yellowstone clearly reflects consistent political interest and influence.[5]

Why is the NPS so vulnerable to political influences? Tradition is one answer to this question. As many ex-NPS directors and scholars have agreed, the NPS has always been politically weak and thus more subject to the whims of political preferences than many other government agencies. This is due in part because the agency is small—it certainly cannot compare to the large size (or political clout) of the Department of Defense or Homeland Security, for instance.[6]

The NPS's political vulnerability also derives from the fact that the agency, since its inception in 1916, has encouraged political support. By building an infrastructure that encourages park visitation, the NPS has succeeded in making parks across America ever more popular, with numerous and thriving gateway (or local) economies developing along the way. Politicians took notice that Americans and visitors from abroad loved the parks and spent money in and around them. In fact, by the 1960s and 1970s the country's national parks were in danger of becoming "loved to death," with high visitor numbers harming the very resources the parks were established to protect. As a result, NPS began trying to curtail such high visitation, worried that this part of its federal mandate was harming the protection of wildlands in the parks. Restricting visitation can, however, limit economic enhancement, the darling child of politics. Thus, increasingly, the political attention that NPS had encouraged now frowns upon its more preservationist policies. The goal of preserving park resources is now often seen as antithetical to economic enhancement and the politicians who embrace a thriving economy react accordingly.[7]

Furthermore, unlike the U.S. Forest Service (USFS), the NPS was only given a directive by the federal government recently (in 1998) to further park protection and visitor experience through scientific research. Consequently, only in the contemporary era has the NPS embraced substantial research projects and research reviews, and sometimes only because it has lost a court battle or political fight over decisions it has made (such as in the Fishing

Bridge Village and snowmobile issues). This late-coming research directive has made the agency more subject to political influence, for politicians seem to have a sixth sense enabling them to determine when a robust research base is lacking (again, such as in the Fishing Bridge and snowmobile cases).[8]

This political influence, unfortunately, can lead at times to compromised resource protection and visitor experiences, as the snowmobile story illustrates. Such influence is the strongest policy-making determinant in the national parks in the contemporary era. The next most influential determinant is the scientific research base—if it is robust, widely accepted as true, and easily understood by the public. Other strong influences are the public's thinking about agency policy-making proposals and their effects on economies and motorized public access, as well as whether the agency has a coalition of support from outside interests and how compellingly all have framed the debate. All six determinants influence policy-making outcomes, and the agency usually needs all six determinants aligned in its favor to succeed. The political determinant often falls into line when the other five determinants are supportive of managers' intentions.

Toward Improved National Park Protection

Looking toward the future, building the policy-making determinants in their favor is the single strongest tool that NPS managers have for achieving success. Park managers throughout the NPS system are working toward that end, improving their already good track record of success in park preservation. Before turning to some examples of such efforts, there are three additional recommendations deriving from this analysis to discuss: park managers will likely achieve even more policy successes by furthering their commitment to scientific *research*, allowing sufficient *time* to work on the determinant alignment, and advancing strong and compelling *visions* toward preservation.

The agency's scientific *research* and resource monitoring deficiencies were brought to light in 1997, by NPS historian Richard West Sellars. NPS director Robert Stanton took Sellars's findings to heart and chartered the Natural Resource Challenge, a multifaceted approach to improving the agency's research and monitoring, its partnership ability with outside researchers, and its ability to make those research results available to the public.[9] (By passing the National Parks Omnibus Management Act in 1998, Congress provided further impetus to facilitate and utilize research efforts.) Toward these ends, the challenge consisted of three things. First was a nationwide Inventory and Monitoring Program for the parks, the first national network to provide comprehensive inventories of NPS natural resources (such as the animal and plant species) and to monitor their status over time. To facilitate university research, the agency developed the Cooperative Ecosystem Studies Units, with staff members stationed at various universities around the country able to use expedited processes to charter university research with NPS funds. And finally, the NPS developed Research Learning Centers, Internet-based platforms making the research and monitoring information accessible to anyone with a computer and web access.[10]

While Congress has not funded the program to the extent the agency would prefer, the Natural Resource Challenge has been fairly successful in transforming NPS's approach to research and monitoring, and the use of such information in park management. Indeed, it was research piloted through this program that helped to inform both the snowmobile and the bison controversies, leading to possible solutions for both.[11]

Continuing and strengthening the commitment to this research program, along with collaborations with colleges and universities, will reap many more rewards for park managers in the future. Among other things, a robust research base can help swing other policy-making determinants in NPS's favor. For example, both the fire and wolf controversies illustrate that a solid scientific base can help park managers frame issues in a simple way that appeals to the public. Also, a strong science base is required for political support, as all the success stories discussed in this book have illustrated. Furthermore, because not all national park research needs are attractive to independent researchers, continuing to fund the Natural Resource Challenge can fill those research gaps. Some subjects, such as fire policy and wolf ecology, are attractive research topics to scholars, who have produced volumes of university-sponsored research, but it took NPS-sponsored programs to get scientists to research the specific effects of wolf reintroduction and snowmobile use on Yellowstone. Finally, focusing some research attention on the world of political science—the realm in which many high-level NPS policies are rendered, as this book indicates—would complement the natural, cultural, and social science investigations that the program has thus far promoted.

In addition to research, having enough *time* to develop support for policy making is an important aspect for park managers to consider. In rushed situations, such as during the snowmobile controversy with its court-imposed deadlines, managers have been unable to build durable coalitions, complete necessary research, or address public fears about loss of park access and potential economic harms. Time and again, park managers, the courts, and others have been tempted to believe that solutions were just a short time away, when in fact good policy making can take a long time—five and one-half years was the average length of time needed for the fire policy review and New World Mine successes (with seventeen years needed for wolf reintroduction!). When rushed to a policy decision like this, the NPS is not as successful in aligning the determinants or in enjoying policy success. While taking sufficient time may come with negative consequences (like the absence of wolves and fires for periods of time in Yellowstone), the ultimate policy outcome is usually worth the wait.

To garner support, the policy-making *vision* also must be strong. Proposing, for example, to reintroduce wolves was considerably more visionary —and more protective in the long run of park resources—than proposing to leave half of Fishing Bridge Village open, even though grizzly bears might be imperiled by that action. Not surprisingly, many environmental groups rallied around the compellingly framed wolf reintroduction, while none supported the agency's proposal to leave part of Fishing Bridge open (a public relations disaster for NPS). The park manager's ability to advance strong vision is, to be certain, often dependent on the contemporary political climate. Yellowstone superintendent Bob Barbee, for example, did not enjoy the climate necessary to advance a strong vision for Fishing Bridge Village. Sometimes waiting for the right political climate to advance a strong vision can pay rich dividends, as in the New World Mine story. Once the political climate shifted and allowed Yellowstone superintendent Mike Finley to oppose the mine, the remaining determinants quickly fell into place in support of the NPS.

Managers contending with policy-making controversies in national parks around the park system have been working to align the determinants in support of their proposals, in efforts past, present, and future. In the recent past, Grand Canyon National Park faced a soundscape issue concerning scenic overflights across the canyon. Thousands of helicopters and small planes take hundreds of thousands of visitors on flightseeing tours over the canyon annually, providing them with a perspective not possible from the park's rim viewpoints. The noise from such flights, which disturbs backcountry hikers, was the focal point of a controversy in this park for decades. As with the snowmobile issue at Yellowstone, Grand Canyon managers struggled to build a coalition of support to quiet the parks (the Federal Aviation

Administration [FAA], which regulates all the country's airspace, tends to promote air travel), procure the necessary research, and convince involved stakeholders that limiting such overflights would not damage local economies. Despite these hurdles, NPS managers at Grand Canyon released an EIS in 2011 proposing to substantially increase backcountry silence throughout the park, a progressive vision complemented by substantial amounts of new research and supported by external interest groups. The agency's persistence in aligning the policy determinants appeared to be paying off. Unfortunately, in 2012, that EIS became moot because Senator John McCain passed a legislative rider compelling the NPS and FAA to retain overflight use at existing levels (possibly ending this debate, though air noise will continue to provoke complaints and probable future policy-making efforts, such as an effort to overturn the rider).[12] McCain's action reminds us that parks exist in a politically charged space.

Presently, NPS managers in Yosemite National Park are working to align the determinants in their favor concerning their longest ongoing controversy: the appropriate level of development and human recreation in the iconic Yosemite Valley. Most recently, this debate has taken the form of a management plan for the Merced River, which flows through the valley and was declared a Wild and Scenic River in 1987. Under the Wild and Scenic Rivers Act, managing agencies must create plans to protect the river by stipulating the kinds and amounts of use they will allow on the river and within one-quarter mile of its banks. Yosemite managers issued one such plan in 2000, with a supplement in 2005. Both were litigated—successfully— by local interest groups displeased with NPS's proposals. Such litigation is testament to the fact that NPS lacked a strong coalition with external interests. Additionally, because the agency's policy proposals involved curtailing some automobile access to Yosemite, NPS's plans were framed by opponents as "anti-automobile" and as potentially harmful to the economy. Relevant scientific data concerning the issue was assembled, but important questions about gaps in the information went unanswered (such as research that linked river water to the natural function of the valley's scenic, moist meadows). Recently, however, the NPS has commissioned extensive amounts of research to fill the knowledge gaps and has discussed some relatively visionary proposals for the valley's future. Such efforts suggest that the agency may be aligning more policy determinants in its favor—but a court-ordered deadline may prevent policy-making success.[13]

Finally, future opportunities also exist for NPS to build policy determinants in its favor. Perhaps the best example is an issue that has been simmering on the back burner in many national parks: noise from motorcycles, particularly Harley-Davidson motorcycles, whose owners have altered their bikes' exhaust systems to produce the characteristic Harley sound. Park managers throughout the national park system have been fielding complaints for years from visitors upset about how this noise detracts from their park experience. In fact, in many parks, Harley-Davidson motorcycles are the single loudest vehicles that travel through the landscape. Most Harley drivers, though, do not tour the parks to destroy the soundscape; they have the same love of nature as most park visitors. To deal with this controversy, park managers could develop a compelling vision of quiet parks with quiet motorcycles and then start building a coalition with Harley-Davidson owners sympathetic to that vision. NPS managers could approach the national Harley-Davidson owner's club toward that end. If a coalition is not possible with that (or similar) groups, park managers could certainly find environmental groups sympathetic to this issue, with whom they could build a coalition and frame a compelling vision.[14]

In addition, in the specific case of Yellowstone, park managers could begin to assemble a scientific research base detailing the impacts of Harley-Davidson noise on park soundscapes. Of all the national parks, Yellowstone has perhaps the best opportunity to build such a research base, as park managers there have been gathering soundscape data year-round—including during the annual Harley-Davidson motorcycle rally in Sturgis, South Dakota, and the annual Honda Gold Wing motorcycle rally in Billings, Montana. Owners of both Harley-Davidsons and Hondas often tour Yellowstone en route to or from these rallies—but Hondas are generally not as noisy as Harley-Davidsons. By analyzing their existing data, Yellowstone managers could build a research base comparing the soundscape impacts of the two motorcycle types and likely show that noise is not a requirement for motorcycle touring of Yellowstone National Park. More important, they could build a park- and issue-specific research base that NPS and other researchers could draw upon for years to come. It could be used when NPS has developed the coalition to quiet Yellowstone and other national parks. By publishing research papers several years in advance of such a policy-making effort, NPS can further ensure that the research findings will be commonly accepted by the public (and that stakeholders in the debate will not reject research based on their values). In such a way, park managers could begin to align the policy-making determinants in their favor.[15]

Park management issues that fester for decades, such as noise in the Grand Canyon and development in Yosemite, have been termed "wicked" by some social scientists. These scientists have found several common threads in such issues: scientific uncertainty, a deep-seated values conflict between involved stakeholders, and resulting agency inability to resolve the issue. Some scientists feel that the best approach to this situation is to acknowledge the issue's intransigence, seek research into problem areas, and change management of the issue incrementally according to the new research.[16] Certainly, the snowmobile, bison, and wolf issues also appear to be "wicked." However, wolf management seems more resolved than the snowmobile or bison issues, perhaps because the NPS did indeed acknowledge the controversial nature of the reintroduction proposal and sought the appropriate research. While park managers in the snowmobile and bison issues have done the same things, they succeeded more with wolf reintroduction—arguably because they advocated a strong vision for the park's future but also because they patiently aligned the policy determinants in their favor. With snowmobiles and bison, park managers have not been so successful, perhaps because their vision has not been as strong, and certainly because the policy determinants have not been aligned. Park managers' success with wolf reintroduction indicates that the incremental approach may not always be the successful one; the radical vision, supported by all six policy determinants, achieved a level of success in that issue that remains to be seen in the bison and snowmobile issues. Some wicked issues, in other words, may be more resolvable than others, given agency commitment to a strong vision (which, as noted above, is not always possible for park managers to advance) and successful alignment of policy determinants. At the very least, some wicked issues may subside into lower-intensity conflicts with the proper alignment of policy determinants— and with the necessary time and a strong agency vision.

Aligning the policy determinants in their favor can take years, as park managers know. This is in part because complete (or nearly complete) alignment of the determinants is necessary for an outcome to be successful— though it should be emphasized that complete alignment is no guarantee of policy-making success. Given the changing political climate, park managers may have to wait a while for a full alignment of determinants; issues may fester and resources may suffer for extended periods, but ultimate policy success and resource protection seem possible for most issues, given the

FIGURE 34: Visitors at Old Faithful, 2008. Park managers have been working diligently in the last two decades to restore quiet to Yellowstone in the winter months. While they have enjoyed some success, oversnow vehicle noise is still prevalent in certain areas of the park, especially at Old Faithful. In addition to the noise, the high cost of touring the park on either snowmobile or snowcoach prohibits many from experiencing the spectacular sights and sounds of Yellowstone in winter. With a more complete alignment of the policy determinants in their favor, Yellowstone managers might one day succeed in making a winter visit both quieter and more affordable for all. Erupting in the background is Lion Geyser; Old Faithful is out of view to the left. Author photo.

long-term vision park managers have. Ultimately, the parks exist in a political world, something park managers have long recognized and a situation about which they are developing more and more expertise.

Along with such expertise, having a healthy dose of persistence, good scientific research, and a compelling vision will result in more policy-making struggles becoming success stories. If that comes to pass, the future Yellowstone visitor might have a different experience than today's visitor. Hearkening back to the visitor touring Yellowstone in this book's introduction, future visitors will still enjoy the sight of wolves and evidence of wildfire activity, and appreciate the absence of the harmful gold mine. They will see wild bison in the park and notice some bison finding safe harbor outside the park in winter. When they travel through the Fishing Bridge area, they might notice meadows and sapling trees thriving in previously trampled areas. They might also be able to tour Yellowstone in winter affordably, either on buses or in their own cars, on snow-plowed roads that were once groomed for noisy oversnow vehicles but now are plowed for quieter and more comfortable travel (figure 34). Such visitors, in short, may find a park whose resources are protected more consistently in the face of an uncertain future, resulting in a visitor experience that is more enriching for all.[17] That Yellowstone would be the park that its managers are constantly working to create, one in which they expertly use the world of politics, the knowledge of scientific studies, and the other policy-making determinants to protect Yellowstone National Park for all time.

Notes

Abbreviations Used in the Endnotes and Bibliography

ARC   American Rivers Collection, CONS 147, Conservation Collection, Denver Public Library, Denver, Colorado

BDC   *Bozeman Daily Chronicle*, Bozeman, Montana

BGZ   *Billings Gazette*, Billings, Montana

CEP   *Cody Enterprise*, Cody, Wyoming

CST   *Casper Star Tribune*, Casper, Wyoming

DCP   Development Concept Plan

DPL   Conservation Collection, Denver Public Library, Denver, Colorado

DSC   Storage Area Box 51, National Park Service Denver Service Center, Technical Information Center, Denver, Colorado. Note that this box will eventually be transferred to the Federal Records Center in Denver.

EPA   Environmental Protection Agency

FWS   Fish and Wildlife Service

GYA   Greater Yellowstone Area

GYC   Greater Yellowstone Coalition, Bozeman, Montana

GYCC   Greater Yellowstone Coordinating Committee

GYCN   Noranda Collection, Greater Yellowstone Coalition files, Bozeman, Montana

GYR   *Greater Yellowstone Report* newsletter, Greater Yellowstone Coalition, Bozeman, Montana

HCN   *High Country News* periodical, Paonia, Colorado

JHNG   *Jackson Hole News and Guide*, Jackson, Wyoming

LVE   *Livingston Enterprise*, Livingston, Montana

MAOF   Management Assistant's Office files, National Park Service, Yellowstone National Park, Mammoth Hot Springs, Wyoming. Note that some of the Management Assistant's Office files were transferred to the Yellowstone National Park Archives shortly after the Yellowstone Heritage Center in Gardiner, Montana, opened in 2005. The scholar pursuing sources cited is welcome to contact the author if he or she cannot find sources at the Heritage Center or in Yellowstone's other file collections.

MST   *Minneapolis Star Tribune*, Minneapolis, Minnesota

NEPA   National Environmental Policy Act

NPCA   National Parks and Conservation Association

NPS   National Park Service

NWF   National Wildlife Federation

NYT   *The New York Times*

SCLDF Sierra Club Legal Defense Fund

SLT   *The Salt Lake Tribune*

TWS   The Wilderness Society Collection, CONS 130, Conservation Collection, Denver Public Library, Denver, Colorado

WSJ   *The Wall Street Journal*

YCR   Yellowstone Center for Resources files, National Park Service, Yellowstone National Park, Mammoth Hot Springs, Wyoming. Note that many YCR files were transferred to the Yellowstone Heritage Center when it opened in Gardiner, Montana, in 2005.

USDA   United States Department of Agriculture, Washington, D.C.

USDI   United States Department of the Interior, Washington, D.C.

USFS   United States Forest Service

YNPA   Yellowstone National Park Archives, Gardiner, Montana

YNPR   Yellowstone National Park Research Library, Gardiner, Montana

YNPV   Yellowstone National Park Research Library vertical files, Gardiner, Montana

Introduction

1. The books are: William R. Lowry, *Repairing Paradise: Restoring Nature in America's National Parks* (Washington, D.C.: The Brookings Institution, 2009); Paul Schullery, *Searching for Yellowstone: Ecology and Wonder in the Last Wilderness* (Boston: Houghton Mifflin, 1997); James A. Pritchard, *Preserving Yellowstone's Natural Conditions: Science and the Perception of Nature* (Lincoln: University of Nebraska Press, 1999); and Richard West Sellars, *Preserving Nature in the National Parks: A History* (New Haven, CT: Yale University Press, 1997).

2. See the following for further discussion on national park managers: Richard A.

Bartlett, *Yellowstone: A Wilderness Besieged* (Tucson: University of Arizona Press, 1986); Michael Frome, *Regreening the National Parks* (Tucson: University of Arizona Press, 1992); Susan G. Clark, *Ensuring Greater Yellowstone's Future: Choices for Leaders and Citizens* (New Haven, CT: Yale University Press, 2008); Schullery, *Searching for Yellowstone*; Alfred Runte, *National Parks: The American Experience* (Lincoln: University of Nebraska Press, 1979); Michael J. Yochim, *Yellowstone and the Snowmobile: Locking Horns over National Park Use* (Lawrence: University Press of Kansas, 2009); Larry M. Dilsaver and William C. Tweed, *Challenge of the Big Trees: A Resource History of Sequoia and Kings Canyon National Parks* (Three Rivers, CA: Sequoia Natural History Association, Inc., 1990); Larry M. Dilsaver, *Cumberland Island National Seashore: A History of Conservation Conflict* (Charlottesville: University of Virginia Press, 2004); Aubrey L. Haines, *The Yellowstone Story: A History of Our First National Park*, rev. ed. (1977; Wyoming: The Yellowstone Association for Natural Science, History & Education, Inc., in cooperation with the University Press of Colorado, 1996); Alfred Runte, *Yosemite: The Embattled Wilderness* (Lincoln: University of Nebraska Press, 1990); and R. Gerald Wright, *Wildlife Research and Management in the National Parks* (Urbana: University of Illinois Press, 1992).

3. From the NPS Organic Act, which is "An Act to Establish a National Park Service, and for Other Purposes," 39 Stat. 535, approved August 25, 1916, as found in Lary M. Dilsaver, *America's National Park System: The Critical Documents* (Lanham, MD: Rowman & Littlefield Publishers, Inc., 1994), 46–47.

4. One good example of the influence such employees have can be found in the conflicting snowmobile policies between Glacier and Yellowstone National Parks. While the former prohibits them, the latter allows them. These policies were determined in part by the predispositions of the superintendents in those parks in the 1970s, both of whom felt they were correctly applying the agency's mandate to their park. See Michael J. Yochim, "Snow Machines in the Gardens: The History of Snowmobiles in Glacier and Yellowstone National Parks," *Montana the Magazine of Western History*, Autumn 2003, 2–15. Also, see the New World Mine and snowmobile controversies explored in chapters 3 and 4 herein. Superintendent Mike Finley and Interior Secretary Gale Norton played pivotal (and very different) roles in these two policy-making issues.

5. Runte, *National Parks*, 25. Authors discussing the history of, and generally the increasing influence of, science and research in the parks include: Sellars, *Preserving Nature in the National Parks*; James Pritchard, *Preserving Yellowstone's Natural Conditions*, 1999; Schullery, *Searching for Yellowstone*; Wright, *Wildlife Research and Management in the National Parks*; Lowry, *Repairing Paradise*; Alice Wondrak Biel, *Do (Not) Feed the Bears: The Fitful History of Wildlife and Tourists in Yellowstone* (Lawrence: University Press of

Kansas, 2006); Hal K. Rothman, *Blazing Heritage: A History of Wildland Fire in the National Parks* (New York: Oxford University Press, 2007); Steven A. Primm and Tim W. Clark, "The Greater Yellowstone Policy Debate: What is the Policy Problem?," *Policy Sciences* 29, no. 2 (1996): 137–66; and Richard Grusin, *Culture, Technology, and the Creation of America's National Parks* (New York: Cambridge University Press, 2004). Authors providing an alternative viewpoint are: Alston Chase, *Playing God in Yellowstone* (New York: Harcourt Brace Jovanovich, 1986); Karl Hess Jr., *Rocky Times in Rocky Mountain National Park: An Unnatural History* (Niwot: University Press of Colorado, 1993); Micah Morrison, *Fire in Paradise: The Yellowstone Fires and the Politics of Environmentalism* (New York: HarperCollins Publishers, Inc., 1993); Charles Kay, "Aboriginal Overkill: The Role of Native Americans in Structuring Western Ecosystems," *Human Nature* 5, no. 4 (1994): 359–98; and Charles Kay, "Are Ecosystems Structured from the Top-Down or Bottom-Up? A New Look at an Old Debate," *Wildlife Society Bulletin* 26, no.3 (1998): 484–98. These authors generally believe NPS ignores science. Chase in particular has seen extensive rebuttals by other scholars; see Schullery, *Searching for Yellowstone*, 44–45, 225, 278; and Holmes Rolston, "Biology and Philosophy in Yellowstone," *Biology and Philosophy* 5 (1990): 241–58. Regarding Kay, see my rebuttal, "Aboriginal Overkill Overstated: Errors in Charles Kay's Hypothesis," *Human Nature* 12, no. 2 (2001): 141–67.

6. Perhaps the best discussion of incorporating locals into park management can be found in: Karl Jacoby, *Crimes Against Nature: Squatters, Poachers, Thieves, and the Hidden History of American Conservation* (Berkeley: University of California Press, 2001); and Lowry, *Repairing Paradise*. Other authors have focused on Native American dispossession, such as Mark David Spence in *Dispossessing the Wilderness: Indian Removal and the Making of the National Parks* (New York: Oxford University Press, 1999); and Barbara J. Morehouse, *A Place Called Grand Canyon: Contested Geographies* (Tucson: University of Arizona Press, 1996).

7. For more information on this subject, see Martin A. Nie, *Beyond Wolves: The Politics of Wolf Recovery and Management* (Minneapolis: University of Minnesota Press, 2003), 26–112; William T. Borrie, Wayne A. Freimund, and Mae A. Davenport, "Winter Visitors to Yellowstone National Park: Their Value Orientations and Support for Management Actions," *Human Ecology Review* 9, no.2 (2002): 41–48; Mae A. Davenport and William T. Borrie, "The Appropriateness of Snowmobiling in National Parks: An Investigation of the Meanings of Snowmobiling Experiences in Yellowstone National Park," *Environmental Management* 35, no. 2 (2005): 151–60; Judith Layzer, *The Environmental Case: Translating Values into Policy* (Washington, D.C.: CQ Press, 2006), 1–25, 223–50; Yochim, *Yellowstone and the Snowmobile*; Stephen Fox, *The American Conservation Movement: John Muir and His Legacy* (Madison: University of Wisconsin Press, 1981); Catherine L. Albanese, *Nature*

Religion in America: From the Algonkian Indians to the New Age (Illinois: University of Chicago Press, 1990); Linda Graber, *Wilderness As Sacred Space* (Washington, D.C.: American Association of Geographers, 1976); and Thomas R. Dunlap, *Faith in Nature: Environmentalism as Religious Quest* (Seattle: University of Washington Press, 2004). Note that "stakeholder" refers to members of the public who choose to involve themselves in federal government policy debates.

8. The ex-NPS directors and their books are: George B. Hartzog, *Battling for the National Parks* (Mount Kisco, NY: Moyer Bell Ltd., 1988); James M. Ridenour, *The National Parks Compromised: Pork Barrel Politics and America's Treasures* (Merrillville, IN: ICS Books, Inc., 1994); and W. C. Everhart, *The National Park Service* (Boulder, CO: Westview Press, 1983). See also Schullery, *Searching for Yellowstone*; Primm and Clark, "The Greater Yellowstone Policy Debate"; and Mary Ann Franke, *To Save the Wild Bison: Life on the Edge in Yellowstone* (Norman: University of Oklahoma Press, 2005).

9. Lowry's two books are *The Capacity for Wonder: Preserving National Parks* (Washington, D.C.: The Brookings Institution, 1994) and *Preserving Public Lands for the Future: The Politics of Intergenerational Goods* (Washington, D.C.: Georgetown University Press, 1998). See also Daniel L. Dustin and Ingrid E. Schneider, "The Science of Politics/The Politics of Science: Examining the Snowmobile Controversy in Yellowstone National Park," *Environmental Management* 34, no. 6 (2005): 761–67.

10. Lowry, *Repairing Paradise*. Primm and Clark, in "The Greater Yellowstone Policy Debate," produce much the same finding.

11. Jason Seawright and John Gerring present a thorough discussion of case study selection techniques in "Case Selection Techniques in Case Study Research," *Political Research Quarterly* 61, no. 2 (June 2008): 294–308. As they note is common in case study research, the controlled comparison in this book is a hybrid of two different techniques: the "most similar" and "most different" methods. See also Alexander L. George and Andrew Bennett, *Case Studies and Theory Development* (Cambridge, MA: MIT Press, 2005).

12. Clark, *Ensuring Greater Yellowstone's Future*, 123–26. As further demonstration that it should be excluded, an examination of the "Vision" document controversy would reveal most, but not all, of the same determinants at play—neither science nor coalitions were at play in the issue. Another example of an issue excluded from my study is oil and gas drilling in the Shoshone National Forest, bordering Yellowstone to the east; the 1990s controversy mainly involved policy making in general on the national forest.

13. James R. Skillen, in *The Nation's Largest Landlord: The Bureau of Land Management in the American West* (Lawrence: University Press of Kansas, 2009), 12, also defines the contemporary policy-making era as beginning with Reagan's inauguration. Peter J. Balint, Ronald E. Stewart, Anand Desai, and Lawrence C. Walters, in their book *Wicked Environmental Problems: Managing Uncertainty*

and Conflict (Washington, D.C.: Island Press, 2011), 212–16, find that many countries experience a shift toward a new policy-making framework in the later stages of industrialization. These authors found that, in the United States, a shift began to occur in the 1960s, which found expression in the passage of the National Environmental Policy Act and other environmental laws of the 1970s; the shift was complete by about 1980.

14. For snowmobiles, see my own work, *Yellowstone and the Snowmobile*. For wolf reintroduction, see Douglas W. Smith and Gary Ferguson, *Decade of the Wolf: Returning the Wild to Yellowstone* (Guilford, CT: Lyons Press, 2005); Hank Fischer, *Wolf Wars: The Remarkable Inside Story of the Restoration of Wolves to Yellowstone* (Helena, MT: Falcon Press, 1995); and Thomas McNamee, *The Return of the Wolf to Yellowstone* (New York: Henry Holt and Company, 1997). For bison, see Franke, *To Save the Wild Bison*.

15. Additionally, in all cases, park managers had to exhibit commitment toward their policy-making goal, one of Lowry's requirements (see Lowry, *Repairing Paradise*). Given the national level of the debates examined in this book, such commitment is assumed and universally present and therefore not carefully examined.

Chapter One

1. Randy Shaw, *The Activist's Handbook: A Primer for the 1990s and Beyond* (Berkeley: University of California Press, 1996), 248–49.

2. Bob Barbee, personal interview with author, Bozeman, Montana, March 24, 2003. Paul Schullery et al., *Fishing Bridge and the Yellowstone Ecosystem, A Report to the Director* (Denver: U.S. Government Printing Office, November 1984), 1, MAOF.

3. The assessment of the influence of environmentalists and Simpson are drawn from the author's personal interviews with: Chris Turk, Denver, Colorado, June 4, 2003; Louisa Willcox, Livingston, Montana, April 9, 2003; Bob Ekey, Bozeman, Montana, April 9, 2003; and Sue Consolo-Murphy, Mammoth Hot Springs, Wyoming, March 25, 2003.

4. Schullery, *Searching for Yellowstone*, 187–90; Schullery et al., *Fishing Bridge and the Yellowstone Ecosystem*; and Paul Schullery, *Nature and Culture at Fishing Bridge: A History of the Fishing Bridge Development in Yellowstone National Park* (Yellowstone National Park, WY: NPS, 2010), 81–85. Note that spawning fish were *potentially* available to grizzly bears, and only in some of Pelican Creek's tributaries; grizzlies were not using any fish habitats in the area in the early 1980s to any significant degree.

5. As found in A. Starker Leopold, S. A. Cain, C. M. Cottam, I. N. Gabrielson, and T. L. Kimball, "Wildlife Management in the National Parks" in *America's National Park System: The Critical Documents*, ed. Larry Dilsaver (Lanham, MD: Rowman & Littlefield, 1994), 239. Olaus Murie's suggestion is from Fishing Bridge Team

Meeting notes, July 8, 1985, File "New Alts. FBDCP," Box "Mid-8os Fishing Bridge History," MAOF; Yellowstone Study Committee, "Yellowstone Master Plan Study," 10–11, YNPV; and USDI-NPS, *Master Plan, Yellowstone National Park* (Denver: NPS, 1974), 17–18, 31.

6. The Leopold report was written by A. Starker Leopold, S. A. Cain, C. M. Cottam, I. N. Gabrielson, and T. L. Kimball, and its official title is "Wildlife Management in the National Parks"; it can be found in *America's National Park System: The Critical Documents*, 237–52. See also William Barmore to Superintendent, November 25, 1968; and William Dunmire to Project Supervisor, May 2, 1972, both in File "Memoranda and correspondence, 1972–1975," Box D-190, YNPA.

7. USDI-NPS, *Master Plan, Yellowstone National Park*, 16–18, 31. While there was some controversy about the master plan's proposal to remove lodging from Yellowstone, there was little focus on the Fishing Bridge proposal.

8. Construction planning and start information is from Sue Consolo-Murphy and Beth Kaeding, "Fishing Bridge: 25 Years of Controversy Regarding Grizzly Bear Management in Yellowstone National Park," *Ursus* 10 (1998): 385–93; and Chase, *Playing God in Yellowstone*, 219–25. For more information on NEPA, see Zygmunt J. B. Plater, Robert H. Abrams, and William Goldfarb, *Environmental Law and Policy: Nature, Law, and Society* (St. Paul, MN: West Publishing Co., 1992), 596–655.

9. Plater et al., *Environmental Law and Policy*, 656–85.

10. Pritchard, *Preserving Yellowstone's Natural Conditions*, 247.

11. Consolo-Murphy and Kaeding, "Fishing Bridge: 25 Years of Controversy," 385–93; Schullery, *Searching for Yellowstone*, 187–90; Pritchard, *Preserving Yellowstone's Natural Conditions*, 237–47; Wright, *Wildlife Research and Management*, 112–16; Sellars, *Preserving Nature in the National Park*, 249–53; and Wondrak Biel, *Do (Not) Feed the Bears*, 86–133.

12. Consolo-Murphy and Kaeding, "Fishing Bridge;" Schullery, *Searching for Yellowstone*, 187–90; Schullery, *Nature and Culture at Fishing Bridge*, 86; and Paul Schullery, e-mail message to author, January 24, 2012.

13. FWS opinion and consultation with John Townsley is from FWS Acting Regional Director, Region 6 (signature illegible) to NPS Regional Director, Rocky Mountain Region, October 31, 1971; Don. W. Minnich to NPS Regional Director, May 3, 1980; Lorraine Mintzmyer to Wally Steucke and Wayne Brewster, September 29, 1980; Roy Slatkavitz to Regional Director, November 25, 1980; FWS Acting Area Manager to Regional Director, December 12, 1980; and John Townsley to Wally Steucke, January 26, 1981, all in File "FWS File," Box "Mid-8os Fishing Bridge History," MAOF. Grizzly bear management plan is from John G. Wood to Regional Director, June 18, 1982, brown folder, Box "FB EIS DCP," MAOF; and USDI-NPS, *Final Environmental Impact Statement, Grizzly Bear Management Program* (Denver, CO: NPS, October 1982), 5.

14. Barbee interview and Consolo-Murphy interview. Bear management plan information is from USDI-NPS, *FEIS: Grizzly Bear Management Program*, October 1982.

15. Bob Barbee, "Superintendent's Annual Report for 1983," 55, YNPR; Mike Strunk to Assistant Manager, June 23, 1983, File "Briefings/NPS Correspondence," Box "Mid-80s Fishing Bridge History," MAOF; "Public Response Form, Lake/Fishing Bridge/Bridge Bay Development Concept Plan, Yellowstone National Park," File "NPS—Yellowstone N. P.—Fishing Bridge Comments," GYC; and Mike Strunk to Team Captain, September 12, 1983, loose in Box "Fishing Bridge EIS General Files," MAOF.

16. William D. Weiss to Bob Barbee, September 30, 1983, File "Public/Congressional Response, 1983 to Fall 1984," Box "Fishing Bridge EIS General Files," MAOF.

17. Robert J. Shelley to Regional Director, September 14, 1983, File "Comments from Public Meetings," Box "Mid-80s Fishing Bridge History," MAOF; and William D. Weiss to Bob Barbee, September 30, 1983, File "Public/ Congressional Response, 1983 to Fall 1984," Box "Fishing Bridge EIS General Files," MAOF.

18. As quoted in Lawrence Wright, "Development Has Grizzlies in a Bear Hug," *HCN*, September 3, 1984.

19. William D. Weiss to Bob Barbee, September 30, 1983, File "Public/Congressional Response, 1983 to Fall 1984," Box "Fishing Bridge EIS General Files," MAOF; Hal Ritchie to Bob Barbee, September 8, 1983, loose in Box "Fishing Bridge EIS General Files," MAOF; and Mike Strunk to Assistant Manager, September 12, 1983, loose in Box "Fishing Bridge EIS General Files," MAOF. See also Lawrence Wright, "Development Has Grizzlies in a Bear Hug," *HCN*, September 3, 1984.

20. An example of congressional inquiries is in the letter Ron Marlenee, George Hansen, and Larry Craig to Russell Dickenson, November 17, 1983, loose in Box "Fishing Bridge EIS General Files," MAOF; in Wright, "Development Has Grizzlies in a Bear Hug"; and in "Briefing Statement for the Director, December 1983," File "Rusbrief/Options," Box "Mid-80s Fishing Bridge History," MAOF.

21. Wright, "Development Has Grizzlies in a Bear Hug"; and Bruce Gilchrist, "Campground Closure at Yellowstone National Park," *Trailer Life* (January 1984): 29. The Gilchrist article is in File "Public/Congressional Response 1983 to Fall 1984," Box "Fishing Bridge EIS General Files," MAOF.

22. Schullery et al., *Fishing Bridge and the Yellowstone Ecosystem*, 2, 110.

23. Ibid., 58–76, 108–10. These actions were part of larger efforts in the early 1970s to promote natural regulation policies in Yellowstone, all part of the fallout from the Leopold report. See Pritchard, *Preserving Yellowstone's Natural Conditions*, 201–50.

24. Schullery et al., *Fishing Bridge and the Yellowstone Ecosystem*, 58–76, 108–10; Roy A. Renkin and Kerry A. Gunther, "Predicting Grizzly Bear Mortality in

Developed Areas of Yellowstone Park," 171–76; and Kerry A. Gunther, M. J. Biel, K. A. Churchill, and R. L. Danforth, "Changing Problems in Yellowstone Bear Management, 23 Years after the Dumps," 85–110, both in *Greater Yellowstone Predators, Proceedings of the Third Biennial Conference on the Greater Yellowstone Ecosystem, September 24–27, 1995* (Jackson, WY: Northern Rockies Conservation Cooperative, 2000). Those same 1970s management actions are responsible in part for a large increase in regional bear populations in the 1990s and 2000s.

25. Dan Wenk, telephone interview with author, April 4, 2003, during which he told the author why Bridge Bay was analyzed separately from Fishing Bridge; and Consolo-Murphy and Kaeding, "Fishing Bridge," in which the authors discuss the problems with analyzing Fishing Bridge separately from the other two areas.

26. Simplistic claims by some modern scholars that national park management should be based solely on scientific research need to reckon with the field's limitations. Chase in *Playing God in Yellowstone* promotes science-based park management, as does Kay in "Aboriginal Overkill" and "Are Ecosystems Structured from the Top-Down or Bottom-Up?"

27. Karen Gibbons to Russell Dickenson, July 30, 1984, File "EIS—Fishing Bridge—1981–1984," Box L-69, YNPA.

28. Bob Barbee to "Friends of Yellowstone," June 8, 1984, File "[Untitled]," Box K-108, YNPA; Karen Gibbons to Russell Dickenson, July 30, 1984, File "EIS—Fishing Bridge—1981–1984," Box L-69, YNPA; Bob Barbee to David A. Smith, June 20, 1985, File "David Smith," Box "Mid-80s Fishing Bridge History," MAOF; and Malcom Wallop, Alan Simpson, and Dick Cheney to Russell Dickenson, September 24, 1984, File "Fishing Bridge DCP/EA Notes," Box "Mid-80s Fishing Bridge History," MAOF.

29. Karen Gibbons to Russell Dickenson, July 30, 1984, File "EIS—Fishing Bridge—1981–1984," Box L-69, YNPA; and Rick Reese, "Greater Yellowstone Coalition to Parties Concerned with Fishing Bridge Issue," August 16, 1984, in File "Fishing Bridge DCP/EA Notes," Box "Mid-1980s Fishing Bridge History," MAOF.

30. Simpson was called "Son of Cody" by Management Assistant Steve Iobst, in author's personal interview with Iobst on April 4, 2003, at Mammoth Hot Springs, Wyoming.

31. "Delegation Wants EIS on Fishing Bridge Campground," press release, July 17, 1984, File "NPS—Yellowstone N.P.—Fishing Bridge Correspondence," GYC; and Malcom Wallop, Alan Simpson, and Dick Cheney to Russell Dickenson, September 24, 1984, File "Fishing Bridge DCP/EA Notes," Box "Mid-1980s Fishing Bridge History," MAOF. Wyoming economic bust and boom information is from Phil Roberts, "Boom and Bust, Again: Wyoming in the 1970s," http://uwacadweb. uwyo.edu/robertshistory/New_History_of_Wyoming_chapter_19.htm, accessed July 26, 2011.

32. See the following articles about this issue in *National Parks* magazine: "Yellowstone Grizzlies—Losing Ground to People" (January–February 1983): 38–39; "Conflict at Yellowstone NP Between Grizzlies and Campers" (May–June 1984): 47; Paul Schullery, "Securing the Grizzly's Small Portion" (July–August 1984): 27–32; "Battling for the Bears at Fishing Bridge Campground" (July–August 1984): 33; "Fishing Bridge and Grizzlies" (May–June 1985): 39; "Yellowstone Backs Down On Fishing Bridge Pact" (January–February 1988): 10; and "Fishing Bridge" (May–June 1988): 9.

33. Planning developments are from 50 *Federal Register* 7495, February 22, 1985; NPS, "National Park Service to Prepare Environmental Impact Statement on Fishing Bridge," press release, March 14, 1985, File "Miscellaneous Documents," Box K-106, YNPA; and Bob Barbee to All Offices, May 20, 1985, File "Miscellaneous Memoranda," Box K-106, YNPA. Records of EIS preparation are from Howie Thompson to Midwest/Rocky Mountain Team Assistant Manager, August 13, 1985; and Howie Thompson to Midwest/Rocky Mountain Team Assistant Manager, August 27, 1985, both in File "Fishing Bridge DCP/ EA Notes," Box "Mid-80s Fishing Bridge History," MAOF. See also Howie Thompson to Assistant Manager, January 14, 1986, File "Meetings and Trip Reports," Box "Mid-80s Fishing Bridge History," MAOF. Public response data is from "Fishing Bridge Public Response Newsletter," File "FB Newsletter," Box "Fishing Bridge EIS General Files," MAOF. Need for congressional approval is from "Consult Solicitors Options," handwritten notes (author unknown), File "FB DEIS," Box "Mid-80s Fishing Bridge History," MAOF.

34. Survey results are from "Results of East Entrance Survey," 1984, File "EIS— Fishing Bridge—1981–1984," Box L-69, YNPA; "Results of Camper Exit Survey," 1984, loose in Box "Fishing Bridge EIS, 2nd Newsletter Response," MAOF; and "Results of RV Park Survey," 1984, File "YCC/Surveys," Box "Mid-80s Fishing Bridge History," MAOF. Reopening consultation is from Lorraine Mintzmyer to FWS Regional Director, July 19, 1985, File "David Smith," Box "Mid-80s Fishing Bridge History," MAOF.

35. Alan Simpson information is from Barbee interview; Iobst interview; and Michael Scott, personal interview with author, Bozeman, Montana, April 16, 2003. See also Donald Loren Hardy, *Shooting from the Lip: The Life of Senator Simpson* (Norman: University of Oklahoma Press, 2011).

36. Alan Simpson to "Bill" (Bill Vehnekamp, a Cody resident), August 19, 1984, File "Correspondence—General, Fall 1984," Box "Fishing Bridge EIS General Files," MAOF.

37. Meeting results are from "Summary of September 26, 1985 'Summit Meeting' on Fishing Bridge," n.d., File "EIS—Fishing Bridge—1985," Box L-69, YNPA; Bob Barbee, "Superintendent's Annual Report for 1985," 35, YNPR; and Robert Ekey, "Fishing Bridge Action Delayed," *BGZ*, October 3, 1985. See also Alan Simpson to "Bill," August 19, 1984, File "Correspondence—General, Fall 1984," Box "Fishing Bridge EIS General Files," MAOF. Information about good speaking

terms is from Barbee interview. By this time, it was clear that the controversy involved only Fishing Bridge, so Bob Barbee also resumed the DCP planning for Bridge Bay and Lake. See Steve Iobst to All Employees, November 1, 1985, File "Miscellaneous Memoranda," Box K-106, YNPA; and Bob Barbee, "Superintendent's Annual Report for 1985," 36, YNPR.

38. Galen Buterbaugh to NPS Regional Director, October 18, 1985; Bob Barbee to Pat Williams, January 29, 1986, both in File "David Smith," Box "Mid-80s Fishing Bridge History," MAOF. See also Jack Neckels to Estelle V. Nojunas, November 14, 1985, File "1621 Mgmt. of Natural Resources and Areas—Threatened and Endangered Species, 1985," Box N-132, YNPA; and Barbee, "Superintendent's Annual Report for 1985," 36.

39. NPS, "Interim Management Plan for Operations at Fishing Bridge and Grant Village," May 1986, YNPV; and "Fishing Bridge Rules Tightened," *LVE*, May 12, 1986. See also Wayne Brewster to Superintendent, May 7, 1986; and Ben Clary (for Robert Barbee) to Wayne Brewster, May 8, 1986, both in File "EIS—Environmental Assessment—Lake/Bridge Bay DCP—1980–91," Box L-69, YNPA. Many of the interim plan closures are still in effect today, including the following: Pelican Valley is closed to human entry prior to July 4 every summer; Pelican Valley is open only 9 a.m. to 7 p.m.; no overnight camping is allowed in Pelican Valley; Heart Lake is closed to human entry before July 1; and Grant Village campground opens annually on June 20.

40. *NWF and Wyoming Wildlife Federation vs. NPS, USFWS, and Department of the Interior, Legal Complaint*, March 27, 1986, File "File 3," Box W-222, YNPA; and Matt Reid, "Controversy at Fishing Bridge," *The Pronghorn* (Wyoming Wildlife Federation newsletter), May 1986.

41. Thomas France to Bob Barbee, June 4, 1985, File "NPS—Yellowstone N.P.—Fishing Bridge Correspondence," GYC. See also Thomas France to Bob Barbee, July 3, 1985; and Bob Barbee to Thomas France, July 23, 1985, both in File "N1621 Mgmt. of Natural Resources & Areas—Threatened & Endangered Species 1985," Box N-132, YNPA. And see *NWF and Wyoming Wildlife Federation vs. NPS, USFWS, and Department of the Interior, Legal Complaint.* Thomas France to Bob Barbee, February 7, 1986; and Thomas France to Dave Mattson, May 20, 1986, both in File "EIS—Fishing Bridge—Interim Management Plan—Litigation—NWF vs. NPS/USFWS—1986," Box W-242, YNPA. And Betsy Marston, "Groups Sue to Close Campground," *HCN*, April 28, 1986. William Penn Mott's involvement is from Thomas France to William Penn Mott, August 22, 1985, File "NPS—Yellowstone N.P.—Fishing Bridge Correspondence," GYC.

42. Margot Zallen to Regional Director, NPS, and Regional Director, FWS, June 4, 1987, File "EIS—Fishing Bridge—Interim Management Plan—Litigation—NWF vs. NPS/UWFWS—1987–88," Box W-242, YNPA; Tom Howard, "Wildlife group looks past 'interim' ruling," *BGZ*, May 29, 1987; and "Campsites Can Open, Judge Says," *BGZ*, May 29, 1987.

43. Scott E. Atkinson, Thomas D. Crocker, and Cliff Nowell, "Socio-Economic Impact Analysis of the Proposed Relocation of Fishing Bridge Facilities in Yellowstone National Park," 2, File "Briefings/NPS Correspondence," Box "Mid-80s Fishing Bridge History," MAOF.

44. Alan Simpson to "Bob" [Barbee], October 9, 1986, File "Socioeconomic 'Comment,'" Box "Fishing Bridge EIS General Files," MAOF.

45. Alan Simpson to "Bob" [Barbee], October 9, 1986, File "Socioeconomic 'Comment,'" Box "Fishing Bridge EIS General Files," MAOF; Craig Johnson, "Study on Fishing Bridge Pleases Conservationists," *BDC*, September 26, 1986; and personal interviews with Turk, Willcox, Barbee, Iobst, Consolo-Murphy, and Wenk.

46. Yochim, *Yellowstone and the Snowmobile*, 137–40; and Nie, *Beyond Wolves*, 29.

47. Delays information is from Jack Neckels to Director, January 10, 1986, loose in Box "Fishing Bridge EIS, 2nd Newsletter Response," MAOF; Ben Clary (for Bob Barbee) to Pete Wilson, December 11, 1986, File "Correspondence," Box K-106, YNPA; and "Fishing Bridge Planning Briefing, July 1986," File "Briefings/ NPS Correspondence," Box "Mid-80s Fishing Bridge History," MAOF. Campsite replacement is from "Public Response Newsletter, April 1986," File "FB DEIS," Box "Mid-80s Fishing Bridge History," MAOF; "Fishing Bridge," *HCN*, April 28, 1986; and Robert Ekey and Tom Howard, "Fishing Bridge Choices: Options Detailed for Campground," *BGZ*, April 10, 1986.

48. Bill Schilling, attachment to April 25, 1986 letter to Bob Barbee, File "Correspondence—General, Fall 1984," Box "Fishing Bridge EIS General Files," MAOF.

49. Bill Schilling to Bob Barbee, April 2, 1986; Ben Clary (for Bob Barbee) to Bill Schilling, April 29, 1986; and Bill Schilling to Bob Barbee, April 25, 1986, all in File "Correspondence—General, Fall 1984," Box "Fishing Bridge EIS General Files," MAOF. See also "Fishing Bridge Issue Grows," *Idaho Falls Post Register*, April 29, 1986; "Closures Opposed at Fishing Bridge," *LVE*, April 28, 1986; and Paul A. Smith, "Park's Fishing Bridge Should Remain Open," *Casper Star Tribune*, November 7, 1986.

50. "Analysis of Public Response to April 1986 Newsletter for the Fishing Bridge Development Concept Plan, Yellowstone National Park," File "F.B. Public Response—April '86," Box "Mid- 80s Fishing Bridge History," MAOF; and "Fishing Bridge Planning Briefing, July 1986," File "Briefings/NPS Correspondence," Box "Mid-80s Fishing Bridge History," MAOF.

51. As quoted in Craig Johnson, "Earth First! protests over Fishing Bridge," *BDC*, March 4, 1986.

52. Untitled information sheet for Public Affairs Officers, July 9, 1985, File "EIS— Fishing Bridge—1985—EF! Arrests," Box L-69, YNPA; Craig Johnson, "Earth First! Protests Over Fishing Bridge," *BDC*, March 4, 1986; "Earth First Chief Arrested in Park Protest," *Idaho Falls Post Register*, July 8, 1986; Joan Haines, "Four Earth First! Protesters Arrested in Park," *BDC*, July 8, 1986; Bob Barbee, "Superintendent's Annual Report for 1986," 28, YNPR; "Earth First

Demonstration, Grant Village, July 7, 1986," Video 091A, YNPA; "Earth First Demonstration, Fishing Bridge, 7–8–86," Video 090A, YNPA; and "Action Plan—Operation 'Earthmover,' May 22–26, 1986," File "EIS—Fishing Bridge—Interim Management Plan—Operation Earth Mover," Box W-242, YNPA. Bob Barbee and his staff were the "bioprostitutes," a label given to them by Earth First! protesters in 1986.

53. Lance Olsen to Bob Barbee, July 25, 1986, File "Correspondence—General, Fall 1984," Box "Fishing Bridge EIS General Files," MAOF; Robert Ekey, "Park workers lobby against development," *BDC*, April 7, 1986. See also Tony Povilitis, "A Voice in the Wilderness" (Campaign for Yellowstone's Bears newsletter, no. 2); "Why Is Fishing Bridge Important to Bears" and "How You Can Help the Grizzly Bears of Yellowstone," both flyers that were disseminated at summer 1986 protests; all in File "Public Demonstrations in YNP," Box K-25, YNPA. And see Richard R. Meis to Bob Barbee, April 30, 1986, File "NPS—Yellowstone N.P.—Fishing Bridge Correspondence," GYC.

54. Barbee interview. USDI-NPS, *Draft Environmental Impact Statement/Development Concept Plan, Fishing Bridge Developed Area, Yellowstone* (Denver: NPS, 1987), iii. Effectiveness of various activist tactics is from Shaw, *The Activist's Handbook*. Several persons involved in the controversy agreed that environmentalist influence was not great; this information is from personal interviews with Iobst, Turk, and Barbee.

55. Information on political pressure is from Robert Ekey, "Park Boss Plans Deal with Cody," *BGZ*, October 27, 1986; and Howie Thompson to Assistant Manager, Central Team, Denver Service Center, October 27, 1986, File "FB Newsletter," Box "Fishing Bridge EIS General Files," MAOF. Planning for the preferred alternative is from Richard A. Strait to Regional Director, n.d., loose in Box "Fishing Bridge EIS, 2nd Newsletter Response," MAOF; "Preliminary Concepts of Preferred Alternative for Fishing Bridge Environmental Impact Statement Released," press release, File "Untitled," Box K-108, YNPA. Final form of preferred alternative is from Ekey, "Park Boss Plans Deal with Cody"; "Fishing Bridge Plan Unveiled," *LVE*, November 7, 1986; and USDI-NPS, *Draft Environmental Impact Statement*, 29–35.

56. Jack Neckels to Deputy Director, August 14, 1986; and William Penn Mott to Jack Neckels, September 4, 1986, both in File "Briefings/NPS Correspondence," Box "Mid-80s Fishing Bridge History," MAOF. Howie Thompson, notes on conference call to discuss modifications to the Preferred Alternative, December 18, 1986, File "Fishing Bridge EIS," Box "Fishing Bridge EIS General Files," MAOF. See also Bob Barbee, "Newsletter: Fishing Bridge Planning Update, Yellowstone National Park, February 1987," File "EIS—Fishing Bridge—1987," Box L-69, YNPA.

57. Howie Thompson, notes on conference call, April 7, 1987, File "Fishing Bridge EIS," Box "Fishing Bridge EIS General Files," MAOF. See also USDI-NPS, *Draft Environmental Impact Statement*, 113–18, 153–200.

58. Bob Barbee, as quoted in "Fishing Bridge," *GYR* (Greater Yellowstone Coalition

newsletter), Fall 1987, 9; Hank Fischer to Ed Lewis, Terri Martin, Tom France, Larry Mehlhaff, Mike Scott, Matt Reid, and Len Carlman, November 13, 1987, File "NPS— Yellowstone N.P.—Fishing Bridge EIS," GYC.

59. Alan Simpson, as quoted in Daniel Wiseman, "Wyoming Delegation Takes Issue with Mott," *JHNG*, June 17, 1987.

60. Wiseman, "Wyoming Delegation Takes Issue with Mott;" Rocky Barker, "Park Service EIS Praised," *Idaho Falls Post-Register*, October 28, 1987; and "National Park Service Releases Draft Fishing Bridge Environmental Impact Statement and Development Concept Plan," press release, October 26, 1987, File "Untitled," Box K-108, YNPA.

61. Chase, *Playing God in Yellowstone*, 295–370.

62. Chase's book received only negative reviews, as noted by Paul Schullery, personal communication with author, April 13, 2004. See also Schullery, *Searching for Yellowstone*, 44–45, 225, 278; and Holmes Rolston, "Biology and Philosophy in Yellowstone," *Biology and Philosophy* 5 (1990): 241–58.

63. USDI-NPS, *Draft Environmental Impact Statement*, 26–84.

64. Ibid., 30, 198; and Wayne Brewster to Regional Director, Rocky Mountain Region, NPS, October 13, 1987, File "Last Two Weeks," Box "Mid-80s Fishing Bridge History," MAOF.

65. USDI-NPS, *Draft Environmental Impact Statement*, 30.

66. Ibid.

67. Alan Simpson, as quoted in Barker, "Park Service EIS Praised."

68. "Jasper" Carlton to Bob Barbee, January 5, 1988, File "NPS—Yellowstone N.P.— Fishing Bridge Comments," GYC. Silence of environmental groups is from Jim Carrier, "Fishing Bridge Site Will Stay Open, to Detriment of Bears," *Denver Post*, January 11, 1988. Environmental group comments are from Duane Howe and Matthew Reid to Bob Barbee, January 5, 1988; Ralph Maughan to Bob Barbee, January 3, 1988; Philip Knight to Bob Barbee, November 14, 1987; and "Environmental Defense Fund Comments on Development at Fishing Bridge in Yellowstone National Park," n.d., all in File "NPS—Yellowstone N.P.—Fishing Bridge Comments," GYC. See also Hank Fischer to Bob Barbee, January 11, 1988, File "Fishing Bridge," GYC; and Louisa Willcox to Bob Barbee, January 15, 1988; and Lance Olsen to Bob Barbee, January 11, 1988, both loose in Box "FB EIS DCP," MAOF.

69. First quote is from Michael Fischer in "Yellowstone Grizzlies Endangered," press release, December 28, 1987, File "NPS—Yellowstone N.P.—Fishing Bridge Comments," GYC; and second quote is from "Fishing Bridge Update," in Grizzly Bear Task Force newsletter, File "NPS—Yellowstone N.P.—Fishing Bridge/Alerts," GYC. Other supporting documents are Phil White, "Park Service Proposal Puts RVs Next to Bears," *CST*, January 13, 1988; David A. Smith, "Killing Grizzly Treats Symptom Instead of Cause," *BDC*, December 16, 1987; Philip Knight to Bob Barbee, November 14, 1987, File "NPS—Yellowstone N.P.—Fishing Bridge Comments," GYC; Thomas McNamee to Bob Barbee, January 5, 1988, File "Fishing

Bridge," GYC; Lance Olsen to Bob Barbee, January 11, 1988, loose in Box "FB EIS DCP," MAOF; and Wright, *Wildlife Research and Management*, 150.

70. Organized campaign information is from Fischer to Lewis, Martin, France, Mehlhaff, Scott, Reid, and Carlman. Some flyers disseminated by environmental groups are: Sierra Club, "Give Fishing Bridge Back to the Bears;" Grizzly Bear Task Force, "Untitled;" GYC, "Let's Give Fishing Bridge Back to the Bears;" and Defenders of Wildlife, "Let the Bears Recreate at Fishing Bridge," all in File "NPS—Yellowstone N.P.—Fishing Bridge/alerts," GYC. See also The Wilderness Society, "Protect Yellowstone National Park: Let's Give Fishing Bridge Back to the Bears," File "Fishing Bridge/Historic," Box "Fishing Bridge EIS, 2nd Newsletter Response," MAOF. The 95 percent figure is from "Summary of Public Response," File "Last Two Weeks," Box "Mid-80s Fishing Bridge History," MAOF.

71. Campaign for letters supporting Alternative A or D are from Louisa Willcox to "Folks concerned about Fishing Bridge," memorandum, December 21, 1987, File "NPS—Yellowstone N.P.—Fishing Bridge Correspondence," GYC; "Deadline Extended for Comments on Fishing Bridge Plan," *BGZ*, December 4, 1987; and "Summary of Public Response," File "Last Two Weeks," Box "Mid-80s Fishing Bridge History," MAOF. Heritage Society information is from "Heritage Society Renewing Fishing Bridge Closure Battle," *CST*, December 29, 1987; "Fishing Bridge Paper Issued," *JHNG*, December 30, 1987; and Wyoming Heritage Society, "Action Alert: Fishing Bridge," File "Fishing Bridge/Historic," Box "Fishing Bridge EIS, 2nd Newsletter Response," MAOF. Other Alternative A support information is from Cody Country Chamber of Commerce, "Fishing Bridge R.V. Campground Needs Help! You Must Take Action Today;" Beverly Edwards, "GSers Asked to Help Save Fishing Bridge RV Facilities," *Hi-Way Herald* (Good Sam Club newsletter), n.d.; and "State Agrees with Park Service over Fishing Bridge," press release, January 26, 1988, all in File "Fishing Bridge/Historic," Box "Fishing Bridge EIS, 2nd Newsletter Response," MAOF. See also Terry Povah to Bob Barbee, January 12, 1988, loose in Box "FB EIS DCP," MAOF. Good Sam Club success is from "Summary of Public Comments to the Fishing Bridge Draft DCP/EIS," File "Last Two Weeks," Box "Mid-80s Fishing Bridge History," MAOF; and Iobst interview.

72. Cody Country Chamber of Commerce, "Fishing Bridge R.V. Campground Needs Help! You Must Take Action Today."

73. Ibid. See also Edwards, "GSers Asked to Help Save Fishing Bridge RV Facilities" and "State Agrees with Park Service over Fishing Bridge."

74. NPS, "Yellowstone Proposes Modification of Fishing Bridge Preferred Alternative in Response to 2,905 Public Comments," press release, n.d., File "NPS—Yellowstone N.P.—Fishing Bridge EIS," GYC; and USDI-NPS, *Final Environmental Impact Statement/Development Concept Plan, Fishing Bridge Developed Area, Yellowstone National Park* (Denver: NPS, 1988), iv, 37–42. According to Chris Turk, in personal interview with author, Alan Simpson prevailed upon Bob Barbee to change the campground replacement trigger to one that would be tripped more easily (but I was unable to confirm her statement).

75. Information on consulting the delegation is from Bob Barbee to Malcom Wallop, Alan Simpson, and Dick Cheney (separately), April 19, 1988, all in File "In-house correspondence since mid-March 1988," Box "Mid-80s Fishing Bridge History," MAOF. Final decision is from JoAn Bjarko, "Park Makes Final Decision on Fishing Bridge," *BDC*, May 25, 1988; and NPS, "Record of Decision Issued on the Final Environmental Impact Statement for the Fishing Bridge Development Concept Plan," press release, May 26, 1988, File "Untitled," Box K-108, YNPA. NWF had by this time lost both its case and an appeal; see *NWF v. NPS* (D. Wyo. 1987), 669 *F. Supp.* 384, 390; David A. Watts to Director, NPS, February 22, 1988, in File "EIS—Fishing Bridge—Interim Management Plan—Litigation—NWF vs. NPS/ USFWS—1987–88," Box W-242, YNPA; Thomas France to Mike Scott, Ed Lewis, Lance Olsen, Larry Mehlhaff, and John Zelasney, August 19, 1988, File "NPS— Yellowstone N.P.—Fishing Bridge Correspondence," GYC; and Matthew M. Reid, "Analysis of Issues Pertaining to Grizzly Bears in the Fishing Bridge Final Environmental Impact Statement," September 22, 1988, File "NPS—Yellowstone N.P.—Fishing Bridge EIS," GYC.

76. Chief Ranger to District and Sub-District Rangers, September 18, 1991, File "N1615—Wildlife, 1991," Box W-196, YNPA; Sue Consolo-Murphy, "Fishing Bridge Cleanup Day Moves (Pieces of) Mountains," *The Buffalo Chip* (Yellowstone's Resource Management newsletter), September-October 1991, YNPA; and Sue Consolo-Murphy and Daniel P. Reinhart, "Restoring Fishing Bridge Campground: The Challenges of 'Undevelopment' in America's Oldest National Park," in *On the Frontiers of Conservation: Proceedings of the 10th Conference on Research and Resource Management in Parks and on Public Lands, The 1999 George Wright Society Conference*, ed. David Harmon (Hancock, MI: The George Wright Society, 1999), 210–14.

77. Dan Sholly to Kevin Brandt, December 26, 1990; and Kevin Brandt to Dan Sholly, March 11, 1991, both in File "N16 Management of Natural Resources and Areas 1990–91," Box W-196, YNPA; Paul Hoffman to Bob Barbee, April 28, 1992, File "Chambers of Commerce," Box A-404, YNPA; and Schullery, *Nature and Culture at Fishing Bridge*, 83–91. Some might question the need for an NPS visitor center in Cody—it already has the popular Buffalo Bill Museum, which includes the new Draper Natural History Museum, the premier exhibit about the "Greater Yellowstone Ecosystem."

78. NPS, "Environmental Impact Statement to Be Prepared for Replacement of Fishing Bridge Campsites in Yellowstone National Park," press release, March 23, 1992, File "NPS—Yellowstone N.P.—Fishing Bridge EIS," GYC; and Mike Finley, "Superintendent's Annual Report for 1994," 55, YNPR.

79. Information on the draft EIS is from Yellowstone interpretive planner Beth Kaeding, personal interview with author, Mammoth Hot Springs, Wyoming, March 25, 2003. Chris Turk, NPS regional environmental quality coordinator, in interview with author, Mammoth Hot Springs, Wyoming, July 9, 2002, mentioned Simpson's retirement, though she only suggested that it might be responsible in

part for the lack of a final EIS on campground replacement. The thoughts on Finley's different management outlook and political climate are the author's.

80. Several interviewees, including Louisa Willcox, discussed the role of scientific research with the author. Bob Barbee, for example, suggested that science is important in court. The idea that scientific research was unable to conclusively prove that bears would die, though, is the author's own conclusion. Research is often controversy driven in the NPS; see, for example, Wright, *Wildlife Research and Management*, 24.

81. The cabin area remains trampled, though Yellowstone managers recently announced plans to restore it. See NPS, "Lake Area Comprehensive Plan/ Environmental Assessment," January 31, 2012, http://parkplanning.nps.gov/document.cfm?parkID=111&projectID=32279&documentID=4551, accessed February 8, 2012. Christopher Servheen and Rebecca Shoemaker, "Delisting the Yellowstone Grizzly Bear: A Lesson in Cooperation, Conservation, and Monitoring," *Yellowstone Science* 16, no. 2 (July 2008): 25–29.

82. Consolo-Murphy interview; and Paul Schullery, e-mail to author, December 1, 2011.

Chapter Two

1. Ralph Regula, quoted in Les Aucoin, "Don't Get Hosed: How Political Framing Influences Fire Policy," in *The Wildfire Reader: A Century of Failed Forest Policy*, ed. George Wuerthner (Washington, D.C.: The Foundation for Deep Ecology by arrangement with Island Press, 2006), 67. The word "Barbeeque," used in the chapter title, is a corruption of Superintendent Barbee's last name; this nickname was commonly heard around Yellowstone in 1988. It was variously spelled, such as "Barbee-Q" in Ted Williams, "Incineration of Yellowstone," *Audubon* (January 1989): 65, and "Barbee-cue" in Brandon Loomis, "Managing Fire," *JHNG*, October 2, 1991. Alan Simpson speech, *Congressional Record*, 100th Congress, 2nd Session, daily ed. (September 14, 1988): S23737.

2. See, for example, Wuerthner, *The Wildfire Reader*; George Wuerthner, *Yellowstone and the Fires of Change* (Salt Lake City: Haggis House Publications, 1988); Rothman, *Blazing Heritage*; Rocky Barker, *Scorched Earth: How the Fires of Yellowstone Changed America* (Washington, D.C.: Island Press, 2005); and Robert Ekey, *Yellowstone on Fire!* (Billings, MT: Billings Gazette, 1989). Micah Morrison presents an account of the summer's events, as well, in *Fire in Paradise: The Yellowstone Fires and The Politics of Environmentalism* (New York: HarperCollins Publishers, Inc., 1993).

3. Historian Hal Rothman includes a short summary of this policy in *Blazing Heritage*, 168–85, but he leaves out many of the crucial details concerning the dominant influences on NPS policy making.

4. For more information, see Leopold et al., "Wildlife Management in the National Parks," 237–52; Sellars, *Preserving Nature in the National Parks*, 204–66; Pritchard,

Preserving Yellowstone's Natural Conditions, 201–50; and Rothman, *Blazing Heritage,* 101–28. The latter (see pages 81–90) discusses pre-Leopold report efforts to reintroduce fire into the Everglades, an effort that illustrates that the Leopold report's recommendations were rooted in some foregoing experience.

5. Leopold et al., "Wildlife Management in the National Parks," 237–52. The Sequoia park information is from Sellars, 254–58; and 53 *Federal Register* 244 (December 20, 1988), 51196–205. Pritchard provides the best account of Yellowstone's move to natural regulation in *Preserving Yellowstone's Natural Conditions,* 201–50. Don G. Despain and Robert E. Sellers recorded the first moves toward a fire program in Yellowstone in "Natural Fire in Yellowstone National Park," *Trends in Natural Resource Management* (April–May–June 1977): 25–29. Fire terminology has a history as complex as NPS's fire policy. Fires that park managers allow to burn under supervision have variously been called "prescribed fires," "wildfire used for resource benefit," "naturally caused fires," and "management fires," depending on the time period and the image that managers wish to convey. I will use the terminology in vogue at the time of the 1988 fires, when "prescribed natural fire" or just "prescribed fire" referred to a fire caused by lightning but permitted to burn under predefined prescriptions, and a "wildfire" referred to a fire caused either by people or by nature, but one that park managers desired to extinguish. In 1988, the term "wildland fire" was not formally used, but is a term I use in general reference to fires—human- or naturally caused—on the undeveloped lands of America, primarily in the West.

6. NPS, "The Yellowstone Fires: A Primer on the 1988 Fire Season," October 1, 1988, 5, YNPV.

7. William Romme, "Fire and Landscape Diversity in Subalpine Forests of Yellowstone National Park," *Ecological Monographs* 52, no. 2 (1982): 199–221; and William Romme and Dennis Knight, "Landscape Diversity: The Concept Applied to Yellowstone Park," *BioScience* 32, no. 8 (1982): 664–70. See also Doug Houston, "Wildfires in Northern Yellowstone National Park," *Ecology* 54, no. 5 (1973): 1111–17; Richard Monastersky, "Lessons from the Flames," *Science News* 134, no. 20 (November 12, 1988): 314–17; and Rothman, *Blazing Heritage,* 171.

8. GYCC, "Greater Yellowstone Area Fire Situation, 1988," n.d., 1–2, YNPV; NPS, "The Yellowstone Fires," 6–7; and Monastersky, "Lessons from the Flames."

9. GYCC, "Greater Yellowstone Area Fire Situation," 2, 47–60; NPS, "The Yellowstone Fires," 7; and Rocky Barker, "How the 1988 Fires Grew," *HCN,* November 7, 1988, 12. As late as July 11, 1988, the National Weather Service was predicting normal precipitation for the month; see John Varley to Bob Haraden, December 6, 1988, File "Fires—1988 Fires—Correspondence," Box Y-286, YNPA. Information relating to shelter deployment and increased July burning is from "Clover-Mist Fire Review," December 1, 1988, File "Fires—1988 Fires—Fire Reviews," Box Y-286, YNPA.

10. Extreme summer weather is from Monastersky, "Lessons from the Flames." Fires on USFS lands is from GYCC, "Greater Yellowstone Area Fire Situation," 1, 36, 47–55; NPS, "The Yellowstone Fires," 9–10; and "Common Errors and

Misunderstandings about the Yellowstone Fires," February 1989, File "Media and Fire," Box Y-263, YNPA.

11. GYCC, "Greater Yellowstone Area Fire Situation," 64–68, 70; and NPS, "The Yellowstone Fires," 7–8. To scholar Hal Rothman, Superintendent Barbee stated, "The joke over in West Yellowstone was what is brown in the middle and black on both sides? A bulldozer line!" For the latter, see Rothman, *Blazing Heritage*, 177.

12. NPS, "The Yellowstone Fires," 8–9.

13. Minimum impact information is from GYCC, "Greater Yellowstone Area Fire Situation," 66–68; NPS, "The Yellowstone Fires," 9; Ed Wright, "Drought Conditions And 'Let Burn' Policy Leave Yellowstone In Shambles," *BlueRibbon Magazine* (November 1988): B3; and Barker, "How the 1988 Fires Grew," 13. Concerning dozer lines in Yellowstone see GYCC, "The Greater Yellowstone Fires of 1988: Questions and Answers," File "Fires—1988 Fires—Area Surveys," Box Y-286, YNPA.

14. As quoted in Scott McMillion, "Biologist Says He's Vindicated over '88's Hottest Media Quote," *BDC*, March 28, 1998.

15. The happy-face story is from Paul Schullery, "The Story Itself: Lessons and Hopes from the Yellowstone Fire Media Event," *The George Wright Forum* 6, no. 3 (1989): 17–25. The "let-burn" policy discussion can be found in Wuerthner, *Yellowstone and the Fires of Change*, 12–13. See also McMillion, "Biologist Says He's Vindicated"; NPS, "The Yellowstone Fires," 10; and the Senate Committee on Energy and Natural Resources and Senate Committee on Agriculture, Nutrition, and Forestry, *Current Fire Management Policies*, 100th Congress, 2nd session, 1988, 12, 74–75.

16. NPS, "The Yellowstone Fires," 9–10; and Joe Zarki, "A Summer to Remember," *Interpretation* (Spring 1989), File "Miscellaneous Materials," Box Y-262, YNPA.

17. Conrad Smith, *Media and Apocalypse* (Westport, CT: Greenwood Press, 1992), 45. See also Conrad Smith, "Media Coverage of the 1988 Yellowstone Fires," *Interpretation* (Spring 1989), File "Miscellaneous Materials," Box Y-262, YNPA; and the various presentations in Glenda Wallace, ed., *The Power of Politics, the Media and the Public to Affect Wildland/Urban Fire Protection Programs in the 1990s: Proceedings from the 1992 National Symposium and Workshop*, (National Wildfire Foundation, 1993).

18. For the loss of business in the region, see Geoffrey O'Gara, "The West Is Burning (But It's Probably Good News)," *HCN*, August 15, 1988, 8–9; and Geoffrey O'Gara, "Yellowstone Businesses Are 'Up in Smoke,'" *The Washington Post*, September 5, 1988. Information on the local complaints is from Patrick Doyle et al. to Bob Barbee, July 26, 1988, File "Petition Fires 1988," Box A-355, YNPA; Scott McMillion, "Anatomy of an Inferno," *BDC*, March 28, 1998; Cliff Stickney to [Donald Hodel], September 5, 1988, File "Y1415 Wildland Fire Mgmt., Correspondence, 1 of 2, 1988," Box Y-219, YNPA; and George Hackett, Michael A. Lerner, and Mary Hager, "Fighting for Yellowstone," *Newsweek* (September 19, 1988): 18–20.

19. *Congressional Record*, 100th Congress, 2nd Session, daily ed. (September 14, 1988): S23736–39. See also Ron Marlenee to Donald Hodel, August 22, 1988; Ron Marlenee to Donald Hodel, September 2, 1988; Ron Marlenee to Donald Hodel,

September 8, 1988; and Donald Hodel to Ron Marlenee, September 23, 1988, all in File "Y1415 Wildland Fire Mgmt., Correspondence, 1 of 2, 1988," Box Y-219, YNPA. See also Dick Cheney to Donald Hodel, September 12, 1988, File "Fire Interpretation, In House Material on Fires," Box Y-263, YNPA.

20. Senate Committee on Energy and Natural Resources et. al., *Current Fire Management Policies*, 4.

21. Ibid., 4–6.

22. Ibid., 67–69, 78–79. Further defenses of park policy are from Bob Barbee, personal interview with author, Bozeman, Montana, March 24, 2003; and the following letters: Donald Hodel to Ron Marlenee, Donald Hodel to Alan Simpson, and Donald Hodel to Dick Cheney, all December 13, 1988, File "Y1415 Wildland Fire Mgmt., Correspondence, 2 of 2, 1988," Box Y-219, YNPA.

23. As found in Senate Committee on Energy and Natural Resources et al., *Current Fire Management Policies*, 79.

24. Ibid., 23, 42–43; and Philip Shabecoff, "Park Service Plans to Revise Fire Recovery Policy," *NYT*, September 15, 1988. Information on other western fires is from Bert Lindler, "More than Yellowstone Burned," *HCN*, November 7, 1988, 17–18.

25. Fire policy review team appointment is from Senate Committee on Energy and Natural Resources et al., *Current Fire Management Policies*, 23, 42–43. See also the following letters: Richard Lyng and Donald Hodel to Peter C. Myers and Earl E. Gjelde, September 28, 1988; and Peter C. Myers and Earl E. Gjelde to Dale Robertson, William Penn Mott, Robert Burford, Frank Dunkle, Pat Ragsdale, and Charles Jarvis, September 28, 1988, both in File "December 15, 1988: Statement on the Fire Policy Report," Box 14:103, TWS, DPL. See also Donald Hodel to Ron Marlenee, December 13, 1988; and Donald Hodel to Alan Simpson, December 13, 1988, both in File "Y1415 Wildland Fire Mgmt., Correspondence, 2 of 2, 1988," Box Y-219, YNPA. The reasons against including private citizens on the committee is from "Feds Name Fire Policy Review Team; Prescribed Burns Pushed," *Federal Parks & Recreation*, October 6, 1988, 6–7, File "Policy & Management of Fires in Yellowstone," Box Y-262, YNPA; and Brad Leonard to Robert Hyde, October 26, 1988, File "Untitled," Storage Box 52, DSC.

26. Early planning is from the following two letters: Bob Barbee to Greater Yellowstone Unified Area Commander, Fire Incident Commanders, August 5, 1988, File "Miscellaneous," Box Y-222, YNPA; and Steve W. (full name not provided) to Fire Crew, September 7, 1988, File "Yellowstone Fire—1988," Box 10:111, TWS, DPL. USFS participation is from George M. Leonard to Regional Foresters, Station Directors, Area Director and WO Staff Directors, September 27, 1988, File "4000—Research," Box A-394, YNPA. The committees' information is from Lorraine Mintzmyer to All Other Regional Directors, Directorate WASO, and Managers Denver Service Center and Harpers Ferry Center, October 12, 1988, File "N1623 Mgmt. of Natural Resources 1988," Box N-132, YNPA; "Yellowstone National Park 1988 Fire Season Recovery Plan, October 1988," File "Recovery Information," Box

Y-262, YNPA; and Sue E. Heggen to R. Williams, e-mail message, September 21, 1988, File "1920—Land and Resource Management Planning," Box A-393, YNPA.

27. The scientists' interest in the fires is from "Briefing Paper: Greater Yellowstone Postfire Research—October, 1989," File "Research (General)," Box Y-262, YNPA; John D. Varley, "Yellowstone's Newest Growth Industry: Postfire Research!," File "Fires—1988 fires—Correspondence," Box Y-286, YNPA; and Andrew Malcolm, "In Ashes of Burned Forests, a Rare Chance to Study Nature's Recovery," *NYT*, September 27, 1988. Scientific support of the policy is from "Scientists Defend Park's 'Let-Burn' Policy,'" *LVE*, January 20, 1989.

28. Articles published at the fire season's peak include: "Taking the Heat," *Los Angeles Times*, September 1, 1988; "Fire Policy Is a Good One," *The Missoulian*, August 28, 1988; Robert Ekey, "Fires Have Bright Side," *BGZ*, July 18, 1988; Ruth Rudner, "Even as It Burns, Yellowstone Is Reborn," *WSJ*, August 25, 1988; and George Wuerthner, "Save the Forests: Let Them Burn," *HCN*, August 29, 1988.

29. Articles appearing that fall included: "Fire-Fighting Policies Should Not Be Added to the Ashes," *Rocky Mountain News*, September 13, 1988; Rupert Cutler, "Fire in Yellowstone, Hot Air in Washington," *MST*, September 15, 1988; Michael Satchell and Peter Dworkin, "Burn Baby Burn! Stop Baby Stop!" *U.S. News & World Report*, September 19, 1988; "When to Let the Forest Burn," *NYT*, September 14, 1988; "The Renewal of Yellowstone Park," *MST*, September 14, 1988; Scott McMurray, "Back to Life: Yellowstone Park Begins Its Renewal," *WSJ*, September 23, 1988; Timothy Egan, "Yellowstone, and Its Sales Pitch, Undergo Rebirth," *NYT*, September 24, 1988; Andrew Malcolm, "In Ashes of Burned Forests, A Rare Chance to Study Nature's Recovery," *NYT*, September 27, 1988; and Jim Carrier, "Yellowstone Fires Burned as Others Were Fought," *Denver Post*, October 17, 1988.

30. Federal assistance information is from William Penn Mott to Rick Loftice, n.d., File "Y1415 Wildland Fire Mgmt., Correspondence, 1 of 2, 1988," Box Y-219, YNPA; and F. A. Dorrell to George Dunlop, November 15, 1988, File "1920—Land and Resource Management Planning," Box A-393, YNPA. For decisions to promote change and learning opportunity, see: "The 1988 Fires of Yellowstone," an undated promotional brochure issued by Wyoming, Montana, and Idaho, File "Media and Fire," Box Y-263, YNPA; and Steve Iobst to Superintendent and Public Affairs Officer, October 17, 1988, File "Fire Interpretation, In House Material on Fires," Box Y-263, YNPA.

31. Gene Bryan to Wyoming Travel Commission State Planning Coordinator, September 20, 1988, File "1560—State, County, and Local Agencies," Box A-393, YNPA.

32. Visitation statistics are from Donald Hodel to Leonard H. Johnson, December 13, 1988, File "Y1415 Wildland Fire Mgmt., Correspondence, 2 of 2, 1988," Box Y-219, YNPA; and "Changes Suggested in Yellowstone Fire Policy," in *Congressman Dick Cheney Reports to Wyoming*, December 1988, 3, Box Y-221, YNPA. Surprise at finding lack of complete devastation is from Smith, *Media and Apocalypse*, 66.

At least one study confirmed that those who visited the park after the fires believed it to be less burned than those who had not visited the park; see David J. Snepenger, "Marketing Yellowstone National Park After the Fires of 1988," unpublished report for NPS, November 15, 1989, YNPV. Gene Bryan to Wyoming Travel Commission State Planning Coordinator, September 20, 1988, File "1560—State, County, and Local Agencies," Box A-393, YNPA. Changes in state attitude are evident in "The 1988 Fires of Yellowstone"; Mario P. Delisio, "Yellowstone: Alive and Well," *Idaho Motorist* (Winter 1988): 10–11, YNPV; and Bob Ekey, Northern Rockies regional director of The Wilderness Society, personal interview with author, Bozeman, Montana, April 9, 2003.

33. For the research consortium see: Linda Wallace to John Varley et al., August 29, 1988; and Linda Wallace to Bob Barbee, October 25, 1988, both in File "Fires—1988—Research—Proposals—1989—National Science Foundation," Box N-354, YNPA. See also "Fire Consortium Update," December 1988, File "Fires—1988—Research—FIRE Consortium," Box N-354, YNPA; James G. Schmitt, "Greater Yellowstone Fire Impact and Recovery Research Workshop, Overview," YNPV; and Roger Lewin, "Ecologists' Opportunity in Yellowstone's Blaze," *Science* 241 (September 30, 1988): 1762–63.

34. "Briefing Paper: Greater Yellowstone Postfire Research—October, 1989," File "Research (General)," Box Y-262, YNPA; and Varley, "Yellowstone's Newest Growth Industry." Scientific support of the policy is from "Scientists Defend Park's 'Let-Burn' Policy.'" Note that Frank Press of the National Research Council offered Donald Hodel his council's review of fire policy revisions. Although Hodel seemed inclined to accept Press's offer, there is no indication that he ever did, perhaps because of the widespread scientific support for the policy; see Frank Press to Donald Hodel, September 23, 1988, and Donald Hodel to Frank Press, December 13, 1988, both in File "Y1415 Wildland Fire Mgmt., Correspondence, 2 of 2, 1988," Box Y-219, YNPA. Note too that the FIRE Consortium was not heard from again, though the momentum it began clearly continued. Ultimately, Linda Wallace summarized this new research in *After the Fires: The Ecology of Change in Yellowstone National Park* (New Haven, CT: Yale University Press, 2004).

35. Thomas Bonnicksen, "Yellowstone Fire Information Update," September 12, 1988, File "Fires—1988 Fires—Correspondence," Box Y-286. His ideas were repeated by Thomas Maugh in "Forest Fires: The Debate Heats Up," *Los Angeles Times*, October 13, 1988.

36. Alston Chase, "Neither Fire Suppression nor Natural Burn Is a Sound Scientific Option," *NYT*, September 18, 1988. Chase's ideas were repeated widely; see, for instance: Donald R. Leal, "Yellowstone Burns as Park Managers Play Politics," *WSJ*, August 26, 1988; Warren Brooks, "Scorched Environmentalism?" *Washington Times*, September 19, 1988; Matt Ridley, "Scorched Earth," *The New Republic*, October 3, 1988, 13–14; Geoffrey O'Gara, "When Nature Runs its Fiery Course," *MST*, October 2, 1988; Roberta Anderson, "From National Treasure To National Disaster," *BlueRibbon Magazine* (November 1988): A8; and Richard Monastersky,

"Taking the Heat: A Policy Under Fire," *Science News* 134, no. 20 (November 12, 1988): 316. Micah Morrison also promoted Chase's ideas in "While Yellowstone Burned," *The American Spectator* (November 1988): 18–22, and in his later book, *Fire in Paradise*. Paul Erlich seconded Chase's notion that Yellowstone was too disturbed by previous management policies and too complex for natural regulation to operate effectively, as reported in James Coates, "Let-It-Burn Policy Puts Heat on Officials," *Chicago Tribune*, November 20, 1988. Erlich is the only other scientist I found that was even close to agreeing with Chase and Bonnicksen.

37. Chase's book allowed him to be seen as authoritative on scientific matters even though he was not a research scientist.

38. The support by Thomas Swetnam, John Varley, and Stephen Pyne is in Monastersky, "Taking the Heat." Other scientist support is described in Tom McKnight, "Yellowstone: Park for All Ages," *Los Angeles Times*, September 17, 1988; in Woodrow to Nathaniel Pryor Reed, November 15, 1988, File "Fires—1988 Fires—Correspondence," Box Y-286, YNPA; and in Dirk Johnson, "Forest Fires Cast a Persistent Pall on Much of West," *NYT*, September 12, 1988. The idea that Native American influence was probably minor is from William R. Romme and Don Despain, "Historical Perspective on the Yellowstone Fires of 1988," *BioScience* 39, no. 10 (November 1989): 695–99. See also Rothman, *Blazing Heritage*, 171, and Thomas R. Vale, ed., *Fire, Native Peoples, and the Natural Landscape* (Washington, D.C.: Island Press, 2002).

39. See "Environment Groups Defend Administration Policy on Forest Fires," *NYT*, September 11, 1988; Michael Milstein, "The Long, Hot Summer," *National Parks* (November–December 1988): 26–27, 50; Michael Frome, "Rebirth in Yellowstone," *Defenders*, November–December 1988, 6–7; and the entire edition of *GYR* (Autumn 1988).

40. Matthiessen, "The Case for Burning," *NYT Magazine*, 41.

41. "Nature's Course," *Los Angeles Times*, December 18, 1988; and Peter Matthiessen, "The Case for Burning," *NYT Magazine*, 38–41, 121–23, 128–29. See also, "Yellowstone Fire Damage Fades into the Backdrop," *BGZ*, November 8, 1988; Tamara Jones, "Yellowstone Fights to Restore Image," *MST*, November 26, 1988; and Ruth Rudner, "Burned but Not Burned Out: Post-Blaze Yellowstone," *WSJ*, November 29, 1988.

42. NPS, "Fire-Soil Monitoring—Fire Intensity," schedule and status report, September 27, 1988; "Presentation by Henry Shovic," November 1, 1988; and Henry Shovic, "Fire-Soil Effects in Yellowstone," hand-out, September 26, 1988, all in File "Soil: Effects of Fire," Box Y-262, YNPA. See also "Preliminary Burned Area Survey of Yellowstone National Park and Adjoining National Forests: Project Summary, October 1988," File "5180—Fire Reports," Box A-394, YNPA. Later estimates are from GYCC, "The Greater Yellowstone Fires of 1988: Questions and Answers," January 25, 1989, File "Fires—1988 Fires—Area Surveys," Box Y-286, YNPA. The estimate of 706,000 acres is from Nancy Kessler, "Reports Support 'Let Burn' but Criticize Implementation," *HCN*, December 19, 1988, 3. See also

Todd Wilkinson, "Yellowstone Fires Spark National Debate," *GYR* (Autumn 1988): 1, 4–5. The 1989 estimate is from Don Despain, Ann Rodman, Paul Schullery, and Henry Shovic, "Burned Area Survey of Yellowstone National Park: The Fires of 1988," December 1989, YNPV.

43. Some of the press reports are: Rudner, "Burned but Not Burned Out;" T. R. Reid, "Yellowstone Fires Reassessed," *Washington Post*, December 3, 1988; and Kessler, "Reports Support 'Let Burn.'"

44. The Bambi reference is from the following: Wuerthner, *The Wildfire Reader*; Tamara Jones, "Yellowstone Fights to Restore Image," *MST*, November 26, 1988; Rocky Barker, "Bambi Versus John Muir," *HCN*, November 7, 1988, 16; and Williams, "Incineration of Yellowstone," 51. The Smokey the Bear information is from Wuerthner, *The Wildfire Reader*; Williams, "Incineration of Yellowstone;" Barker, "Bambi Versus John Muir;" Donald Dickmann to Director, January 30, 1989, File "Untitled," Storage Area Box 51, DSC; and Bill Morris to Rod Miller, February 9, 1989, File "FAM/letters," DSC. Many other sources mention both Bambi and Smokey the Bear.

45. Francis J. Singer et al., "Impacts of the 1988 Fires upon Elk and their Habitats," November 15, 1988, File "Elk—1988," Box N-351, YNPA; NPS, "Final Assessment of Fire Effects on Park Wildlife Announced," press release, November 10, 1988, File "Mammals and the Effects of Fire," Box Y-263, YNPA; and Francis J. Singer and Paul Schullery, "Yellowstone Wildlife: Populations in Process," *Western Wildlands* 15, no. 2 (Summer 1989): 18–22. Another eighty-eight elk, thirty-two deer, ten moose, and six black bears were killed on USFS lands surrounding Yellowstone; see: GYCC, "The Greater Yellowstone Fires of 1988: Questions and Answers," January 25, 1989, File "Fires—1988 Fires—Area Surveys," Box Y-286, YNPA. For results from elsewhere in Wyoming, see Wyoming Game & Fish Department, "Status Report on the Fire Situation in Wyoming as it Relates to the Wildlife Resource and Associated Recreation," September 19, 1988, File "1560—State, County, and Local Agencies," Box A-393, YNPA. The final resource assessment report was issued in March 1989; see: GYCC, *The Greater Yellowstone Postfire Assessment*, Susan Mills, ed., March 1989, YNPV.

46. "Clover-Mist Fire Review," December 1, 1988, 12.

47. "Clover-Mist Fire Review," December 1, 1988; and "Yellowstone Fire Management Review: North Fork and Wolf Lake Fires, November 14–17, 1988," 13, both in File "Fires—1988 Fires—Fire Reviews," Box Y-286, YNPA; and USDA and USFS and USDI-NPS, "Coordination and Management Review," January 1989, YNPV. See also the Snake River Complex, Hellroaring and Storm Creek (combined into one report), and Fan Fire Reviews in File "Fires—1988 Fires—Fire Reviews," Box Y-286, YNPA; as well as Kessler, "Reports Support 'Let Burn'"; and Allegations Review Task Force, "Northern Rocky Mountain Fires of 1988, Final Report," February 20 to March 3, 1989, File "5100—Fire Coordination—GYA Interagency Fire Mgmt. Planning," Box A-394, YNPA.

48. 53 *Federal Register* 244 (December 20, 1988): 51196–205. See also USDI,

"Secretaries Hodel and Lyng Receive Forest Fire Review Team Report, Ask for Public Review," press release, December 15, 1988, File "Fire Management Policy Review Team," Box Y-263, YNPA; and Bruce M. Kilgore, "Review Team Finds Fire Policy Sound But 'Application Needs Changing,'" YNPV.

49. 53 *Federal Register* 244 (December 20, 1988): 51199.

50. 53 *Federal Register* 244 (December 20, 1988): 51199.

51. 53 *Federal Register* 244 (December 20, 1988): 51196–205. See also Rothman, *Blazing Heritage*, 171–76.

52. Bill Morris to Rod Miller, State Planning Coordinator's Office, February 9, 1989, File "FAM/letters," DSC.

53. Steve Cowper to Dale Robertson, February 24, 1989, File "FAM/letters," DSC.

54. William Locke to Steve Hodapp, February 2, 1989; and Jack Kirkley to Steve Hodapp, February 6, 1989, both in File "Untitled," DSC. See also the following letters: Bill Morris to Rod Miller, State Planning Coordinator's Office, February 9, 1989; Steve Cowper to Dale Robertson, February 24, 1989; and Bruce Vento to Peter Myers, February 9, 1989, all in File "FAM/letters," DSC. And see Jim Sweaney to USFS Chief, February 20, 1989, File "FAM/letters," DSC; and Allen Kreger to Bob Barbee, February 10, 1989, File "letters," DSC. Note that Wyoming governor Mike Sullivan disagreed with some of Morris's more strident criticisms, especially the one about local residents needing to recognize the fire history and ecology implications of their native homes (see Mike Sullivan to Dale Robertson, February 22, 1989, File "FAM/letters," DSC). At least one other person in the hearings echoed Morris's concern that some recommendations appeared to be a "witch hunt"; see Marty Huebner, "Fire Policy Review Hearing," Idaho Falls, February 8, 1989, 38, DSC (the unpublished transcripts for these hearings, which have long, varying titles and different authors, can be found loose within the DSC. I have chosen to abbreviate them in this manner: "Fire Policy Review Hearing," place, date, DSC).

55. The Wilderness Society, "Statement by George T. Frampton, Jr., President of The Wilderness Society, on the Fire Policy Report," press release, December 15, 1988, File "December 15, 1988: Statement on the Fire Policy Report," Box 14:103, TWS. Other expressions of support from the environmental community can be found in: Douglas Jehl, "Moratorium on 'Let It Burn' Policy Urged," *Los Angeles Times*, December 16, 1988; Jim Carrier, "Cut Dry-Year Fires, Panel Reviewing Parks' Policy Urges," *Denver Post*, December 16, 1988; Philip Shabecoff, "Report Finds Flaws in Fire Planning But Backs Policies as Basically Sound," *NYT*, December 16, 1988; William Cottrell to William Penn Mott, January 5, 1989, File "P letters," DSC; Allan Crail to Senator James McClure, February 14, 1989, File "P letters," DSC; Wyoming Wildlife Federation, "For the Record of Public Comment on Interagency Fire Management Policy," February 20, 1989, File "FAM/letters," DSC; John Hopkins to William Penn Mott, February 15, 1989, File "P letters," DSC; and Brien Culhane to Dale Robertson, February 21, 1989, File "Letters," DSC.

56. E. Thomas Tuchmann to Dale Robertson, February 21, 1989; James B. Roberts

to Dale Robertson, February 8, 1989; and L. Gary Lundvall, Dan L. Taylor, and Dennis J. Smith to USFS Chief and NPS Director, February 14, 1989, all in File "FAM/letters," DSC. See also Richard E. Sanderson to William Penn Mott, February 21, 1989, File "P letters," DSC. Concerning NPS support, see: Thomas Ritter to Associate Director, February 22, 1989; H. Gilbert Lusk to Director, February 21, 1989; and F. Eugene Hester to Operations Associate Director, February 28, 1989, all in File "P letters," DSC. Information on USFS support is from James F. Torrence to Chief, February 7, 1989; and John Mumma to Chief, February 22, 1989, both in File "FAM/letters," DSC.

57. This was tallied from all the letters in DSC.

58. Hearings were held in Tallahassee, FL; Missoula, MT; Washington, D.C.; Sacramento, CA; Salt Lake City, UT; Anchorage, AK; Jackson, WY; Idaho Falls, ID; Albuquerque, NM; Seattle, WA; and Cody, WY. For GYC testimony by Hank Phibbs see "Fire Policy Review Hearing," Jackson, FL, February 7, 1989, 45–48, DSC; and by Louisa Willcox, "Fire Policy Review Hearing," Cody, WY, February 14, 1989, 112–18, DSC. For examples of experts see: Dale Taylor, "Fire Policy Review Hearing," Anchorage, AK, February 7, 1989, 13–19, DSC; Deb Patla, "Fire Policy Review Hearing," Jackson, FL, February 7, 1989, 56–61, DSC; and Jay Anderson, "Fire Policy Review Hearing," Idaho Falls, ID, February 8, 1989, 29–32. For a summary of the Missoula hearing, see Bruce Farling, "Few sparks fly at hearing on forest fires," *HCN*, February 27, 1989, 4.

59. "Fire Policy Review Hearing," Cody, WY, February 14, 1989, 53.

60. "Fire Policy Review Hearing," Cody, WY, February 14, 1989, 69.

61. An extremist in the Jackson hearings was Harold Turner, "Fire Policy Review Hearings," Jackson, WY, February 7, 1989, 13–20, DSC. For Alan Simpson's testimony (6–9), and Reuben Bullock's testimony (103–7), see "Fire Policy Review Hearing," Cody, WY, February 14, 1989.

62. John E. Cook, "Fire Policy Review Hearing," Albuquerque, NM, February 9, 1989, 23; and USDI and USDA, "Summary of Public Comments on the Fire Management Policy Report," April 1989, YNPV.

63. Although this was a congressional hearing, I have been unable to locate a published transcript. Fortunately, the YNPA has copies of most testimonies in File "Fires—1988—Congressional Hearing—Statements—January 31, 1989," Box Y-286. Dennis Knight's quote is from his testimony at this meeting.

64. Forestry personnel who spoke included Society of American Foresters Executive Director William Banzhaf, National Association of State Foresters State Forester of Oregon James Brown, and American Forestry Association Director of Resource Policy Dr. Gerald J. Gray. Other speakers included: James M. Peek, University of Idaho professor of wildlife management; James K. Agee, University of Washington chairman of the Forest Resources Management Division; and Norman L. Christensen Jr., Duke University professor of botany and forestry and environmental studies. Environmental organization representatives who spoke were: Lynn Greenwalt, National Wildlife Federation vice president; Louisa Willcox,

GYC program director; and George Frampton, The Wilderness Society president. See also Andrew Melnykovynch, "Diatribes on fires may yield to facts this spring," *HCN*, February 27, 1989, 7, in which he focuses primarily on Marlenee's rhetoric and factual mistakes as chair of the hearing.

65. Ron Marlenee, quoted in Melnykovynch, "Diatribes on Fires," 7.

66. Gregg D. Fauth, "The Information Connection—Fire Interpretation Team," March 1989, File "F.I.R.E. Team," Box Y-263, YNPA; and "Yellowstone Fires '88—Slide Program—Fire Team," n.d., File "Scripts for Programs," Box Y-262, YNPA.

67. Tamara Jones, "Yellowstone Fights to Restore Image," *MST*, November 26, 1988. Bob Barbee's speaking abroad from Barbee interview.

68. Division of Interpretation, "Fire Interpretation Plan Status Report," February 8, 1989, File "Interpretation of Fires," Box Y-263, YNPA; and NPS, "New Exhibit to Open at Grant Village Visitor Center in Yellowstone National Park," press release, June 8, 1989, File "Untitled," Box K-108, YNPA. See also NPS, "Yellowstone National Park 1988 Fire Season Recovery Plan, October 1988," File "Recovery Information," Box Y-262, YNPA.

69. NPS, "The Yellowstone Fires," YNPV; "Common Errors and Misunderstandings about the Yellowstone Fires," February 1989, File "Media and Fire," Box Y-263, YNPA. See also Jack de Golia to "Friend," n.d.; and NPS, "Yellowstone Fires, 1988," handout, n.d., both in File "Handouts (Public)," Box Y-263, YNPA. And see: "Readings About Fire, January 1989," File "Fire Management Policy Review Team," Box Y-263, YNPA; Bob Barbee to All NPS Units, August 15, 1989, File "Fire—1988 Fires—Correspondence," Box Y-286, YNPA; "Children's Slide Show," n.d., File "Scripts for Programs," Box Y-262, YNPA; NPS, "New Curriculum on Wildland Fire Ecology Available to Teachers," press release, April 19, 1990, File "Fire Policies," GYC; "Fire Ecology Game—Fire Team," File "Scripts for Programs," Box Y-262, YNPA; and Jack de Golia, "The Endless Summer of '88 at Yellowstone: Madness, Macintoshes, and Mail," *Interpretation* (Spring 1989), File "Miscellaneous Materials," Box Y-262, YNPA. The Forest Service and Greater Yellowstone Coordinating Committee (a group of USFS and NPS managers overseeing most of the GYA's forests and parks) also distributed information, including USFS, "Fire Recovery," Spring 1989, and "Wildfire," *Northern Region Wildfire Information Series*, Summer 1989, both in YNPV; and GYCC, "The Greater Yellowstone Fires of 1988: Questions and Answers," January 25, 1989, File "Fires—1988 Fires—Area Surveys," Box Y-286, YNPA.

70. Williams, "Incineration of Yellowstone," 38–85; Geoffrey O'Gara, "Beyond the Burn," *Sierra*, (January–February 1989): 40–51; and George Wuerthner, "The Flames of '88," *Wilderness* (Summer 1989): 41–54; and the entire edition of the *GYR* (Autumn 1988).

71. "What the Fires Mean to Yellowstone's Friends," *Yellowstone Fires 1988: A Special Supplement to Yellowstone Today*, May 1990, YNPV. Phil Perkins, personal interview with author, Mammoth Hot Springs, Wyoming, December 3, 2002; Barbee interview; and Bob Barbee to Director, n.d., File "Fire Interpretation, In House Material on Fires," Box Y-263, YNPA.

72. Concerning the $33 million, see GYCC, "The Greater Yellowstone Fires of 1988." The Wyoming sales tax information is from Wyoming Department of Administration and Fiscal Control Division of Research and Statistics, "The Yellowstone Fires of 1988: An Analysis Based on Sales Tax Collections and Various Park Related Data," February 1989, YNPV. The concern of Wyoming officials is from Gene Bryan to Rod Miller, February 6, 1989, File "FAM/letters," DSC; and Rick H. to Dan P., February 1, 1989, File "FAM/letters," DSC. See also Bruce Farling, "Forest Fire-Fighting Is Just Another Form of (Roast) Pork," *HCN*, February 27, 1989, 16; Clynn Phillips and David Taylor, "An Assessment of the 1988 Fire Suppression Expenditure Impacts on the Greater Yellowstone Region Economy," November 1989, YNPV; and Ann Arbor Miller, "Visits Dropped During Fires, but Rebounded," *BDC*, March 28, 1998.

73. The study suggesting increased visitation is in Richard Trahan, "Impact of the Yellowstone Fires on Planned Public Visitation"; the report was presented to Kenneth Hornback, NPS Statistical Office, June 1, 1989, File "Visitor Info—Fire," MAOF. See also Williams, "Incineration of Yellowstone," 80; and David J. Snepenger, "Marketing Yellowstone National Park After the Fires of 1988," November 15, 1989, YNPV.

74. David Jeffery, "Yellowstone: The Great Fires of 1988," *National Geographic* (February 1989): 255–73. See also Williams, "Incineration of Yellowstone," 38–85; O'Gara, "Beyond the Burn," 40–51; Wuerthner, "The Flames of '88," 41–54; Tom McNamee, "On Wilderness and Gardening," *GYR* (Winter 1989): 3, 18; Tom Harpole, "Yellowstone Revival," *Outdoor Photographer* (April 1989): 40–48; and M. John Fayhee, "Yellowstone: Was the Fire a Devastating Conflagration or a Beneficial Act of Nature?" *Backpacker* (January 1989): 42–46.

75. USDA/USDI, "Final Report on Fire Management Policy," May 5, 1989, YNPV. Concerning Manuel Lujan's actions, see USDI, "New U.S. Fire Management Recommendations Approved by Secretaries of Interior and Agriculture," press release, June 1, 1989, YNPV; and NPS Acting Director to Directorate, Field Directorate, WASO Division Chiefs and Park Superintendents, July 12, 1989, File "Fire Management Plan," MAOF.

76. Rocky Barker, "The Message Is: 'Nature Is a Good Thing,'" *HCN*, June 19, 1989, 5; and "GYC Conference Attracts Record Crowd," *GYR* (Summer 1989): 9.

77. The information on reporters' visits is in "PAO [Public Affairs Office] Calendar for April 1989," April 10, 1989, File "Pending Requests," Box Y-262, YNPA. Some articles include: Paul A. Witteman, "Springtime in the Rockies," *Time* (May 29, 1989): 94–95; Michael Satchell, "Yellowstone Lives!" *U.S. News and World Report* (May 15, 1989): 24–26; and "Yellowstone a Year Later," *Sunset: the Magazine of Western Living* (May 1989): 108–19.

78. For more on George Bush's visit, see Brett Prettyman, "Keeper of the Wild," *SLT*, September 14, 2003; and Barbee interview. Subsequent visitation is from John Varley, "The Status of Yellowstone's New Fire Plan," *Renewable Resources Journal* (Spring 1993): 20–21; John Varley, testimony in House Committee on Agriculture,

Subcommittee on Forests, Family Farms, and Energy, *Recovery of Forest Resources from the Greater Yellowstone Wildfires, Exxon Valdez Oilspill, and the Mount St. Helens Eruption*, 102nd Congress, 1st Session, 1991, 13; and Ann Arbor Miller, "Visits Dropped During Fires." Phil Perkins, during my personal interview with him, seconded the idea that resurging visitation largely erased concerns that fires damaged local economies.

79. Schullery, "The Story Itself," 17–25; Alistair James Bath, "Attitudes Toward Fire and Fire Management Issues in Yellowstone National Park," (PhD diss., University of Calgary, 1993), iii–iv; and Perkins interview.

80. The Student Conservation Association, "Greater Yellowstone Recovery Corps," informational brochure, n.d., File "Recovery Information," Box Y-262, YNPA.

81. "Wilderness and Parks Fire Conference, Montana State University," May 23–26, 1989, and "Agenda: Greater Yellowstone Coalition's 1989 Annual Meeting," May 19–21, 1989, both in File "Fires—1988 Fires—Area Surveys," Box Y-286, YNPA. See also "Examining the Greater Yellowstone Ecosystem: A Symposium on Land and Resource Management" abstracts, April 13–15, 1989; and "Symposiums, Books, Videos and Documentaries on the GYA," April 3, 1989, both in File "1360—Meetings," Box A-392, YNPA. Holmes Rolston's testimony is from Barker, "The Message Is," 5; Rolston shortly thereafter published his response to Chase in "Biology and Philosophy in Yellowstone," *Biology and Philosophy* 5 (1990): 241–58.

82. See, for example, William Romme and Don Despain, "The Long History of Fire in the Greater Yellowstone Ecosystem," *Western Wildlands* 15 (Summer 1989): 10–17; Romme and Despain, "Historical Perspective on the Yellowstone Fires of 1988," 695–99; Norman L. Christensen et al., "Interpreting the Yellowstone Fires of 1988," *BioScience* 39, no. 10 (November 1989): 678–85; Paul Schullery and Don Despain, "Prescribed Burning in Yellowstone National Park: A Doubtful Proposition," *Western Wildlands* 15 (Summer 1989): 30–34; Bonnicksen, "Fire Gods and Federal Policy," *American Forests* (July-August 1989): 14–16, 66–68; and Robert Barbee, "Replies from the Fire Gods," and Nathan L. Stephenson, David J. Parsons, and Howard T. Nichols, "Replies from the Fire Gods," (two different articles under that same title), both in *American Forests*, (March/April 1990): 34–35, and 35, 70, respectively.

83. Christensen et al., "Interpreting the Yellowstone Fires of 1988," 678-85 (quote pp. 684-85).

84. Christensen et al., "Interpreting the Yellowstone Fires of 1988," 678–85. Bob Ekey suggested that Christensen's objective support and level-headedness helped retain the use of fire by park managers (Bob Ekey personal interview with author, Bozeman, MT, December 9, 2003). See also Varley, "The Status of Yellowstone's New Fire Plan," 20–21; Howard T. Nichols, "Policy in Practice: U.S. Parks," *Forum for Applied Research and Public Policy* (Summer 1989): 50–53; Peter Matthiessen, "Our National Parks: The Case for Burning," *NYT Magazine*, December 11, 1988, 128; Barbee, "Replies from the Fire Gods," 34–35; Singer

and Schullery, "Yellowstone Wildlife: Populations in Process," 18–22; and the comments of Idaho U.S. senator James A. McClure in *Western Wildlands* 15 (Summer 1989): 57–60.

85. Conference proceedings can be found in Jason M. Greenlee, ed., *The Ecological Implications of Fire in Greater Yellowstone: Proceedings, Second Biennial Conference on the Greater Yellowstone Ecosystem* (Fairfield, WA: International Association of Wildland Fire, 1996).

86. The release and public input summary are from NPS, "Scoping Statement, Yellowstone National Park: Revision of Wildland Fire Management Plan," press release, July 5, 1990, File "Fires—Management—Environmental Assessment—1975–90," Box Y-286, YNPA; "Public Input Report, Revision of Wildland Fire Management Plan," October 1990, File "Public Input Report/Scoping," MAOF; "Update: Revision of Wildland Fire Management Plan," November 1990, File "Fire Management Plan," MAOF; Jeanne-Marie Souvigney to Bob Barbee, October 5, 1990, File "Untitled," MAOF; and Joan Haines, "Conservationists Endorse Let-Burn Policy," *BDC*, October 7, 1990.

87. USDI-NPS, *Yellowstone National Park Wildland Fire Management Plan* (Yellowstone National Park, WY: NPS, June 1991); USDI-NPS, *Draft Environmental Assessment for Wildland Fire Management Plan* (Yellowstone National Park, WY: NPS, June 1991); and John Varley and Paul Schullery, "Reaching the Real Public in the Public Involvement Process: Practical Lessons in Ecosystem Management," *The George Wright Forum* 13, no. 4 (1996): 72, 74.

88. NPS, "Draft Wildland Fire Management Plan and Environmental Assessment Available for Public Comment," press release, July 13, 1991, File "Untitled," Box K-108, YNPA; 56 *Federal Register* 148 (August 1, 1991): 36831; "Printing Specifications, YNP Wildland Fire Management Plan Report and Comment Form," n.d., File "Printing Info. for WFMP/EA," MAOF; "Report and Comment Form, July 1991: Yellowstone National Park Wildland Fire Management Plan," YNPV; Michael Milstein, "Yellowstone's New Fire Plan Proposes Prescribed Burns," *BGZ*, July 16, 1991; Angus M. Thuermer Jr., "Park Fire Plan Zones for Blazes," *JHNG*, July 17, 1991; and "Yellowstone Outlines Fire-Fighting Plan," *CST*, July 16, 1991.

89. Richard R. Bahr to Bob Barbee, memorandum, November 13, 1991, in File "Wildland Fire Management," Box W-195, YNPA; "Executive Summary: Wildland Fire Management in Yellowstone National Park," n.d., File "Fires—Management—1992–95," Box Y-286, YNPA; and "Agencies/Interest Groups" (a summary of public comments), September 11, 1991, File "Public Comments on Draft WFMP/EA—Status Report on Comments," MAOF.

90. House Committee on Government Operations, Subcommittee on Environment, Energy, and Natural Resources, *Federal Fire Management Policy: Evaluation of Changes Made after Yellowstone*, 101st Congress, 2nd Session, 1990; House Committee on Agriculture, Subcommittee on Forests, Family Farms, and Energy, *Recovery of Forest Resources from the Greater Yellowstone Wildfires, Exxon Valdez*

Oilspill, and the Mount St. Helens Eruption, 102nd Congress, 1st Session, 1991, 6–17, 30–45; Marit Sawyer, "Simpson, Thomas Give Cautious Support to Prescribed Fires," *CST*, January 24, 1991; Diane Eastridge, "Delegation Embraces New Fire Policy," *JHNG*, February 27, 1991; and "Wallop Likes New Fire Management Plan," *Powell Tribune*, May 12, 1992.

91. Information relating to fire behavior since 1988 is from Ridenour, *The National Parks Compromised*, 149–51; "Former Park Director Took Low-Key Approach to 1991 Yellowstone Fire," *CEP*, November 21, 1994; and Mary Ann Franke, *Yellowstone in the Afterglow* (Mammoth Hot Springs, WY: NPS, 2000), 45.

92. Fire plan approval information is from Bob Barbee to Regional Director, March 12, 1992, File "Fire–FONSI," MAOF; Scott McMillion, "Yellowstone: Let Some Burn?" *BDC*, May 5, 1992; "New Yellowstone Fire Plan Limits 'Let Burn,'" *CST*, May 6, 1992; and "Yellowstone Fire Plan Updated," *JHNG*, May 13, 1992. The new fire plan information can be found in Yellowstone National Park, *Yellowstone National Park Wildland Fire Management Plan* (Yellowstone National Park, WY: NPS, March 1992). For the first fire, see: NPS, "Prescribed Natural Fire Burning in Yellowstone National Park," press release, July 2, 1992, File "Fires," Box 10:102, TWS. Concerning the acreage, see: "Superintendent's Annual Report, 1992," 46, YNPR.

93. Phil Perkins' opinion is from Scott McMillion, "Policy Holds Up, with Fine-Tuning," *BDC*, March 28, 1998; and Perkins interview. John Varley's opinion is from Williams, "Incineration of Yellowstone," 59.

94. Phil Perkins, personal communication with author, telephone conversation, March 30, 2004; and Michael J. Yochim, "Compromising Yellowstone: The Interest Group-National Park Service Relationship in Modern Policy-making," (PhD diss., University of Wisconsin-Madison, 2004), 208–9. Note that some fires in any year escape control.

95. Pat Williams, quoted in Oliver Staley, "Political Fires Burned Nearly as Hot," *BDC*, March 28, 1998.

96. The ideas on removing the fire policy review to higher levels is from Bob Ekey, personal interview with author, Bozeman, MT, April 9, 2003.

Chapter Three

1. President Bill Clinton, as quoted in Associated Press, "Clinton vows to preserve national parks," August 26, 1995. Bruce Babbitt as quoted by Mike Finley, in telephone interview with author, June 24, 2003; and in Mike Finley, "Never Running From a Fight: Interview with Mike Finley," *Yellowstone Science* 9, no. 3 (Summer 2001): 9–19. Alex Balogh as quoted by GYC program director, Louisa Willcox, in her notes from a conversation with him, in Louisa [Willcox] to File, November 3, 1992, loose in GYCN.

2. Brooks M. Beard, "The Old World Meets the New World: Mining Interests and

Environmental Protection in the 90's" unpublished manuscript, 14, 18–19, File 20, Box 70, ARC; and Mike Clark, personal interview with author, Bozeman, Montana, April 16, 2003.

3. Ralph Glidden, "Exploring the Yellowstone High Country: A History of the Cooke City Area," n.d., 81–88, File "Historical Info about New World Area," YCR. See also Mark David Spence, *Dispossessing the Wilderness: Indian Removal and the Making of the National Parks* (New York: Oxford University Press, 1999).

4. Aubrey L. Haines, *The Yellowstone Story: A History of Our First National Park*, rev. ed. (Yellowstone National Park, WY: The Yellowstone Association for Natural Science, History, and Education, Inc., in cooperation with the University Press of Colorado, 1996), 108–30; Paul Schullery and Lee Whittlesey, *Myth and History in the Creation of Yellowstone National Park* (Lincoln: University of Nebraska Press, 2003); and Chris Magoc, *Yellowstone: The Creation and Selling of an American Landscape, 1870–1903* (Albuquerque: University of New Mexico Press, 1999), 2–12.

5. General Mining Law of 1872, 30 U.S.C.A., 22–39; An Act to Set Apart a Certain Tract of Land Lying Near the Headwaters of the Yellowstone River as a Public Park, Approved March 1, 1872, 17 Stat. 32; and Gordon Morris Bakken, *The Mining Law of 1872: Past, Politics, and Prospects* (Albuquerque: University of New Mexico Press, 2008).

6. Richard A. Bartlett, *Yellowstone: A Wilderness Besieged* (Tucson: University of Arizona Press, 1985), 91; Glidden, "Exploring the Yellowstone High Country," 89–100; and USFS and State of Montana, *New World Project Newsletter*, June 1995, 2, File "FS Newsletter," YCR.

7. Information on Noranda Minerals Corporation is from Jack Doyle, "Tarnished Giant: The Business and Environmental Practices of the Noranda/Edper Complex" (unpublished research paper for the GYC, December 1994), File "Jack Doyle on Noranda," GYCN. The corporate hierarchy of this company was complicated. According to Brooks Beard, in "The Old World Meets the New World":

> Crown Butte Mines, Inc. is a wholly owned subsidiary of a Canadian corporation, Crown Butte Resources, Ltd., which, in turn, is 60 percent owned by Hemlo Gold Mines, Inc. A 1987 agreement between Noranda Inc., also a Canadian corporation, and Crown Butte provided the New World project funding and briefly made Crown Butte Resources a 60 percent Noranda subsidiary in early 1991. Noranda sold its gold properties, including Crown Butte, to Hemlo Gold Mines, Inc. later that year. Hemlo Gold Mines, in turn is 46 percent owned by Noranda Minerals, Inc., a Canadian corporation based in Toronto. Next, Noranda Minerals is a wholly owned subsidiary of Noranda, Inc. Finally, Brascan Limited, a highly diversified Canadian company operating in natural resources, financial services and utility sectors, owns 49 percent of Noranda, Inc. (11)

As the controversy unfolded, the press and public commonly referred to the primary company promoting the mine as either Crown Butte or Noranda. Because both names, per Beard, have validity, and to avoid confusion, I have chosen to use Noranda Minerals Corporation or Noranda as the name for the primary mining proponent.

8. John Skow, "Mother Lode vs. Mother Nature," *Time* (November 22, 1993), 58. See also James E. Elliott, Allan R. Kirk, and Todd W. Johnson, "Field Guide: Gold-Copper-Silver Deposits of the New World District," n.d., File "Misc. Info about Noranda/CBMI;" and Crown Butte Mines, Noranda Minerals Corporation, and Hydrometrics, Inc., "New World Project, Park County, Montana, Project Description," July 1989, File "[Untitled]," both in YCR. And see Tom Shands, "Gold, Copper Mine Proposed near Cooke City," *LVE*, August 24, 1989.

9. Montana Metal Mine Reclamation Act is MCA 82-4-301, et seq.; Montana Environmental Policy Act is MCA 75-1-101, et seq. See also Robin Patten, "Development and Potential Impacts of the New World Project," April 1992, loose in YCR; Beartooth Alliance, "The New World Project: Hard Rock Mining Near Yellowstone National Park and the Absaroka-Beartooth Wilderness," fact sheet, June 1991, File "Untitled," YCR. Montana's mine favoritism is from Yellowstone National Park briefing statement, "New World Mine Proposal," May 1994, File "Completed Congressionals," YCR; and Janis E. Johnston, "Contested Terrain: A Sociological Analysis of Natural Resource Conflict" (master's thesis, University of Wyoming, 1998), 39.

10. Beartooth Alliance, "The New World Project."

11. Beartooth Alliance, "The New World Project"; Patten, "Development and Potential Impacts of the New World Project"; Don Bachman, "For a 'Pound of Gold': Noranda Submits Plans to Mine Above Yellowstone Watersheds," *GYR* (Winter 1991); and Jim Robbins, "Some See It as a 'Mine from Hell'; Others Say It Will Heal Old Mining Scars," *HCN*, November 4, 1991, 9. See also Crown Butte Mines, Noranda Minerals Corp., and Hydrometrics, Inc., "New World Project;" and Tom Turner, *Justice on Earth: Earthjustice and the People It Has Served* (Oakland, CA: Earthjustice, 2002), 24.

12. USFS and State of Montana, *New World Project Newsletter*, 2.

13. Turner, *Justice on Earth*, 23–25; Amy Irvine, *Making a Difference: Stories of How Our Outdoor Industry and Individuals Are Working to Preserve America's Natural Places* (Guilford, CT: Falcon Press, 2001), 129–35; Johnston, "Contested Terrain," 82–85; and Beard, "The Old World Meets the New World," 7–8. See also "Letter from the Chairman" in *The Alliance* (Beartooth Alliance newsletter), n.d.; and Beartooth Alliance, "New World Project: Questions and Answers," fact sheet, n.d., both in File "Untitled," YCR.

14. Beartooth Alliance, "The New World Project"; Patten, "Development and Potential Impacts of the New World Project"; Bachman, "For a 'Pound of Gold'"; Beartooth Alliance, "New World Project: Questions and Answers"; Todd Wilkinson, "A Clash Between Two Kinds of Wealth," *HCN*, June 4, 1990, 11; and

Daniel P. Reinhart and David J. Mattson, "Grizzly Bear and Black Bear Habitat Use in the Cooke City, Montana, Area 1990–1991" (unpublished report, May 30, 1992), File "CEM & Biological Assessment," YCR.

15. Beartooth Alliance, "The New World Project"; Patten, "Development and Potential Impacts of the New World Project"; Bachman, "For a 'Pound of Gold'"; Beartooth Alliance, "New World Project: Questions and Answers"; and Wilkinson, "A Clash Between Two Kinds of Wealth."

16. Turner, *Justice on Earth*, 24–26; Bachman, "For a 'Pound of Gold'"; Beard, "The Old World Meets the New World," 7–9; Patten, "Development and Potential Impacts of the New World Project"; Heidi Barrett, personal interview with author, Bozeman, Montana, April 9, 2003; and Louisa Willcox, personal interview with author, Livingston, Montana, April 9, 2003.

17. Turner, *Justice on Earth*, 25; and Irvine, *Making a Difference*, 139.

18. Don Bachman, "New World Mining Project: Incomplete Application Stalls Permitting Process," *GYR* (Spring 1991): 14. See also Robin [Patten] to Noranda, memorandum, June 25, 1992; and Robin [Patten] to Louisa [Willcox] and Jeanne-Marie [Souvigney], June 24, 1992, both in File "Memos—Patten," GYCN. And see Noranda, "No Cyanide or Open Pits for New World: Revised Plan Cuts Costs, Minimizes Impacts," *New World News* (Noranda newsletter, July, 1992), File "Mining—Crown Butte Mines—File 2," Box L-67, YNPA; and Beartooth Alliance, "New World Project Update," *The Alliance* (Beartooth Alliance newsletter), September 1992, File "Untitled," YCR.

19. Yellowstone superintendent Bob Barbee to Clint Erb, December 28, 1990, loose in YCR; and Mary Hektner, "List of NPS or DOI correspondence to lead agencies regarding the New World Mine," n.d., File "Denver Meeting July 16–17, 1996," YCR. See also the following correspondence: Bob Barbee to Clint Erb, August 5, 1991; Bob Barbee to Clint Erb, March 23, 1992; Bob Barbee to Mike DaSilva, July 31, 1992; Bob Barbee to Mike DaSilva, December 4, 1992; and Bob Barbee to Mike DaSilva, March 29, 1993, all in File "Completeness Reviews," YCR. Correspondence with GYC is from Robin Patten to Mary Hektner, June 4, 1992, File "Noranda Correspondence—Patten," GYCN; and Confidential Memo re: New World Project Gardiner Meeting, June 3, 1992, File "Memos—Patten," GYCN. And see "Summary Briefing Paper," March 18, 1992, File "Mining-Crown Butte Mines—File 1," Box L-67, YNPA. Concerning the creation of YCR see: YCR, *Yellowstone Center for Resources Annual Report, 2001* (Mammoth Hot Springs, WY: NPS, 2002). Staff professionalization information is from Paul Schullery, email message to author, December 1, 2011.

20. Louisa [Willcox] to GYC Board Program Committee, November 11, 1991, File "Strategy Memos—New World Project," GYCN; Louisa Willcox to Teresa Erickson, November 19, 1991, loose in GYCN; and Louisa Willcox to New World Project Activists, April 29, 1992, File "Untitled," YCR.

21. Louisa Willcox to New World Project Activists, April 29, 1992, loose in GYCN; and Turner, *Justice on Earth*, 26–27.

22. Louisa Willcox to New World Project Activists; Philip M. Hocker to Louisa Willcox, Richard Parks, Wade King, and Will Patric, May 5, 1992, File "Correspondence—General," GYCN; Blair to Dale Pontius and Tom Cassidy, memorandum, August 1, 1992, File 15, Box 70, ARC; Robin Patten to John Randolph, October 7, 1992, and Robin Patten to Connie Wilbert, October 2, 1992, both in File "Noranda Correspondence—Patten," GYCN; Robin [Patten] to Louisa [Willcox] and Ed [Lewis] re: Meeting with Trout Unlimited, File "Memos—Patten," June 30, 1992, GYCN; and Paul Pritchard to Dale Robertson, September 9, 1993, File "Untitled," YCR.

23. "B[eartooth]A[lliance] Slide Show in Cody," *The Alliance*, July 1992, File "Untitled," YCR; LaMar Empey to Park County Resident, August 16, 1991, File "Citizen Letters," GYCN; and Beartooth Alliance, "Help Stop the New World Mine!," flyer distributed outside a public meeting on the mine in Cody, Wyoming, May 25, 1993, author's personal collection. Park County position is from L. Gary Lundvall to Sherm Sollid, January 13, 1992; and Paul Hoffman to David Rovig, September 28, 1992, both in File "Correspondence—General," GYCN.

24. The Toronto trip and Noranda environmental concerns are from Louisa [Willcox] to File, November 3, 1992, loose in GYCN. See also "Crown Butte Holds Public Meeting at Cooke City," New World News newsletter, August 1992, File "Untitled," YCR. The application completion information is from Sandra J. Olsen and Sherm Sollid to Dan McLaughlin, April 2, 1993, File "Completeness Reviews," YCR; and Todd Dvorak, "Battle Over Mine Heated Up in 1993," *LVE*, December 31, 1993.

25. Ed Lewis to GYC Executive Committee, June 23, 1993, File "Noranda Memos," GYCN.

26. Peter Aengst to Nick Rahall, March 30, 1993, File "Peter's '93 Letters—Out," GYCN; and Peter Aengst to Dale Bumpers, March 30, 1993, File "Untitled," YCR. See also Ed Lewis to GYC Board Executive Committee, June 23, 1993, memorandum; and Gretchen Long Glickman to GYC Executive Committee, June 23, 1993, both in File "Noranda Memos," GYCN. And see Peter Aengst to Mike Sullivan, September 27, 1993, File "Peter's '93 letters—OUT," GYCN. Conservationists seemed to have overlooked the State of Montana's requirement that reclamation be included in the mining application.

27. American Rivers, "North America's Most Endangered and Threatened Rivers of 1994," File "Am. R. Correspondence & Information," GYCN; "The 1872 Mining Law: A License to Steal" pamphlet, August 1993, File "Fan Mail Stuff," GYCN; "No Mines Near Yellowstone," *NYT*, August 29, 1994; and Bakken, *The Mining Law of 1872*, 159–63.

28. The interaction between Bruce Babbitt and Bob Barbee is from Finley interview; and Finley, "Never Running from a Fight," 9–19. For information on the progress of reforms on the 1872 law, see also James R. Skillen, *The Nation's Largest Landlord: The Bureau of Land Management in the American West* (Lawrence: The University Press of Kansas, 2009), 148–49.

29. Thomas J. Cassidy Jr. to Sherm Sollid, July 30, 1993, File 16, ARC.

30. David P. Garber to Bob Barbee, March 15, 1993, File "Mining—Crown Butte Mines—File 2," Box L-67, YNPA; "Yellowstone National Park Issues Being Analyzed in the New World Project EIS" fact sheet, n.d., File "Extra Copies of Various NPS Correspondence to Lead Agencies on New World," YCR; and "Park Concerned About Water, Tailings, Many Other Issues," *CEP*, June 30, 1993.

31. Bob Barbee to Sherm Sollid, August 1, 1993, File "Completeness Reviews," YCR.

32. Coleman's bristling is from Stu [Coleman] to Superintendent [Bob Barbee], May 3, 1994, handwritten note, File "L3023 Mining: New World Mine Project Correspondence: Agencies," YCR.

33. Various iterations of the quote appeared in Bob Ekey, "Noranda Mine," *Trout* (Spring 1994): 26; Todd Wilkinson, "Fool's Gold," *National Parks* (July–August 1994): 31; Lauren McKeever and Mark Haynes, "Yellowstone Mine: Some Say It'll Bring Glitter, Some Say Tarnish," *SLT*, March 6, 1994; and Hugh Jackson, "Official Laments Lack of Control Over Mine Plan," *CST*, April 19, 1993.

34. Noranda's complaint is from Mark W. Petersmeyer to Roger Kennedy, April 8, 1994; and NPS's response is from Roger Kennedy to Mark W. Petersmeyer, n.d., both in File "Mining—Crown Butte Mines—File 1," Box L-67, YNPA.

35. Reinhart and Mattson, "Grizzly Bear and Black Bear Habitat Use"; and Diana F. Tomback, "Gold and Grizzlies: A Bad Combination," *HCN*, December 3, 1990, 11.

36. Peter Aengst to Noranda New World Activists, June 13, 1993, memorandum; and Peter Aengst to Louisa Willcox, Doug Honnold, Gordon Atkinson, and Gretchen Stroud, May 13, 1993, memorandum, both in File "'93 Memos," GYCN. See also Peter Aengst and Louisa Willcox to Pat Williams, July 6, 1993, File "Peter's '93 letters—Out," GYCN; and Peter Aengst to Noranda New World Mine Activists, memorandum, January 1994, File "January 1994 Update," GYCN. EPA's position can be found in Robert DeSpain to David Garber and Bud Clinch, September 26, 1993; and Stephen Hoffman to Peter Aengst, November 10, 1993, both in File "Scoping," GYCN. See also Louisa Willcox to Bill Yellowtail, January 3, 1993 [*sic*] (should be 1994), File "Cooper's Work," GYCN; Bill Yellowtail to Louisa Willcox, February 15, 1994, File "1994 Correspondence—In," GYCN; and Max Dodson to Dan Fraser, December 22, 1993, File "Peter's '93 Letters—In," GYCN. Note that in these discussions with the EPA, the idea of buying out Noranda's mineral rights came up, an idea that would be more fully discussed later.

37. Turner, *Justice on Earth*, 41; Gretchen Stroud to Managing Agents for Seven Crown Butte, Noranda, or Hemlo Gold Mine affiliates, July 7, 1993, File "Court Cases/ Decisions, File 1," Box A-407, YNPA; "Law Suit Possible Over Water Quality Issues at New World Mine," July 7, 1993, press release, File "Cooper's Work," GYCN; "Lawsuit Filed Over Water Quality Issues at New World Mine," September 16, 1993, press release, File "Complaint," GYCN; and Peter Aengst to Noranda New World Mine Activists, memorandum, January 1994, File "January 1994 Update," GYCN.

38. Stephen Hoffman to Peter Aengst, November 10, 1993, File "Scoping," GYCN; Hugh Jackson, "EPA Official Unloads on Noranda Plan," *CST*, December 4, 1993;

Peter Aengst to Noranda New World Mine Activists, memorandum, January 1994, file "January 1994 Update," GYCN; Bob Ekey, "Noranda Mine," *Trout* (Spring 1994): 25–29; and American Rivers, "North America's Most Endangered and Threatened Rivers of 1994."

39. Yellowstone National Park, "The New World Gold Mine," 1994, booklet loose in YCR files.

40. Max Baucus to Alex Balogh, October 25, 1993, with attached "Transcript of President Clinton's Response to the June 1, 1995, Billings, Montana, Town Meeting Question Concerning the Controversial New World Gold Mine," File "Mining— Crown Butte Mines—File 2," Box L-67, YNPA. Baucus also asked Balogh to consider adverse effects of the mine on Yellowstone in the EIS: to refrain from strip mining or using cyanide leaching, to develop a reclamation plan that used technology with a proven track record of success at such high elevations, and to carefully protect the water resources of the area.

41. Roger Kennedy to Max Baucus, December 16, 1993, File "Mining—Crown Butte Mines—File 1," Box L-67, YNPA. See also Max Baucus to Alex Balogh, October 25, 1993.

42. Max Baucus to Alex Balogh, October 25, 1993. See also Roger Kennedy to Max Baucus, December 6, 1993; Roger Kennedy to Max Baucus, December 16, 1993; and Dan McLaughlin to Roger Kennedy, December 30, 1993, all in File "Mining— Crown Butte Mines—File 1," Box L-67, YNPA. And see Peter Aengst to John Reynolds, December 2, 1993, File "Peter's '93 letters—OUT," GYCN; and Peter Aengst to Noranda New World Mine Activists, memorandum, January 1994, file "January 1994 Update," GYCN.

43. Peter Aengst to Mike Sullivan, September 27, 1993, File "Peter's '93 letters—Out," GYCN; Mark Bagne, "State Ready to Muscle Noranda," *CEP*, December 1, 1993; and Peter Aengst, "Lining Up To Fight Noranda's Proposed Gold Mine," *GYR* (Winter 1994): 10–11. See also Ron Cooper to Dan Heilig et al., February 10, 1994, File "Cooper's Work," GYCN.

44. Water sample results are from Lee Rozaklis and Ed Armbruster to Louisa Wilcox [*sic*], July 29, 1993, File "Noranda," Box A-366, YNPA.

45. Todd Wilkinson, "Cutting the Beartooths," *Backpacker* (August 1993): 12; Ekey, "Noranda Mine," 28; and Wilkinson, "Fool's Gold," 30–35. See also "Opposition Builds to Proposed Gold Mine," *National Parks* (January–February 1994): 16.

46. Bob Ekey, "Noranda Mine," 28.

47. "American Rivers Enters the Fight to Save the Yellowstone," *American Rivers* (Fall 1993): 7; and "Michael Keaton Kicks Off American Rivers Yellowstone Campaign," *American Rivers* (Winter 1994): 5; American Rivers, "North America's Most Endangered and Threatened Rivers of 1994;" and American Rivers, "American Rivers Yellowstone Campaign," [1994], all in File 17, Box 71, ARC. NPCA involvement is from Terri Martin and Rod Greenough to Paul Pritchard, memorandum, October 29, 1993, File "NPCA," GYCN; and Peter Aengst to Noranda New World Mine Activists, memorandum, January 1994, File

"January 1994 Update," GYCN. See also Kevin Coyle to Ian Bayer, April 19, 1994; and Kevin Coyle to David Kerr, April 19, 1994, both in File 18, Box 70, ARC.

48. Thomas J. Cassidy and Polly Dement to Kevin, Randy, memorandum, October 22, 1993; and "American Rivers Campaign Targets Threat to Source Tributaries of Yellowstone River on Edge of World's Oldest National Park," November 5, 1993, press release, both in File 16, Box 70, ARC. The emphasis on Yellowstone is from Louisa [Willcox] to Peter [Aengst], Ed [Lewis], Jeanne-Marie [Souvigney], Brian, Ron, Bob, Mary Stuart, and Ken, memorandum, January 26, 1994, loose in GYCN; and Johnston, "Contested Terrain," 85. NPS prodding is from Clark interview and Mary Hektner, interview with author, Mammoth Hot Springs, WY, April 14, 2003. World Heritage Site information is from "World Heritage Convention," http://whc.unesco.org/en/list, accessed July 26, 2011.

49. "No Mines near Yellowstone," *NYT*, August 29, 1994.

50. Ibid.; "Blocking the Yellowstone Mine," *NYT*, September 18, 1994; and Clark interview. Robert Semple eventually won a Pulitzer Prize for his series of editorials opposing the mine; see American Rivers, "*New York Times'* Robert B. Semple Jr. Received Pulitzer for Editorials Opposing Gold Mine Near Yellowstone National Park," April 10, 1996, press release, File 14, Box 71, ARC; and Irvine, *Making a Difference*, 140.

51. D. B. Rovig to Crown Butte Shareholder, April 1, 1993; and Crown Butte Resources, Ltd., *Annual Report, 1993*, both in File "Misc. Info about Noranda/CBMI," YCR. See also Hemlo Gold Mines, Inc., "Annual Report 1993," File 10, Box 71, ARC; and Crown Butte Mines, "Summary of the New World Project," File "New World Project Briefing Folder," Box N-266, YNPA.

52. Finley interview; Skillen, *The Nation's Largest Landlord*, 148–49; and Crown Butte Resources, Ltd., *Annual Report 1994*, File 16, Box 70, ARC.

53. Finley interview and Finley, "Never Running from a Fight."

54. Clark interview.

55. Sherm Sollid and Mike DaSilva to Mary Hektner, October 12, 1994, File "L3023 Mining: New World Mine Project PDEIS," YCR.

56. Both Park County, Montana, commissioners and Montana governor Marc Racicot supported the mine. See Jake Ellison, "Commissioners Favor Mine," *LVE*, July 20, 1994; Marc Racicot to Mike Finley, June 24, 1996, File "Noranda," Box A-366, YNPA; Mike Finley to Marc Racicot, July 15, 1996, File "Noranda," Box A-366, YNPA; and Turner, *Justice on Earth*, 35. "Stopping the Yellowstone Mine," *NYT*, March 27, 1995; and "Stop this Gold Mine—The Right Way," *BGZ*, April 24, 1995. See also Michael Satchell, "A New Battle over Yellowstone Park," *U.S. News & World Report* (March 13, 1995): 35–36, 41–42.

57. For conservation publicity, see: GYC, "'Mine From Hell' Threatens Yellowstone," broadside, n.d., with associated article "They Get the Gold and We Get the Shaft," File "New World Mine—GYC Fact Sheets," YCR; "Yellowstone Values, Wildlife Defended," *National Parks* (March–April 1995): 10–11; Jessica Maxwell, "The New World Blues," *Audubon* (September–October 1995): 82–89; and seven articles in

the Autumn 1995 issue of *Clementine* (magazine published by the Mineral Policy Center, Washington, D.C.). Endangered river designation is from American Rivers, "American Rivers Announces Continent's Most Endangered Rivers of 1995," press release, April 18, 1995; and "Clarks Fork of the Yellowstone River," both in green folder, YCR.

58. Jim Geringer to Marc Racicot, March 23, 1995, File "Dick Horner, NOR Shareholders Meeting Statement," GYCN.

59. Jim Geringer to Marc Racicot, March 23, 1995, File "Dick Horner, NOR Shareholders Meeting Statement," GYCN; Jim Geringer to Dennis M. Williams, July 21, 1995, File "Betty—1995 Correspondence," GYCN; and Paul House to Boyd Bernard, June 2, 1995, File "Team Noranda 1995 Letters—Out," GYCN. Park County concerns can be found in Jim Geringer to Jack Winninger, October 31, 1995, File "Socio-economic issues," YCR; and Beverly A. Reece, "Who Will Pay?" *Clementine* (Autumn 1995): 10–11.

60. June Brown to Conrad Burns, April 19, 1995, File 19, Box 70, ARC; and Florence Zundel, Joan Humiston, and Loretta Long to Fellow Snowmobilers, April 12, 1995, File "Snowmobiler Support Letters 5/95," GYCN.

61. Peter [Aengst] to Mike [Clark] and Louisa [Willcox], memorandum, April 30, 1995, File "1995 Memos—GYC," GYCN; GYC, "New World Mine Fact Sheets," Spring 1995, File "NW Work Groups," YCR; and GYC, "Gold Mine Threatens Yellowstone," fact sheet, n.d., File "Fact Sheet for Faxing," GYCN. Additionally, although Noranda's application to mine proposed placing the tailings pile in Fisher Creek, the proposal left open the possibility of placing it in Miller Creek should the other site be found unusable. That switch was a distinct possibility, given the potential that the EPA would prohibit the destruction of wetlands by the tailings pile in Fisher Creek.

62. Lobbyist information is from Betty Stroock to GYC Board of Directors, memorandum, August 22, 1995, File "Betty 1995 Correspondence," GYCN; Birch Bayh to Roger G. Kennedy, July 20, 1995, File "Peter's 1995 Letters—In," GYCN; and Meredith Cohn, "Crown Butte Making Its Case," *BGZ*, April 11, 1995. Noranda defenses information is from Crown Butte Mines, Inc., "New World Mine: The Real Story," fact sheet, n.d., File "Pro-mine Publication: New World Mine—The Real Story," YCR; Crown Butte Resources, Ltd., *Annual Report, 1995*, File "Misc. Info about Noranda/CBMI," YCR; Crown Butte Mines, Inc., Joseph J. Baylis to Max Baucus, June 21, 1995, File "Baucus/Kennedy/CBMI/State of Montana letters," YCR; and Joseph J. Baylis, "Mine Project Design Insures No Threat to Yellowstone Park," letter to the editor, September 8, 1995, *NYT*; and Cohn, "Crown Butte Making Its Case."

63. Crown Butte Mines, Inc., "New World Mine."

64. Ibid.

65. Betty Stroock, "The Wrong Place for a Mine," *Clementine* (Autumn 1995): 3–5; Jack Doyle, "Noranda Minerals' Family of Companies," *Clementine* (Autumn 1995): 12–13; Philip M. Hocker, "New World Bravery," *Clementine* (Autumn 1995): 14–16;

Paul House to "all participants in the activist meeting on Noranda's New World Project," memorandum, January 26, 1995, File "Team Noranda 1995 Letters Out," GYCN; GYC, "New World v. Mineral Hill Side-by-side Comparison," fact sheet, n.d., File "Mineral Hill/N. World," GYCN; Betty Stroock to Ken Barrett, August 9, 1995, File "Betty—1995 Correspondence," GYCN; Doug Honnold and Jim Angell to Plaintiffs in *Beartooth Alliance, et al. v. Crown Butte Mines, et al.,* memorandum, April 20, 1994, File "Open Meetings Suit," GYCN; SCLDF, "Conservationists Sue to Stop Secret Deal," May 3, 1994, press release, File "Open Meetings Suit," GYCN; and Turner, *Justice on Earth,* 40.

66. "Yellowstone Park Officials Unfair, Miners Tell Clinton," *BDC,* August 30, 1995. In part, the USFS disposition toward mining was due to the Gallatin National Forest's 1988 forest plan, which placed exploration and development of mineral resources in the area above Cooke City as the highest priority there. See USDA and USFS, *Gallatin National Forest/Forest Plan* (Bozeman, MT: USFS, 1988), iii–67. Don Bachman also notes, however, that while he was a GYC representative he learned of a possible cozy relationship between Sherm Sollid and David Rovig with whom he went to college at Montana Tech in Butte. Rovig went on to become president of Crown Butte Mines (Don Bachman, pers. com. with author, Bozeman, Montana, May 28, 2011).

67. "Mine No Threat to Yellowstone, Racicot Told," *BDC,* August 30, 1995.

68. Mike Finley, as quoted in Lynne Bama, "Yellowstone: A Park Boss Goes to Bat for the Land," *HCN,* April 29, 1996, 1, 8–12; "NPS Concerns: Proposed New World Mine/Yellowstone, July 1995," File "Cost Estimates/Buyout," YCR; "Discussion points with the Forest Service," n.d., File "Meeting w/USFS, 8/31/95," YCR; Michael Milstein, "Park Chief Defends Mine Review Process," *BGZ,* September 12, 1995 (Note that the article's title incorrectly reflects Finley's opinion); and Don Bachman, GYC representative from 1989 to 1991, e-mail to author, December 18, 2010.

69. Geologic Resources Division, NPS, "New World Mine Buyout Cost Estimate," July 1995; and USDI-NPS, "Acquisition of New World Mineral Rights by Land Exchange," both internal briefing papers, File "Baucus letter," YCR. See also Paul Bedard, "Clinton May Visit Yellowstone Mine Site," *Washington Times,* August 23, 1995.

70. President Bill Clinton, as quoted in "New World Mine Plan Draws Clinton's Fire," *JHNG,* June 7, 1995. See also "Transcript of President Clinton's Response to the June 1, 1995, Billings, Montana, Town Meeting Question Concerning the Controversial New World Gold Mine," File "Mining—Crown Butte Mines— File 2," Box L-67, YNPA.

71. Clark interview; Bob Ekey, personal interview with author, Bozeman, Montana, April 9, 2003; Tom Turner, *Justice on Earth,* 43; "Mr. Clinton Can Save Yellowstone," *NYT,* August 14, 1995; "Mr. Clinton Acts on Yellowstone," *NYT,* August 29, 1995; "Mine Project Threatens Yellowstone Park Disaster," *Denver Post,* September 7, 1995; "Stop Mineral Giveaways," *USA Today,* August 31, 1995; and Beard,

"The Old World Meets the New World," 19. See also "Canceling the New World Mine," *NYT*, December 10, 1995.

72. Finley interview; "Briefing Statement," August 21, 1995, File "New World Mine—Briefing Statement, 8/95," YCR; and Beard, "The Old World Meets the New World," 20–21.

73. Bill Clinton quote from Clark interview. See also Allan Robinson, "Clinton Limits Mining Claims," *Toronto Globe and Mail*, August 28, 1995 (Noranda Minerals had its headquarters in Toronto); Bob Ekey, "Clinton Tours New World Mine: Historic Meeting With Conservationists," *GYR* (Summer 1995): 1, 4; Todd Dvorak, "Mine Comes Under President's Scrutiny," *LVE*, August 28, 1995; "Mr. Clinton Acts on Yellowstone," *NYT*, August 29, 1995; and Beard, "The Old World Meets the New World," 21.

74. "Noranda Officials Thumb Nose At President Clinton—Stake 38 New Claims," *GYR* (Summer 1995): 5; Mineral Policy Center, "A Sneak Attack on Yellowstone," press release, n.d., File "Mineral Policy Center," GYCN; 60 *Federal Register* 170 (September 1, 1995): 45732; Michael Milstein, "Crown Butte Files More Claims," *BGZ*, September 6, 1995; and American Rivers, Beartooth Alliance, GYC, and NPCA, "New Mining Claims Attacked," press release, September 5, 1995, green folder, YCR.

75. Paul C. Pritchard, Mike Clark, et al. to Adul Wichiencharoen, February 28, 1995, File "Bingaman letter/World Heritage," YCR; Nadia White, "Noranda Mine Foes Look to UN for Help," *CST*, March 1, 1995; Marcus Lowes, "Groups Ask U.N. to Help Block Mine Near Park," *BGZ*, March 1, 1995; Hektner interview; Bernd von Droste to George Frampton, March 6, 1995, loose in YCR; and George Frampton to Bernd von Droste, n.d., File "L3023 Mining: New World Mine Project—World Heritage Committee," YCR.

76. World Heritage Committee, "UNESCO Convention Concerning the Protection of the World Cultural and Natural Heritage," December 4–9, 1995, File "World Heritage Correspondence," YCR. See also Paul C. Pritchard et al. to Adul Wichiencharoen, September 6, 1995, File "Resource Management—Significant Resource Problems," Box N-365, YNPA; NPCA, "Prominent Americans Urge Protection of Yellowstone National Park from New World Mine," September 7, 1995, press release, File "Completed Congressionals," YCR; and NPCA, "NPCA Leads Conservation Testimony Against Yellowstone Mine Project," September 8, 1995, press release, green folder, YCR. The endangered recommendation is from George Frampton to Bernd von Droste, June 27, 1995, loose in YCR; and from Robbie Robinson (delegation member), "Yellowstone National Park World Heritage Review," November 20, 1995; and World Heritage Committee, "UNESCO Convention Concerning the Protection of the World Cultural and Natural Heritage," December 4–9, 1995, both in file "World Heritage Correspondence," YCR. And see Michael Milstein, "Group: Mine Plan Endangers Park," *BGZ*, December 6, 1995; Bernd von Droste to William McIlhenny, January 8, 1996, File "Completed Congressionals," YCR; and Schullery, *Searching for Yellowstone*, 213.

77. The conservationists' response is from NPCA, American Rivers, Beartooth Alliance, and GYC, "Yellowstone Declared 'In Danger,'" December 5, 1995, press release, File "Completed Congressionals," YCR; and Karin Ronnow, "Yellowstone Found to Be 'In Danger,'" *LVE*, December 5, 1995.

78. Joseph Baylis quoted in "Yellowstone Added to 'Danger' List," *National Parks* (March–April 1996): 13.

79. Conrad Burns, "Burns Pans Park Designation," December 5, 1995, press release, File "L3023 Mining: New World Mine project—World Heritage Committee," YCR.

80. Information and quote on the American Policy Center is from its website, http://www.americanpolicy.org/about/main.htm, accessed March 13, 2005.

81. "Clinton Illegally Implementing United Nations' Green Agenda," *Insider's Report*, newsletter, November 1995, 1, 3–4.

82. NPS's response is from Office of the Secretary, "Statement by Department of Interior on Designation of Yellowstone National Park as a World Heritage Site in Danger," December 5, 1995, press release, loose in YCR; and Mike Finley to Senator Thad Cochran, June 19, 1996, File "Correspondence," Box A-360, YNPA. Don Young's actions and Mike Finley's reaction can be found in Finley, "Never Running from a Fight," 15.

83. *Beartooth Alliance et al. v. Crown Butte Mines, et al.*, 904 F. Supp. 1168 (D. Mont. 1995).

84. Ibid. See also SCLDF, "Federal Judge Holds Noranda/Crown Butte in Violation of Clean Water Act at New World," October 13, 1995, press release, File "Beartooth Alliance vs. Crown Butte Lawsuit," YCR; "Mine Near Park Violating Clean Water Act," *BDC*, October 15, 1995; and Warren Cornwall, "Bad Luck for New World Mine," *HCN*, October 30, 1995, 3. And see SCLDF, "Crown Butte/Noranda Faces Judgment Day," March 5, 1996, press release, File "SCLDF," GYCN; and Turner, *Justice on Earth*, 46.

85. Mike Clark, quoted in Bama, "Yellowstone: A Park Boss Goes to Bat for the Land," 10; Doug Honnold and Susan Daggett to Noranda Clients, September 5, 1995, File "SCLDF," GYCN; and Mary Hektner to James Pipkin, memorandum, June 6, 1996, File "Misc. Info about Noranda/CBMI," YCR.

86. Mike Finley to Sherm Sollid, February 13, 1996, File "Extra copies of various NPS Correspondence to Lead Agencies on New World," YCR. See also Mike Finley to Sherm Sollid, March 8, 1996; Mike Finley to Sherm Sollid, March 29, 1996 (might vs. will discussion); and Mike Finley to Sherm Sollid, April 9, 1996, all three letters in File "L3023 Mining: New World Mine Project PDEIS," YCR.

87. Mike Finley, "A Few Words from Yellowstone National Park," press release, June 1, 1996, File "L3023 Mining: New World Mine Project: Statements/Press, Briefs," YCR.

88. "Park Head Blasts Mine Review Process," *LVE*, June 6, 1996; Marc Racicot to Mike Finley, June 24, 1996, File "Noranda," Box A-366, YNPA; Mike Finley to Marc Racicot, July 15, 1996, File "Noranda," Box A-366, YNPA; Mary Hektner to Susan Rieff and Brooks Yeager, memorandum, July 1, 1996, File "Mad at Mike," YCR; and

John E. Cook to Senator Kempthorne, October 2, 1996, File "Correspondence," Box A-360, YNPA. See also Stu Coleman, "Potential Threats to Yellowstone National Park by the New World Mine Proposal," attached to Gary L. Thor to Stu Coleman, February 29, 1996, File "L3023 Mining: New World Mine Project: Statements/Press, Briefs," YCR; and "Simpson Beleaguers Finley," *JHNG*, June 19, 1996.

89. American Rivers, "American Rivers Announces Continent's Most Endangered Rivers of 1996," April 17, 1996, press release, File "Am. R. Correspondence & Information," GYCN. See also "The Future of the Clarks Fork," *American Whitewater* (February 1996): 50; and Todd Wilkinson, "Global Warning," *National Parks* (March–April 1996): 35–40. Poll information is from Jerry J. Vaske, Glenn E. Haas, Doug Whittaker, Paul Pritchard, and Kathryn Westra, "American Views on National Park Issues," 1996, Box 72, ARC; and Betty Stroock to New World Mine Campaign Supporter, memorandum, April 1996, File "Betty—1996 Correspondence," GYCN.

90. Senator Craig Thomas, as quoted in "Thomas Opposes Gold Mine near Yellowstone," July 23, 1996, press release, File 15, Box 71, ARC.

91. Mike Clark testimony at House Committee on Resources, Subcommittee on Energy and Mineral Resources, *New World Mine Proposed Buyout*, 105th Congress, 1st session, 1997, 77.

92. Mike Clark to Kathleen McGinty, memorandum, November 20, 1995, File "Betty—1995 Correspondence," GYCN. See also Skillen, *The Nation's Largest Landlord*, 151, for more information detailing Clinton's thinking in making a prominent statement of environmental protection leading up to the 1996 elections.

93. Clark testimony, *New World Mine Proposed Buyout*, 75–77; Kathleen McGinty testimony, *New World Mine Proposed Buyout*, 12–17, 53–60; Rocky Barker, "Grassroots Grit Beat 'The Mine from Hell,'" *HCN*, September 2, 1996, 16; Bob Ekey, "Victory for Yellowstone: Historic Agreement Stops the New World Mine," *GYR* (Summer 1996): 1, 4; Erin P. Billings, "Gold Firm May Drop Mine Plan," *BGZ*, July 20, 1996; Turner, *Justice on Earth*, 46; and "Baucus: Mine, Government Talking," *LVE*, July 26, 1996.

94. President Bill Clinton, "Remarks by the President in Announcing Agreement to Save National Park from Mine Development," August 12, 1996, press release, File "Noranda," Box A-366, YNPA; "The Clinton Event on Soda Butte Creek," August 12, 1996, Video 220A, YNPA; Clark interview; and Schullery, *Searching for Yellowstone*, 214.

95. Agreement between and among Crown Butte Mines, Inc. et al., GYC et al., and the United States of America, August 12, 1996, File 2, Box 71, ARC; Brian Kuehl, "Deal Protects Yellowstone, Cleans Up Site and Ensures Public Participation," *GYR* (Summer 1996): 6; Chris Wester, "Clinton Lauds Deal Halting New World Mine," *LVE*, August 12, 1996; and Angus M. Thuermer Jr., "Clinton Stops Yellowstone Mine," *JHNG*, August 14, 1996. President Clinton used a similar exchange of federal land and funds to consolidate federal land holdings and prevent a coal mine from being developed in his newly designated Escalante-Grand Staircase National Monument. See Skillen, *The Nation's Largest Landlord*, 256n104.

96. Mike Clark, "Stopping the New World Mine—A Victory for the Grassroots," *GYR* (Summer 1996): 3.

97. Mike Finley, as quoted in Angus M. Thuermer Jr., "Clinton Stops Yellowstone Mine," *JHNG*, August 14, 1996. See also "Victory at Yellowstone," *NYT*, August 13, 1996; "Time to Fix the Mining Law," *The Washington Post*, August 16, 1996; and Bruce Babbitt, "What the Mining Law Needs: Reform," letter to the editor, *The Washington Post*, September 17, 1996.

98. "Record of Decision: Cooke City Area Mineral Withdrawal, Custer and Gallatin Forest Plan Amendments," August 1997, loose in YCR. The fact that there were some private lands in the mix (see notes 100 and 101) is one reason the federal government pursued a buyout, rather than contesting the mine through administrative action, such as by selecting an EIS alternative that would have turned down the mine project. See Tony Davis, "Hardrock Showdown: Will the Forest Service Finally Say No to Mining?" *HCN*, November 22, 2010.

99. Lois J. Schiffer to Karl Elers, March 11, 1997, File 20, Box 70, ARC; Beartooth Alliance, "Update on NWM Agreement," *The Alliance*, March 1997, File "Untitled," YCR; Heather Abel, "Yellowstone Mine Swap Is in a Very Deep Pit," *HCN*, April 28, 1997, 3; Max Baucus to Mike Finley, June 4, 1997, File "Working Copy Preliminary Draft EIS, Crown Butte," YCR; Erin P. Billings, "Hill Offers New Mine Buyout Bill," *BGZ*, June 18, 1997; and Caroline Byrd, "Congress Must Make Deal to Stop Mine," *CEP*, October 8, 1997.

100. Abel, "Yellowstone Mine Swap," 3; and "Mine Deal Delayed," *LVE*, August 12, 1997.

101. Heidi Hagemeier, "Reeb Strikes Mine Deal," *LVE*, September 26, 1997; "Clinton OKs Mine Buyout," *LVE*, November 17, 1997; Erin P. Billings, "Enviros Criticize New World Mine Deal," *BGZ*, October 24, 1997; Scott McMillion, "Crown Butte Buyout Signed," *BDC*, November 15, 1997; Scott McMillion, "Deal Reached to Protect Land Near Park," *BDC*, March 18, 2008; and GYC, "New World Mine Reclamation: A Success Story," http://greateryellowstone.org/issues/lands/Feature.php?id=65, accessed July 1, 2010.

102. Finley interview; and Hektner, personal communication with author, January 22, 2003. Some might say that because environmentalists led the charge, this policy-making controversy does not belong in this book. No matter who led the charge, this still was a major policy-making issue for Yellowstone, one whose outcome would have a large bearing on the natural and cultural resources of the park.

103. Finley, "Never Running From a Fight," 9–19.

104. Ibid. See also Finley interview and Barrett interview. Another indication that the two Mikes enjoyed working together on conservation causes is that Mike Clark returned to become GYC's executive director in 2008 (after stepping down from the same post after the New World Mine controversy concluded), while Mike Finley joined the same group's board of directors in 2010 (Don Bachman, personal communication with author, June 12, 2011).

105. American Rivers specifically identified Noranda as one of several "bad guys" in Thomas J. Cassidy to Kevin, Dale, Michael, memorandum, January 5, 1994, File 18,

Box 70, ARC. Heidi Barrett, who was active in the Beartooth Alliance at the time, also identified Noranda as a bad guy (Barrett interview).

106. EPA, "Site Assessment Summary and Sampling Activities Report," September 11, 1998, loose in Box N-274, YNPA. Tracer dyes injected on the Fisher Creek side of Henderson Mountain showed up in Miller Creek, a tributary to Soda Butte Creek that flows into Yellowstone National Park.

107. June Brown to Conrad Burns, April 19, 1995, File 19, Box 70, ARC; and Florence Zundel, Joan Humiston, and Loretta Long to Fellow Snowmobilers, April 12, 1995, File "Snowmobiler Support Letters 5/95," GYCN.

108. Finley, "Never Running From a Fight," 9–19; and Finley interview.

109. Skillen, *The Nation's Largest Landlord*, 168.

Chapter Four

1. Hank Fischer, *Wolf Wars: The Remarkable Inside Story of the Restoration of Wolves to Yellowstone* (Helena, MT: Falcon Press, 1995), 94; Hillary Prugh, "To Sled or Not to Sled: The Snowmobiling Saga in Yellowstone National Park," *Northwest Journal of Environmental Law and Policy* 11 (2004–2005), 149–80; and Mike Finley, quoted in Todd Wilkinson, "No Home on the Range," *HCN*, February 17, 1997.

2. Fischer, *Wolf Wars*; Thomas McNamee, *The Return of the Wolf to Yellowstone* (New York: Henry Holt and Company, 1997); Lowry, *Repairing Paradise*; Smith and Ferguson, *Decade of the Wolf*; Franke, *To Save the Wild Bison*; and Yochim, *Yellowstone and the Snowmobile*.

3. Fischer, *Wolf Wars*, 158–63 (see also the photographs on 75–82); and Schullery, *Searching for Yellowstone*, 242–44.

4. Lowry, *Repairing Paradise*, 21–22; Fischer, *Wolf Wars*, 19–23; Schullery, *Searching for Yellowstone*, 81, 125–26, 148–73; Pritchard, *Preserving Yellowstone's Natural Conditions*, 147–200; Paul Schullery and Lee Whittlesey, "The Documentary Record of Wolves and Related Wildlife Species in the Yellowstone National Park Area Prior to 1882," in *Wolves for Yellowstone? A Report to the United States Congress: Volume IV Research and Analysis*, ed. John D. Varley and Wayne G. Brewster (Yellowstone National Park, WY: NPS, 1992), 1-3 to 1-174.

5. Fischer, *Wolf Wars*, 38–43; Lowry, *Repairing Paradise*, 22–25; Smith and Ferguson, *Decade of the Wolf*, 29; and John Weaver, *The Wolves of Yellowstone* (Washington, D.C.: U.S. Government Printing Office, 1978).

6. Fischer, *Wolf Wars*, 72–74, 103–5, 165; Smith and Ferguson, *Decade of the Wolf*, 25; McNamee, *The Return of the Wolf to Yellowstone*, 32–33; and Bob Barbee, "Barbee Retrospective: Yellowstone Wolf Restoration," *Yellowstone Science* 13, no.1 (Winter 2005): 5. The wolf study was broken into four volumes, released in pairs in 1990 and 1992: Yellowstone National Park, FWS, University of Wyoming, University of Idaho, Interagency Grizzly Bear Study Team, and University of Minnesota

Cooperative Park Studies Unit, *Wolves for Yellowstone? A Report to the United States Congress, Volumes I and II* (Mammoth, WY: NPS, 1990); John D. Varley and Wayne G. Brewster, eds., *Wolves for Yellowstone? A Report to the United States Congress, Volume III, Executive Summary* (Yellowstone National Park, WY: NPS, 1992); and *Wolves for Yellowstone? A Report to the United States Congress Volume IV, Research and Analysis* (Yellowstone National Park, WY: NPS, 1992).

7. McNamee, *The Return of the Wolf to Yellowstone*, 33; Fischer, *Wolf Wars*, 80, 88–93, 119–29, 141–42, 156, 162–63; Lowry, *Repairing Paradise*, 26–27, 43–46; Smith and Ferguson, 45–46; and USDI-FWS, *The Reintroduction of Gray Wolves to Yellowstone National Park and Central Idaho* (Helena, MT: FWS, 1994).

8. Lowry, *Repairing Paradise*, 46–47, 52, 58–59; Douglas W. Smith, "Ten Years of Yellowstone Wolves, 1995–2005," *Yellowstone Science* 13, no. 1 (Winter 2005): 18, 20; and Hal Herring, "Wolf Whiplash," *HCN*, May 30, 2011.

9. Lowry, *Repairing Paradise*, 48–49; Schullery, *Searching for Yellowstone*, 242–44, 263–65; and the entire issue of *Yellowstone Science* 13, no. 1 (Winter 2005) (see in particular the bibliography of wolf literature since 1995).

10. Fischer, *Wolf Wars*, 68, 84–88, 94–95, 146; McNamee, *The Return of the Wolf to Yellowstone*, 21, 32–33; and Lowry, *Repairing Paradise*, 28–29.

11. Lowry, *Repairing Paradise*, 28–29, 41–42; Fischer, *Wolf Wars*, 84–88; and USDI-FWS, *The Reintroduction of Gray Wolves to Yellowstone*.

12. David Mech, as quoted in Fischer, *Wolf Wars*, 64; and Lowry, *Repairing Paradise*, 53.

13. Lowry, *Repairing Paradise*, 28, 35; and Fischer, *Wolf Wars*, xiii.

14. The conservation reaction to Reagan is from "Environmental Movement," http://www.answers.com/topic/environmental-movement, accessed February 5, 2011. Information on both films is from Wikipedia, http://en.wikipedia.org/wiki/, accessed February 5, 2011; and the impact of both films is from Lowry, *Repairing Paradise*, 33.

15. Fischer, *Wolf Wars*, 167.

16. Lowry, *Repairing Paradise*, 42–47; Fischer, *Wolf Wars*, 167; and Smith and Ferguson, *Decade of the Wolf*.

17. Fischer, *Wolf Wars*, 62–63, 94; Nie, *Beyond Wolves*, 98–99.

18. Fischer, *Wolf Wars*, 57; and P. J. White, Douglas W. Smith, John W. Duffield, Michael Jimenez, Terry McEneaney, and Glenn Plumb, "Yellowstone After Wolves: Environmental Impact Statement Predictions and Ten-Year Appraisals," *Yellowstone Science* 13, no. 1 (Winter 2005): 34–41.

19. Fischer, *Wolf Wars*, 97–103, 107.

20. Fischer, *Wolf Wars*, 113–14. The statistics are from "Defenders of Wildlife Wolf Compensation Trust," http://www.defenders.org/resources/publications/programs_and_policy/wildlife_conservation/solutions/statistics_on_payments_from_the_defenders_wildlife_foundation_wolf_compensation_trust.pdf, accessed February 5, 2011. The transition to the federal program information is from "Defenders of Wildlife Wolf Compensation Trust," http://www.defenders.org/programs_and_policy/wildlife_conservation/solutions/wolf_compensation_

trust/, accessed July 19, 2011. Note that the figure represents costs only through 2009; more recent figures are not yet available.

21. Ed Bangs, as quoted in "Defenders of Wildlife Wolf Compensation Trust," http://www.defenders.org/resources/publications/programs_and_policy/ wildlife_conservation/solutions/statistics_on_payments_from_the_defenders_ wildlife_foundation_wolf_compensation_trust.pdf, accessed February 5, 2011. See also McNamee, *The Return of the Wolf to Yellowstone*, 21, 32–33; and Lowry, *Repairing Paradise*, 39–41. To be eligible for full market value compensation, a rancher must demonstrate proof that wolves were responsible for a kill. If such evidence is lacking, a rancher is still eligible for 50 percent of market value. Such reimbursements do not account for the time necessary to track down missing animals. Nonetheless, the program has commonly been seen as fair.

22. Lowry, *Repairing Paradise*, 39–41; Fischer, *Wolf Wars*, viii, 164. See also Gloriann Klein's testimony at public hearing and Hank Fischer, "Supply-Side Environmentalist and Wolf Recovery in the Northern Rockies," both in *War Against the Wolf: America's Campaign to Exterminate the Wolf*, ed. Rick McIntyre (Stillwater, MN: Voyageur Press, 1995), 390, 410–15.

23. Lowry, *Repairing Paradise*, 54–55; White et al., "Yellowstone After Wolves"; and John W. Duffield, Chris J. Neher, and D. A. Patterson, "Wolf Recovery in Yellowstone," *Yellowstone Science* 16, no. 1 (Winter 2008): 22.

24. L. David Mech, "Returning the Wolf to Yellowstone," *The Greater Yellowstone Ecosystem: Redefining America's Wilderness Heritage*, ed. Robert B. Keiter and Mark S. Boyce (New Haven, CT: Yale University Press, 1991), 309–22.

25. Fischer, *Wolf Wars*, 125–27; Lowry, *Repairing Paradise*, 28, 30; McNamee, *The Return of the Wolf to Yellowstone*, 36; Mech, "Returning the Wolf to Yellowstone"; and Adolph Murie, *The Wolves of Mount McKinley* (Washington, D.C.: U.S. Government Printing Office, 1944).

26. Fischer, *Wolf Wars*, 154; and Lowry, *Repairing Paradise*, 38.

27. There are at least two excellent summaries of post-reintroduction events and research: Smith and Ferguson, *Decade of the Wolf*, and the entire issue of *Yellowstone Science* 13, no. 1 (Winter 2005). See also Lowry, *Repairing Paradise*, 52–53.

28. Fischer, *Wolf Wars*, 67–68; Lowry, *Repairing Paradise*, 26–27; and McNamee, *The Return of the Wolf to Yellowstone*, 35.

29. Fischer, *Wolf Wars*, 103–5.

30. Ibid., 90–93, 119–29.

31. Ibid., 129.

32. Ibid., 129. See also McNamee, *The Return of the Wolf to Yellowstone*, 33–38, 198–99; and Smith and Ferguson, *Decade of the Wolf*, 25.

33. Lowry, *Repairing Paradise*, 31–32; McNamee, *The Return of the Wolf to Yellowstone*, 84–86, 96–97, 198–99, 267; and Fischer, *Wolf Wars*, 94.

34. Fischer, *Wolf Wars*, 68–69, 144. For politics of wolf recovery, see Nie, *Beyond Wolves*, 53–54, 67–112. For Idaho grizzly reintroduction, see Nie, *Beyond Wolves*, 155, 161. See also, Wright, *Wildlife Research and Management in the National Parks*,

146; Environment News Service, "Grizzly Bears Will Not Be Reintroduced into U.S. West," June 21, 2001, http://www.ens-newswire.com/ens/jun2001/2001–06–21–03.asp, accessed February 6, 2011; and Rob Roy Smith, "Unbearable? Bitterroot Grizzly Bear Reintroduction and the George W. Bush Administration," *Golden Gate University Law Review* 33, no. 3 (2003): 384–417. As of 2012, grizzly bears are still absent from northern Idaho, the only large block of wilderness in the northern Rockies without them.

35. Symbolism and polarity of wolves is from Nie, *Beyond Wolves*, 52.

36. Fischer, *Wolf Wars*, 169–70; McNamee, *The Return of the Wolf to Yellowstone*, 216–25; and Smith and Ferguson, *Decade of the Wolf*, 27.

37. Yochim, *Yellowstone and the Snowmobile*, 53–86. See also Yochim, "Snowmachines in the Gardens," 2–15; Michael J. Yochim, "The Recent Winter Use History of Yellowstone National Park: How Should the National Park Service Envision Its Dual Mission?" *Annals of Wyoming* 73 (2001): 33–46; Michael J. Yochim, "The Development of Snowmobile Policy in Yellowstone National Park," *Yellowstone Science* 7 (Spring 1999): 2–10; and Michael J. Yochim, "Snowplanes, Snowcoaches and Snowmobiles: The Decision to Allow Snowmobiles into Yellowstone National Park," *Annals of Wyoming* 70 (Summer 1998): 6–23.

38. Yochim, *Yellowstone and the Snowmobile*, 90, 115–19, 127–28, 138–40, 151.

39. Ibid., 5, 73, 90, 127–28. See also GYC, "Yellowstone National Park Sound Survey," President's Day Weekend, 2000, File "Greater Yellowstone Coalition," MAOF.

40. Yochim, *Yellowstone and the Snowmobile*, 116–17, 123–26; Cormack Gates, B. Stelfox, T. Muhly, T. Chowns, and R. J. Hudson, *The Ecology of Bison Movements and Distribution In and Beyond Yellowstone National Park: A Critical Review with Implications for Winter Use and Transboundary Population Management* (Calgary, Alberta: University of Calgary, 2005): 236–39; USDI-NPS, *Winter Use Plans Environmental Assessment* (Yellowstone National Park, WY: NPS, November 2008), 3-2 to 3-6; and NPS, *Winter Use Plans Final Environmental Impact Statement, Yellowstone and Grand Teton National Parks, John D. Rockefeller, Jr. Memorial Parkway* (Yellowstone National Park, WY: NPS, 2007), 111–21.

41. Yochim, *Yellowstone and the Snowmobile*, 123–210.

42. Ibid., 178–82. See also NPS, *Winter Use Plans Environmental Assessment*, 2-17 to 2-32, 3-1 to 3-77.

43. New EIS information is from USDI-NPS, "Yellowstone Completes Winter Use Environmental Impact Statement," press release, November 3, 2011, author's personal collection. Holes in research information is from D. Mary Foley, "Scientific Assessment of Yellowstone National Park Winter Use, March 2011," http://www.nps.gov/yell/parkmgmt/reports.htm, accessed May 9, 2011. Environmentalist position is from Yochim, *Yellowstone and the Snowmobile*, 200–01; and from GYC, "Yellowstone Winter Use: Phasing Out Snowmobiles," http://www.greateryellowstone.org/issues/lands/Feature.php?id=40, accessed January 9, 2011. Snowcoach numbers are from NPS, "Yellowstone Winter Visitor Figures a Mixed Bag," press release, April 5, 2010; and "Modest Increase in Yellowstone Oversnow

Holiday Visitation," press release, January 6, 2011, both in 4th EIS Collection, MAOF. Their impacts and the plowing of roads as a management alternative is from Yochim, *Yellowstone and the Snowmobile*, 195–201; and Foley, "Scientific Assessment," 19–25, 48–49, 71, 94. Continued political interest is from Yochim, *Yellowstone and the Snowmobile*, 202–8.

44. Yochim, *Yellowstone and the Snowmobile*, 123–210.

45. Ibid., 149–50, 164–72, 189–90. See also "Wyoming Appeals in Case on Yellowstone Snowmobiles," *SLT*, January 29, 2011.

46. Yochim, *Yellowstone and the Snowmobile*, 123–210; and Foley, "Scientific Assessment," 19–25, 48–49, 71, 94.

47. Yochim, *Yellowstone and the Snowmobile*, 130–37, 151; Borrie et al., "Winter Visitors to Yellowstone National Park," 41–48; Davenport and Borrie, "The Appropriateness of Snowmobiling in National Parks," 151–60; Layzer, *The Environmental Case*, 1–25, 223–50; Albanese, *Nature Religion in America*; Graber, *Wilderness As Sacred Space*; and Dunlap, *Faith in Nature*.

48. Continued public support for snowcoaches is from NPS, "Yellowstone National Park Winter Use Plan/Environmental Impact Statement Draft Public Scoping Comment Analysis Summary," July 2010, http://www.nps.gov/yell/parkmgmt/loader.cfm?csModule=security/getfile&PageID=492177, accessed January 15, 2011. The support for snowcoaches is also from the author's own personal experience, since his departure from Yellowstone in 2009. He personally worked on the snowmobile issue for the NPS from 2005 to 2009. Since then, he has worked for the NPS in Grand Canyon and Yosemite national parks. In his personal discussions with NPS employees—an audience generally seen as more knowledgeable about national parks than the general public—he has observed a consistent impression that the situation in Yellowstone is still dominated by two-stroke snowmobiles polluting Yellowstone's air and soundscape, with wildlife still suffering harassment. This suggests that the public still has a similar perception and that the environmentalists' framing of the issue is still effective. See also www.greateryellowstone.org, accessed regularly during the winter of 2008–2009.

49. Yochim, *Yellowstone and the Snowmobile*, 130–37, 151; Borrie et al., "Winter Visitors to Yellowstone National Park;" Davenport and Borrie, "The Appropriateness of Snowmobiling in National Parks;" Layzer, *The Environmental Case*, 1–25, 223–50; Albanese, *Nature Religion in America*; Graber, *Wilderness As Sacred Space*; and Dunlap, *Faith in Nature*.

50. USDI-NPS, *Winter Use Plans Environmental Assessment*, 3-44, 3-67 to 3-70, 4-43 to 4-44. Visitation by wheeled vehicles to the plowed roads in Yellowstone's northern areas is not included in these figures.

51. Dean Nelson, as quoted in Darcy L. Fawcett, "Colonial Status: The Search for Independence in West Yellowstone, Montana," (professional paper, Montana State University, 1993), 27.

52. Yochim, *Yellowstone and the Snowmobile*, 82–83, 89, 118, 128, 146, 157; and USDI-NPS, *Winter Use Plans Environmental Assessment*, 3-33 to 3-43, 4-27.

53. Yochim, *Yellowstone and the Snowmobile*, 169, 173; and USDI-NPS, *Winter Use Plans Environmental Assessment*, 3-33 to 3-43, 3-67 to 3-70.

54. Yochim, *Yellowstone and the Snowmobile*, 128, 194, 200; and USDI-NPS, *Winter Use Plans Environmental Assessment*, 4-43 to 4-44.

55. For an example of such messaging, see USDI-NPS, *Winter Use Plans Environmental Assessment*, 3-33 to 3-44, 4-26 to 4-33. For an example of how slow the economic argument is to die, see Associated Press, "Wyoming Appeals in Case on Yellowstone Snowmobiles," *SLT*, January 29, 2011, wherein socioeconomic arguments were used as a reason to continue litigation.

56. Yochim, *Yellowstone and the Snowmobile*, 118–19; Borrie et al., "Winter Visitors to Yellowstone National Park"; Davenport and Borrie, "The Appropriateness of Snowmobiling in National Parks"; and Layzer, *The Environmental Case*, 1–25, 223–50.

57. Yochim, *Yellowstone and the Snowmobile*, 140–41; USDI-NPS, *Winter Use Plans Environmental Assessment*, 3-8; John J. Borkowski, P. J. White, Robert A. Garrott, Troy Davis, Amanda R. Hardy, and Dan. J. Reinhart, "Behavioral Responses of Bison and Elk in Yellowstone to Snowmobiles and Snow Coaches," *Ecological Applications* 16, no. 5 (2006): 1911–25; Amanda Hardy, "Bison and Elk Responses to Winter Recreation in Yellowstone National Park" (master's thesis, Montana State University, 2001); John Bruggeman, "Spatio-Temporal Dynamics of the Central Bison Herd in Yellowstone National Park" (PhD diss., Montana State University, 2006); and Foley, "Scientific Assessment," 5–6, 118–27.

58. Yochim, *Yellowstone and the Snowmobile*, 181; USDI-NPS, *Winter Use Plans Environmental Assessment*, 3-4 to 3-6; Craig McClure and Troy Davis, "Wildlife Responses to Motorized Winter Recreation in Yellowstone," 2008, http://www.nps.gov/yell/parkmgmt/upload/2008wildlife_final.pdf, accessed January 26, 2011; and Foley, "Scientific Assessment," 118–27.

59. Yochim, *Yellowstone and the Snowmobile*, 118–19, 138–39; USDI-NPS, *Winter Use Plans Environmental Assessment*, 3-44 to 3-56; Terry M. Spear, Julie Hart, and Dale J. Stephenson, "Yellowstone Winter Use Personal Exposure Monitoring," 2006, http://www.nps.gov/yell/parkmgmt/upload/personal_exposure.pdf, accessed January 26, 2011; Terry M. Spear and Dale J. Stephenson, "Yellowstone Winter Use Personal Exposure Monitoring," 2005, http://www.nps.gov/yell/parkmgmt/upload/personalexposure05.pdf, accessed January 26, 2011; and Foley, "Scientific Assessment," 26–72.

60. Yochim, *Yellowstone and the Snowmobile*, 127–28, 137–38; USDI-NPS, *Winter Use Plans Environmental Assessment*, 3-17 to 3-31; Shan Burson, "Natural Soundscape Monitoring in Yellowstone National Park," 2008, http://www.nps.gov/yell/parkmgmt/upload/soundscape_monitoring_2008(1).pdf, accessed January 26, 2011; and Shan Burson, personal communication with author, October 2008.

61. Yochim, *Yellowstone and the Snowmobile*, 195–96; USDI-NPS, *Winter Use Plans Environmental Assessment*, 3-30 to 3-31; Burson, "Natural Soundscape Monitoring in Yellowstone National Park," 42; and *Greater Yellowstone Coalition, et al., v. Dirk Kempthorne, et al., and National Parks Conservation Association v. USDI/NPS,*

memorandum opinion, September 15, 2008, https://ecf.dcd.uscourts.gov/cgi-bin/show_public_doc?2007cv2112–71, accessed January 26, 2011.

62. For Barry's letter and discussion, see Yochim, *Yellowstone and the Snowmobile*, 143–49. See also USDI-NPS, *Winter Use Plan Draft Environmental Impact Statement* (Yellowstone National Park, WY: NPS, July 1999), 21–78; USDI-NPS, *Winter Use Plans Final Environmental Impact Statement* (Denver, CO: NPS, October 2000), xii–xix; and 66 *Federal Register* 7260–68, January 22, 2001.

63. Quotes by Randy Jones ("personally interested") and Rick Frost ("come away") in "Future of Winter Use, June 3–5, 2002," meeting minutes, SEIS Administrative Record, 51401–25, MAOF.

64. Yochim, *Yellowstone and the Snowmobile*, 150–66, 189–91 (note the extensive table on pages 158–63, detailing political interest in Yellowstone snowmobile policy making). See also Kurt Repanshek, "Former Park Service Director Mainella: Interior Department Called Yellowstone Snowmobile Decisions," November 29, 2007, www.NationalParksTraveler.com, accessed December 11, 2007; and NPS, *Winter Use Plans Final Supplemental Environmental Impact Statement* (Yellowstone National Park, WY: NPS, February 2003).

65. Jeffrey Bissegger, "Snowmobiles in Yellowstone: Conflicting Priorities in Setting National Parks Policy and the Paradox of Judicial Activism for Recreational Business," *Journal of Land, Resources, and Environmental Law* 25 (2005): 109–18; and Prugh, "To Sled or Not to Sled," 149–80.

66. Yochim, *Yellowstone and the Snowmobile*; Michael J. Yochim, "Yellowstone City Park: The Dominating Influence of Politicians in National Park Service Policymaking," *Journal of Policy History* 23, no. 3 (2011): 381–98; NPS, *Winter Use Plans Final Environmental Impact Statement* (Yellowstone National Park, WY: NPS, 2007), vol. 1: 36–37, 105–8 and vol. 2: F-8; and NPS, "Sylvan Pass Operational Risk Management Assessment," October 2007, http://www.nps.gov/yell/parkmgmt/upload/ORMA%20report_Final.pdf, accessed January 28, 2011. A more recent estimate of the cost was $325,000 annually—see USDI-NPS, *Yellowstone National Park Draft Winter Use Plan/Environmental Impact Statement* (Yellowstone National Park, WY: NPS, 2011), 180.

67. Cody mayor Roger Sedam et al. to Suzanne Lewis, December 5, 2006; Temple Stevenson to Suzanne Lewis, January 5, 2007; Ken Volker to John Sacklin, December 18, 2006; Craig Thomas, Michael B. Enzi, and Barbara Cubin to Winter Use Planning Team, May 2, 2007; and Wyoming governor Dave Freudenthal to Suzanne Lewis, May 3, 2007, all in Third EIS Collection, MAOF. See also Mike Stark, "Lawmakers Push to Keep Pass Open," *BGZ*, May 3, 2007; and Ruffin Prevost, "500 Attend Cody Forum on Sylvan Pass Proposals," *BGZ*, March 23, 2007.

68. Dick Cheney, as quoted in Jared Miller, "Vice President Defends his Record," *CST*, December 28, 2009.

69. Yochim, *Yellowstone and the Snowmobile*, 202–8; Yochim, "Yellowstone City Park." NPS, "Winter Use Plans Record of Decision," November 20, 2007, 6; NPS, "Winter Use Plans Record of Decision Amendment, Sylvan Pass Management," 3–5,

both at http://www.nps.gov/yell/planyourvisit/upload/rod_sylvanpass_7-08.pdf, accessed January 28, 2011. See also Jim Drinkard, "White House Reverses Experts on Yellowstone Policy," *San Jose Mercury News*, July 24, 2008; "White House Overruled Experts on Sylvan Pass," *BDC*, July 25, 2008; and Cory Hatch, "Parks Sled Plan in Limbo," *JHNG*, November 20, 2007.

70. Yochim, *Yellowstone and the Snowmobile*, 178–88. See also Nie, *Beyond Wolves*, 29.

71. NPS, *Brucellosis Remote Vaccination Program for Bison in Yellowstone National Park: Draft Environmental Impact Statement* (Yellowstone National Park, WY: NPS, 2010), 2–4, 155–58; Lee H. Whittlesey, "Cows All Over the Place," *Annals of Wyoming* 66 (Winter 1994–1995): 42–57; and Franke, *To Save the Wild Bison*, 267–68.

72. Franke, *To Save the Wild Bison*, 67–68, 90, 130–31; NPS, *Brucellosis Remote Vaccination*, 55; Mary Meagher, "Evaluation of Boundary Control for Bison of Yellowstone National Park," *Wildlife Society Bulletin* 17, no. 1 (1989): 15–19; APHIS, "Brucellosis and Yellowstone Bison," http://www.aphis.usda.gov/animal_health/animal_dis_spec/cattle/downloads/cattle-bison.pdf, accessed December 18, 2010; Gates et al., *The Ecology of Bison Movements and Distribution*, 68. Late in 2011, Montana officials began discussing ways to minimize the brucellosis transmission potential from elk; see Matthew Brown, "Panel to Seek Ways to Better Manage Elk Herds Infected with Brucellosis," *BGZ*, December 8, 2011.

73. Franke, *To Save the Wild Bison*, 68, 80, 109–11, 120, 158; NPS, *Brucellosis Remote Vaccination*; Gates et al., *The Ecology of Bison Movements and Distribution*, 67–72; Meagher, "Evaluation of Boundary Control"; and Mary Meagher, "Yellowstone's Bison: A Unique Wild Heritage," *National Parks and Conservation Magazine* 48 (May, 1974): 9–14; and Whittlesey, "Cows All Over the Place."

74. Franke, *To Save the Wild Bison*, 109–11, 118–19; and Gates et al., *The Ecology of Bison Movements and Distribution*, 93–96.

75. Franke, *To Save the Wild Bison*, 109–15; Meagher, "Evaluation of Boundary Control"; and Meagher, "Yellowstone's Bison"; Whittlesey, "Cows All over the Place"; and Doug Peacock, "The Yellowstone Massacre," *Audubon* 99 (May-June 1997): 42–49.

76. Franke, *To Save the Wild Bison*, 138–46; and Peacock, "The Yellowstone Massacre."

77. USDI-NPS, USDA-USFS, and APHIS, "Record of Decision for Final Environmental Impact Statement and Bison Management Plan for the State of Montana and Yellowstone National Park," December 20, 2000, http://www.nps.gov/yell/parkmgmt/upload/yellbisonrod.pdf; and NPS, *Remote Vaccination DEIS*, accessed December 9, 2010.

78. Franke, *To Save the Wild Bison*, 142–70; USDI-NPS, USDA-USFS, and APHIS, "Record of Decision for Final Environmental Impact Statement and Bison Management Plan"; Matthew Brown, "Bison Slaughter Moratorium Sought," *BDC*, April 11, 2008; Sarah Gilman, "Can Good Fences Make Good Neighbors?" *HCN*, May 16, 2011; "Montana, Feds Negotiating Areas for Buffalo to Roam," *BGZ*, March 9, 2011; and "Colorado, South Dakota Eyed for Yellowstone Bison," *BGZ*, December 14, 2011. This last article reported that Schweitzer reissued his executive order in December 2011, and provided some of the logic for both orders.

79. Chapter four note 79. Gilman, "Can Good Fences Make Good Neighbors?";
Montana Fish, Wildlife and Parks and Montana Department of Livestock,
*Draft Joint Environmental Assess-ment: Adaptive Management Adjustments to
the Interagency Bison Management Plan*, December 2011, http://fwp.mt.gov/
news/publicNotices/environmentalAssessments/ plans/pn_0011.html, accessed
January 30, 2012; and Montana legislature information on brucellosis from
search function at http://leghlngoogle.leg.mt.gov/search?restrict=2011_
Bills&q=brucellosis&site=prod_index&output=xml_no_dtd&client=prod_index
&btnG=MT+Legislature+Search&access=p&ip=64.118.120.106&proxystylesheet=
prod_index&oe=UTF-8&filter=p, accessed September 20, 2011.

80. Gilman, "Can Good Fences Make Good Neighbors?"; "Yellowstone Bison Get More
Room to Roam in Montana," *BGZ*, March 17, 2011; Interagency Bison Management
Plan Agencies to Files, memorandum, March 31, 2011, http://billingsgazette.com/
news/state-and-regiona/montana/pdf., accessed May 9, 2011; "Agreement Close
on Letting Yellowstone Bison Roam in Montana," *BGZ*, April 5, 2011; "Agencies,
Tribes Endorse Plan for Bison to Roam," *BGZ*, April 14, 2011; and Montana Fish,
Wildlife and Parks and Montana Department of Livestock, *Draft Joint Environmental
Assessment*.

81. Tom France, as quoted in Gilman, "Can Good Fences Make Good Neighbors?"

82. Montana Fish, Wildlife and Parks and Montana Department of Livestock, *Draft Joint
Environmental Assessment*; Gilman, "Can Good Fences Make Good Neighbors?";
"Park County Officials Want Roaming Bison Reined In," *BGZ*, April 18, 2011;
"Wandering Bison Causing Trouble in Gardiner," *BGZ*, April 21, 2011; "Montana
Sued for Letting Yellowstone Bison Roam," *BGZ*, May 6, 2011; and "Montana,
Park County Discussing Bison Settlement," *BGZ*, October 26, 2011. That it was in
limbo was reflected in two *Billings Gazette* articles published in December 2011:
"Federal and Montana Agencies Hit Deadlock on Yellowstone Bison Exodus," *BGZ*,
December 1, 2011, followed by "Montana Plans to Let Bison Back into Gardiner
Basin Outside Yellowstone Park," *BGZ*, December 16, 2011. No similar decision has
yet been reached for the West Yellowstone area, but with no cattle present there any
more, a similar agreement seems possible.

83. Free-roaming information is from NPS, "About Bison," http://www.nps.gov/
yell/naturescience/upload/297BisonNatHist8–17–10.pdf, accessed July 30,
2011; and Defenders of Wildlife, "Bison Management and Policy," http://www.
defenders.org/programs_and_policy/wildlife_conservation/imperiled_species/
bison/management_and_policy.php, accessed July 30, 2011. Genetically-pure
bison information is from Peter A. Dratch and Peter J. P. Gogan, "Bison
Conservation Initiative: Bison Conservation Genetics Workshop, Report and
Recommendations," 2010, http://www.westernwatersheds.org/ thewildlifenews/
wp-content/uploads/2010/11/bison_genetics_report.pdf, accessed July 30, 2011.

84. Franke discusses the various framings in *To Save the Wild Bison*, 171–79, 188, 242–
46, 274. The "babies" framing was something the author heard from a BFC member
on a tour of their facilities in May 2003; and "wild" framing is from the author's

personal experience in Yellowstone as a guide from 1996 through 2004, and from the NPS, http://www.nps.gov/yell/naturescience/bisonqa.htm.

85. Franke, *To Save the Wild Bison*, 147–61; and Gates et al., *The Ecology of Bison Movements and Distribution*, 70.

86. NPS, *Brucellosis Remote Vaccination*, 35–37. See quote by Mike Finley at the start of this chapter as demonstration that NPS would do things differently if left to its own devices.

87. Franke, *To Save the Wild Bison*, 143, 148, 171–79, 237–41, 265–66.

88. Ibid., 130–37, 168–70; and Jason Alan Brininstool, "Legacy? An in Depth Perspective on the Interagency Bison Management Plan and the Potential for Collaboration" (master's thesis, University of Montana, 2009). APHIS rules are from Debbi A. Donch and Donald A. Gertonson, "Status Report—Fiscal Year 2008, "Cooperative State-Federal Brucellosis Eradication Program," http://www.aphis.usda.gov/animal_health/animal_diseases/brucellosis/downloads/yearly_rpt.pdf, accessed December 18, 2012. Statistics on the ranching portion of Montana's economy are from Montana Department of Commerce, "Census and Economic Information Center," http://ceic.mt.gov/Economic/BEA/StateREIS/BEAemployment_2006.pdf, accessed December 18, 2010. The most recent figures in the latter appear to be for 2006, with ranching lumped in with all forms of agriculture.

89. Mary Meagher, *The Bison of Yellowstone National Park* (Washington, D.C.: U.S. Government Printing Office, 1973); see also Gates et al., *The Ecology of Bison Movements and Distribution*, 87–121.

90. Mary Meagher, "Winter Recreation-Induced Changes in Bison Numbers and Distribution in Yellowstone National Park," 1993, unpublished paper provided to NPS, Yellowstone National Park files, Mammoth Hot Springs, WY. The advent of snowmobile road grooming is from Yochim, *Yellowstone and the Snowmobile*, 69–70. See also Franke, *To Save the Wild Bison*, 116–19; and Gates et al., *The Ecology of Bison Movements and Distribution*.

91. Gates et al., *The Ecology of Bison Movements and Distribution* (see especially 93–100); J. A. Fuller, R. A. Garrott, and P. J. White, "Emigration and Density Dependence in Yellowstone Bison," *Journal of Wildlife Management* 71, no. 6 (2007): 1924–33; Dan D. Bjornlie and Robert A. Garrott, "Effects of Winter Road Grooming on Bison in Yellowstone National Park," *Journal of Wildlife Management* 65, no. 3 (2001): 560–72; Franke, *To Save the Wild Bison*, 109–11, 210; and P. J. White, Glenn E. Plumb, Michael B. Coughenour, and Rick L. Wallen, "Carrying Capacity and Movements of Yellowstone Bison," *Yellowstone Science* 19, no. 1 (March 2011): 8–14.

92. Brininstool makes much the same argument in his master's thesis, "Legacy?."

93. NPS, *Brucellosis Remote Vaccination*, 2.

94. Conrad Burns, as quoted in Franke, *To Save the Wild Bison*, 144. See also U.S. Senate, 104th Congress, 1st session, S. 745, May 3, 1995.

95. Mike Finley, as quoted in Franke, *To Save the Wild Bison*, 147 (see also pages 137–38, 144, and 154); Gates et al., *The Ecology of Bison Movements and Distribution*, 69–70; and David Bidwell, "Bison, Boundaries, and Brucellosis: Risk Perception

and Political Ecology at Yellowstone," *Society and Natural Resources* 23 (2010): 14–30.

96. "Deal Opens Corridor to Bison," *JHNG*, April 18, 2008, http://www.jhnewsandguide. com/article.php?art_id=2968, accessed December 9, 2010; "Yellowstone Bison Get More Room to Roam in Montana," *BGZ*, March 17, 2011; Interagency Bison Management Plan Agencies to Files, memorandum, March 31, 2011, http:// billingsgazette.com/news/state-and-regiona/montana/pdf., accessed May 9, 2011; "Agreement Close on Letting Yellowstone Bison Roam in Montana," *BGZ*, April 5, 2011; "Agencies, Tribes Endorse Plan for Bison to Roam," *BGZ*, April 14, 2011; "Park County Officials Want Roaming Bison Reined In," *BGZ*, April 18, 2011; "Wandering Bison Causing Trouble in Gardiner," *BGZ*, April 21, 2011; "Montana Sued for Letting Yellowstone Bison Roam," *BGZ*, May 6, 2011; and GYC, "Yellowstone Bison Under Attack," http://www.greateryellowstone.org/issues/wildlife/Feature.php?id=288, accessed March 3, 2011.

Conclusion

1. John Sacklin, as quoted in Lowry, *Repairing Paradise*, 56.

2. Hektner, personal communication with author; and remarks by Ed Bangs in "Defenders of Wildlife Wolf Compensation Trust," http://www.defenders.org/ resources/publications/programs_and_policy/wildlife_conservation/solutions/ statistics_on_payments_from_the_defenders_wildlife_foundation_wolf_ compensation_trust.pdf, accessed February 5, 2011.

3. Lowry, *Repairing Paradise*, 9–16. Lowry examined only coalitions, framing, economies, science, and agency commitment in his book.

4. Wright, *Wildlife Research and Management*, 181; Smith, "Unbearable? Bitterroot Grizzly Bear Reintroduction," 385–417; Environment News Service, "Grizzly Bears Will Not Be Reintroduced into U.S. West;" and Paul Schullery, *Nature and Culture at Fishing Bridge: A History of the Fishing Bridge Development in Yellowstone National Park* (Yellowstone National Park, WY: NPS, 2010), 83–91.

5. See Kai Lee, *Compass and Gyroscope: Integrating Science and Politics for the Environment* (Washington, D.C.: Island Press, 1993): 7–12, for a discussion of the relationship between politics and science in public decision making.

6. Lowry, *The Capacity for Wonder*; Lowry, *Preserving Public Lands for the Future*; George B. Hartzog Jr., *Battling for the National Parks* (Mount Kisco, NY: Moyer Bell Ltd., 1988); Ridenour, *The National Parks Compromised*; and Everhart, *The National Park Service*.

7. Sellars, *Preserving Nature in the National Parks*; Schullery, *Searching for Yellowstone*; Pritchard, *Preserving Yellowstone's Natural Conditions*; and Runte, *National Parks: The American Experience*.

8. USFS research directive is from USFS, "Research and Development," http://www. fs.fed.us/research/, accessed March 6, 2011. NPS research and science history is

from Sellars, *Preserving Nature in the National Parks*; Schullery, *Searching for Yellowstone*; and Pritchard, *Preserving Yellowstone's Natural Conditions*.

9. Sellars, *Preserving Nature in the National Parks*, 291–308; and Kimberly Hirai, "A Park Service Scribe," *HCN*, January 23, 2012. Sellars's book was the most recent and probably the most successful effort to push the agency toward embracing scientific research. Sellars records many earlier efforts, including those by George Wright in the 1930s, the Robbins Report of 1962, and other more recent efforts. See in particular Wright, *Wildlife Research and Management in the National Parks*, 182–89, in which he makes a similar plea for more consistent use of research in park policy making.

10. For information on the Inventory and Monitoring Program, see: http://science. nature.nps.gov/im/index.cfm, accessed August 3, 2011. For information on the Research Learning Centers, see: http://www.nature.nps.gov/learningcenters/, accessed August 3, 2011.

11. Some studies funded through Cooperative Ecosystem Studies Units include the following: Borkowski et al., "Behavioral Responses of Bison and Elk in Yellowstone to Snowmobiles and Snow Coaches," 1911–25; Bruggeman, "Spatio-Temporal Dynamics of the Central Bison Herd in Yellowstone National Park"; Fuller et al., "Emigration and Density Dependence in Yellowstone Bison," 1924–33; and Bjornlie and Garrott, "Effects of Winter Road Grooming on Bison," 560–72.

12. Lucy Moore, "Grand Canyon Working Group Comprehensive Report," August 2008, NPS files, Grand Canyon National Park; Stacey M. S. Gunther, "Overflights in Wilderness: Their Uses, Need and Appropriateness," March 16, 2010, unpublished paper in author's possession; Michael Catanzaro, "Babbitt Limits Flights over Grand Canyon," *BlueRibbon Magazine* (March 1997); Associated Press, "McCain Offers Guidelines for Noise at Grand Canyon," March 17, 2010; and John Dougherty, "Under the Flight Path," *HCN*, June 13, 2011. USDI-NPS, *Special Flight Rules Area in the Vicinity of Grand Canyon National Park: Actions to Substantially Restore Natural Quiet* (Grand Canyon National Park, AZ: NPS, 2011) (the proposed reduction was from about 94,000 flights annually to no more than 65,000 flights annually). McCain's recent action from Cyndy Cole, "Grand Canyon overflights set for increase," *Arizona Daily Sun*, June 30, 2012.

13. Alfred Runte, *Yosemite: The Embattled Wilderness* (Lincoln: University of Nebraska Press, 1990); and Lowry, *Repairing Paradise*, 63–105. See also NPS, *Merced Wild and Scenic River Comprehensive Management Plan and Final Environmental Impact Statement* (Yosemite National Park, CA: NPS, 2000); and *Merced Wild and Scenic River Revised Comprehensive Management Plan and Supplemental Environmental Impact Statement* (Yosemite National Park, CA: NPS, 2005), both available at http://www.nps.gov/yose/parkmgmt/mrp_archive.htm. And see NPS, "Yosemite Valley Groundwater Assessment and Conservation Planning;" and NPS, "Merced River and Meadows Condition Assessment," both available at http://www.nps.gov/ yose/parkmgmt/mrp_research.htm. For the following case, *Friends of Yosemite Valley, et al., v. Ken L. Salazar, et al., Settlement Agreement*, September 29, 2009,

see: http://www.nps.gov/yose/parkmgmt/upload/mrpsettlementagreement.pdf; and NPS, "Yosemite Merced River Litigation Settled after 10 Years," http://www.nps.gov/yose/parknews/mrpsettlement.htm, accessed March 6, 2011. Information on new ideas for management is from NPS, "Preliminary Alternative Concepts Workbook," Spring 2012, http://www.nps.gov/yose/parkmgmt/mrp.htm, accessed on March 22, 2012.

14. See, for example, David G. Havlick, *No Place Distant: Roads and Motorized Recreation on America's Public Lands* (Washington, D.C.: Island Press, 2002), 44–45, 93–94; Sean McDermott, "South Park Attacks Harley Davidson in Episode Titled 'The F Word,'" http://bestscenicroutes.com/south-park-attacks-harley-davidson-in-episode-titled-E2%80%9Cthe-f-word%E2%80%9D/; "Muffle that Bike of Yours, Okay?," http://hikeclimbsurfrun.com/2010/09/21/556/; NPS, "Soundscape/Noise," http://www.nps.gov/pore/naturescience/soundscape.htm; and Ben Beach, "Peace and Quiet: Can You Still Find It in our National Parks?," http://wilderness.org/content/peace-and-quiet-can-you-still-find-it-our-national-parks. All websites accessed March 6, 2011. For the Harley Owner's Group, see: http://www.harley-davidson.com/en_US/Content/Pages/HOG/HOG.html, accessed March 6, 2011. Potential sympathy among Harley owners is from Jim McCaslin, "Something We Never Want to Lose," a speech by Harley-Davidson president and chief operating officer on the need to quiet bikes down, http://www.harley-davidson.com/wcm/Content/Pages/2006_Campaigns/noise_popup.jsp.

15. Existing soundscapes data base is from Burson, "Natural Soundscape Monitoring in Yellowstone National Park," 17, 56. The idea that research findings need to be publicly vetted before a controversy erupts is from Yochim, *Yellowstone and the Snowmobile*, 137–40; and Nie, *Beyond Wolves*, 29.

16. For an excellent overview of "wicked" problems, see Balint et al., *Wicked Environmental Problems*.

17. USDI-NPS, *Lake Area Comprehensive Plan/Environmental Assessment* (Yellowstone National Park, WY: NPS, 2012). For an enjoyable critique of the agency's need to address climate change, see William C. Tweed, *Uncertain Path: A Search for the Future of National Parks* (Berkeley: University of California Press, 2010).

Bibliography

Archival Collections

ARC — American Rivers Collection, CONS 147, Conservation Collection, Denver Public Library, Denver, Colorado

DSC — Denver Service Center, Technical Information Center, National Park Service, Denver, Colorado

GYC — Greater Yellowstone Coalition files, Bozeman, Montana

GYCN — Noranda Collection, Greater Yellowstone Coalition, Bozeman, Montana

MAOF — Management Assistant's Office files, National Park Service, Yellowstone National Park, Mammoth Hot Springs, Wyoming.

TWS — The Wilderness Society Collection, CONS 130, Conservation Collection, Denver Public Library, Denver, Colorado

YCR — Yellowstone Center for Resources files, National Park Service, Yellowstone National Park, Mammoth Hot Springs, Yellowstone

YNPA — Yellowstone National Park Archives, Gardiner, Montana

YNPR — Yellowstone National Park Research Library, Gardiner, Montana

Books and Articles

Albanese, Catherine L. *Nature Religion in America: From the Algonkian Indians to the New Age.* Chicago: University of Chicago Press, 1990.

Aucoin, Les. "Don't Get Hosed: How Political Framing Influences Fire Policy." In *The Wildfire Reader: A Century of Failed Forest Policy*, edited by George Wuerthner, 67–74. Washington, D.C.: The Foundation for Deep Ecology by arrangement with Island Press, 2006.

Bakken, Gordon Morris. *The Mining Law of 1872: Past, Politics, and Prospects.* Albuquerque: University of New Mexico Press, 2008.

Balint, Peter J., Ronald E. Stewart, Anand Desai, and Lawrence C. Walters. *Wicked Environmental Problems: Managing Uncertainty and Conflict.* Washington, D.C.: Island Press, 2011.

Barbee, Bob. "Barbee Retrospective: Yellowstone Wolf Restoration." *Yellowstone Science* 13, no. 1 (Winter 2005): 5.

Barker, Rocky. *Scorched Earth: How the Fires of Yellowstone Changed America.* Washington, D.C.: Island Press, 2005.

Bartlett, Richard A. *Yellowstone: A Wilderness Besieged.* Tucson: University of Arizona Press, 1985.

Bath, Alistair James. "Attitudes Toward Fire and Fire Management Issues in Yellowstone National Park." PhD diss., University of Calgary, 1993.

Bidwell, David. "Bison, Boundaries, and Brucellosis: Risk Perception and Political Ecology at Yellowstone." *Society and Natural Resources* 23 (2010): 14–30.

Biel, Alice Wondrak. *Do (Not) Feed the Bears: The Fitful History of Wildlife and Tourists in Yellowstone.* Lawrence: University Press of Kansas, 2006.

Bissegger, Jeffrey. "Snowmobiles in Yellowstone: Conflicting Priorities in Setting National Parks Policy and the Paradox of Judicial Activism for Recreational Business." *Journal of Land, Resources, and Environmental Law* 25 (2005): 109–18.

Bjornlie, Dan D., and Robert A. Garrott. "Effects of Winter Road Grooming on Bison in Yellowstone National Park." *Journal of Wildlife Management* 65, no. 3 (2001): 560–72.

Borkowski, John J., P. J. White, Robert A. Garrott, Troy Davis, Amanda R. Hardy, and Dan. J. Reinhart. "Behavioral Responses of Bison and Elk in Yellowstone to Snowmobiles and Snow Coaches." *Ecological Applications* 16, no. 5 (2006): 1911–25.

Borrie, William T., Wayne A. Freimund, and Mae A. Davenport. "Winter Visitors to Yellowstone National Park: Their Value Orientations and Support for Management Actions." *Human Ecology Review* 9 (2002): 41–8.

Brininstool, Jason Alan. "Legacy? An in Depth Perspective on the Interagency Bison Management Plan and the Potential for Collaboration." M.A. thesis, University of Montana, 2009.

Bruggeman, John. "Spatio-Temporal Dynamics of the Central Bison Herd in Yellowstone National Park." PhD diss., Montana State University, 2006.

Chase, Alston. *Playing God in Yellowstone.* New York: Harcourt Brace Jovanovich, 1986.

Christensen, Norman L., and James K. Agee, Peter F. Brussard, Jay Hughes, Dennis H. Knight, G. Wayne Minshall, James M. Peek, et al. "Interpreting the Yellowstone Fires of 1988." *BioScience* 39 (November 1989): 678–85.

Clark, Susan G. *Ensuring Greater Yellowstone's Future: Choices for Leaders and Citizens.* New Haven, CT: Yale University Press, 2008.

Davenport, Mae A., and William T. Borrie. "The Appropriateness of Snowmobiling in National Parks: An Investigation of the Meanings of Snowmobiling Experiences in Yellowstone National Park." *Environmental Management* 35, no. 2 (2005): 151–60.

Despain, Don G., and Robert E. Sellers. "Natural Fire in Yellowstone National Park." *Trends in Natural Resource Management*, April/May/June 1977, 25–29.

Dilsaver, Lary M. *America's National Park System: The Critical Documents.* Lanham, MD: Rowman & Littlefield Publishers, Inc., 1994.

———. *Cumberland Island National Seashore: A History of Conservation Conflict.* Charlottesville: University of Virginia Press, 2004.

Dilsaver, Lary M., and William C. Tweed. *Challenge of the Big Trees: A Resource History of Sequoia and Kings Canyon National Parks.* Three Rivers, CA: Sequoia Natural History Association, Inc., 1990.

Duffield, John W., Chris J. Neher, and D. A. Patterson. "Wolf Recovery in Yellowstone." *Yellowstone Science* 16, no. 1 (2008): 22.

Dunlap, Thomas R. *Faith in Nature: Environmentalism as Religious Quest.* Seattle: University of Washington Press, 2004.

Dustin, Daniel L., and Ingrid E. Schneider. "The Science of Politics/The Politics of Science: Examining the Snowmobile Controversy in Yellowstone National Park." *Environmental Management* 34, no. 6 (2005): 761–67.

Ekey, Robert. *Yellowstone on Fire!* Billings, MT: Billings Gazette, 1989.

Everhart, W. C. *The National Park Service.* Boulder, CO: Westview Press, 1983.

Finley, Mike. "Never Running From a Fight: Interview with Mike Finley." *Yellowstone Science* 9, no. 3 (Summer 2001): 9–19.

Fischer, Hank. "Supply-Side Environmentalist and Wolf Recovery in the Northern Rockies." In *War Against the Wolf: America's Campaign to Exterminate the Wolf,* ed. Rick McIntyre, 411–14. Stillwater, MN: Voyageur Press, 1995.

———. *Wolf Wars: The Remarkable Inside Story of the Restoration of Wolves to Yellowstone.* Helena, MT: Falcon Press, 1995.

Fox, Stephen. *The American Conservation Movement: John Muir and His Legacy.* Madison: University of Wisconsin Press, 1981.

Franke, Mary Ann. *To Save the Wild Bison: Life on the Edge in Yellowstone.* Norman: University of Oklahoma Press, 2005.

Frome, Michael. *Regreening the National Parks.* Tucson: University of Arizona Press, 1992.

Fuller, J. A., R. A. Garrott, and P. J. White. "Emigration and Density Dependence in Yellowstone Bison." *Journal of Wildlife Management* 71, no. 6 (2007): 1924–33.

Gates, Cormack, B. Stelfox, T. Muhly, T. Chowns, and R. J. Hudson. *The Ecology of Bison Movements and Distribution In and Beyond Yellowstone National Park: A Critical Review with Implications for Winter Use and Transboundary Population Management.* Calgary, Alberta: University of Calgary, 2005.

George, Alexander L., and Andrew Bennett. *Case Studies and Theory Development.* Cambridge, MA: MIT Press, 2005.

Graber, Linda. *Wilderness As Sacred Space.* Washington, D.C.: American Association of Geographers, 1976.

Greenlee, Jason M., ed. *The Ecological Implications of Fire in Greater Yellowstone: Proceedings, Second Biennial Conference on the Greater Yellowstone Ecosystem.* Fairfield, WA: International Association of Wildland Fire, 1996.

Grusin, Richard. *Culture, Technology, and the Creation of America's National Parks.* New York: Cambridge University Press, 2004.

Gunther, M., J. Biel, K. A. Churchill, and R. L. Danforth. "Changing Problems in Yellowstone Bear Management, 23 Years after the Dumps." In *Greater Yellowstone*

Predators, Proceedings of the Third Biennial Conference on the Greater Yellowstone Ecosystem, September 24–27, 1995, ed. David Harmon, 85–110. Jackson, WY: Northern Rockies Conservation Cooperative, 2000.

Haines, Aubrey L. *The Yellowstone Story: A History of Our First National Park*. rev. ed. Yellowstone National Park, WY: The Yellowstone Association for Natural Science, History, and Education, Inc., in cooperation with the University Press of Colorado, 1996.

Hardy, Amanda. "Bison and Elk Responses to Winter Recreation in Yellowstone National Park." MA thesis, Montana State University, 2001.

Hardy, Donald Loren. *Shooting from the Lip: The Life of Senator Alan Simpson*. Norman: University of Oklahoma Press, 2011.

Hartzog, G. B., Jr. *Battling for the National Parks*. Mount Kisco, NY: Moyer Bell Ltd., 1988.

Havlick, David G. *No Place Distant: Roads and Motorized Recreation on America's Public Lands*. Washington, D.C.: Island Press, 2002.

Hess, Karl, Jr. *Rocky Times in Rocky Mountain National Park: An Unnatural History*. Niwot: University Press of Colorado, 1993.

Houston, Doug. "Wildfires in Northern Yellowstone National Park." *Ecology* 54, no. 5 (1973): 1111–17.

Irvine, Amy. *Making a Difference: Stories of How Our Outdoor Industry and Individuals Are Working to Preserve America's Natural Places*. Guilford, CT: Falcon Press (An imprint of The Globe Pequot Press), 2001.

Jacoby, Karl. *Crimes Against Nature: Squatters, Poachers, Thieves, and the Hidden History of American Conservation*. Berkeley: University of California Press, 2001.

Johnston, Janis E. "Contested Terrain: A Sociological Analysis of Natural Resource Conflict." MA thesis, University of Wyoming, 1998.

Kay, Charles. "Aboriginal Overkill: The Role of Native Americans in Structuring Western Ecosystems." *Human Nature* 5, no. 4 (1994): 359–98.

———. "Are Ecosystems Structured from the Top-Down or Bottom-Up? A New Look at an Old Debate." *Wildlife Society Bulletin* 26, no. 3 (1998): 484–98.

Layzer, Judith. *The Environmental Case: Translating Values into Policy*. Washington, D.C.: CQ Press, 2006.

Lee, Kai. *Compass and Gyroscope: Integrating Science and Politics for the Environment*. Washington, D.C.: Island Press, 1993.

Leopold, A. Starker, S. A. Cain, C. M. Cottam, I. N. Gabrielson, and T. L. Kimball. "Wildlife Management in the National Parks." In *America's National Park System: The Critical Documents*, ed. Lary Dilsaver, 237–52. Lanham, MD: Rowman & Littlefield, 1994.

Lewin, Roger. "Ecologists' Opportunity in Yellowstone's Blaze." *Science* 241 (September 30, 1988): 1762–63.

Lowry, William R. *The Capacity for Wonder: Preserving National Parks*. Washington, D.C.: The Brookings Institution, 1994.

———. *Preserving Public Lands for the Future: The Politics of Intergenerational Goods*. Washington, D.C.: Georgetown University Press, 1998.

——. *Repairing Paradise: Restoring Nature in America's National Parks*. Washington, D.C.: The Brookings Institution, 2009.

Magoc, Chris. *Yellowstone: The Creation and Selling of an American Landscape, 1870–1903*. Albuquerque: University of New Mexico Press, 1999.

McNamee, Thomas. *The Return of the Wolf to Yellowstone*. New York: Henry Holt and Company, 1997.

Meagher, Mary. "Evaluation of Boundary Control for Bison of Yellowstone National Park." *Wildlife Society Bulletin* 17, no. 1 (1989): 15–19.

Mech, L. David. "Returning the Wolf to Yellowstone." In *The Greater Yellowstone Ecosystem: Redefining America's Wilderness Heritage*, ed. Robert B. Keiter and Mark S. Boyce, 309–22. New Haven, CT: Yale University Press, 1991.

Monastersky, Richard. "Lessons from the Flames." *Science News* 134, no. 20 (November 12, 1988): 314–17.

——. "Taking the Heat: A Policy Under Fire." *Science News* 134, no. 20 (November 12, 1988): 316.

Morehouse, Barbara J. *A Place Called Grand Canyon: Contested Geographies*. Tucson: University of Arizona Press, 1996.

Morrison, Micah. *Fire in Paradise: The Yellowstone Fires and The Politics of Environmentalism*. New York: Harper Collins Publishers, Inc., 1993.

Murphy, Sue Consolo, and Beth Kaeding. "Fishing Bridge: 25 Years of Controversy Regarding Grizzly Bear Management in Yellowstone National Park." *Ursus* 10 (1998): 385–93.

Murphy, Sue Consolo, and Daniel P. Reinhart. "Restoring Fishing Bridge Campground: The Challenges of 'Undevelopment' in America's Oldest National Park." In *On the Frontiers of Conservation: Proceedings of the 10th Conference on Research and Resource Management in Parks and on Public Lands, The 1999 George Wright Society Conference*, ed. David Harmon, 210–14. Hancock, MI: The George Wright Society, 1999.

Nie, Martin A. *Beyond Wolves: The Politics of Wolf Recovery and Management*. Minneapolis: University of Minnesota Press, 2003.

Plater, Zygmunt J. B., Robert H. Abrams, and William Goldfarb. *Environmental Law and Policy: Nature, Law, and Society*. St. Paul, MN: West Publishing Co., 1992.

Primm, Steven A., and Tim W. Clark. "The Greater Yellowstone Policy Debate: What Is the Policy Problem?" *Policy Sciences* 29, no. 2 (1996): 137–66.

Pritchard, James A. *Preserving Yellowstone's Natural Conditions: Science and the Perception of Nature*. Lincoln: University of Nebraska Press, 1999.

Prugh, Hillary. "To Sled or Not to Sled: The Snowmobiling Saga in Yellowstone National Park." *Northwest Journal of Environmental Law and Policy* 11 (2004–05): 149–80.

Renkin, Roy A., and Kerry A. Gunther, "Predicting Grizzly Bear Mortality in Developed Areas of Yellowstone Park." In *Greater Yellowstone Predators, Proceedings of the Third Biennial Conference on the Greater Yellowstone Ecosystem, September 24–27, 1995*, ed. A. Peyton Curlee, Anne-Marie Gillesberg, and Denise Casey, 171–76. Jackson, WY: Northern Rockies Conservation Cooperative, 2000.

Ridenour, James M. *The National Parks Compromised: Pork Barrel Politics and America's Treasures*. Merrillville, IN: ICS Books, Inc., 1994.

Rolston, Holmes. "Biology and Philosophy in Yellowstone." *Biology and Philosophy* 5 (1990): 241–58.

Romme, William. "Fire and Landscape Diversity in Subalpine Forests of Yellowstone National Park." *Ecological Monographs* 52, no. 2 (1982): 199–221.

Romme, William, and Don Despain. "Historical Perspective on the Yellowstone Fires of 1988." *BioScience* 39, no. 10 (November 1989): 695–99.

———. "The Long History of Fire in the Greater Yellowstone Ecosystem." *Western Wildlands* 15 (Summer 1989): 10–17.

Romme, William, and Dennis Knight. "Landscape Diversity: The Concept Applied to Yellowstone Park." *BioScience* 32, no. 8 (September 1982): 664–70.

Rothman, Hal K. *Blazing Heritage: A History of Wildland Fire in the National Parks*. New York: Oxford University Press, 2007.

Runte, Alfred. *National Parks: The American Experience*. Lincoln: University of Nebraska Press, 1979.

———. *Yosemite: The Embattled Wilderness*. Lincoln: University of Nebraska Press, 1990.

Schullery, Paul. *Searching for Yellowstone: Ecology and Wonder in the Last Wilderness*. Boston: Houghton Mifflin, 1997.

———. "The Story Itself: Lessons and Hopes from the Yellowstone Fire Media Event." *The George Wright Forum* 6, no. 3 (1989): 17–25.

Schullery, Paul, and Don Despain. "Prescribed Burning in Yellowstone National Park: A Doubtful Proposition." *Western Wildlands* 15 (Summer 1989): 30–4.

Schullery, Paul, and Lee Whittlesey. "The Documentary Record of Wolves and Related Wildlife Species in the Yellowstone National Park Area Prior to 1882." In *Wolves for Yellowstone? A Report to the United States Congress: Volume IV Research and Analysis*, ed. John D. Varley and Wayne G. Brewster, 1-3 to 1-174. Yellowstone National Park, WY: National Park Service, 1992.

———. *Myth and History in the Creation of Yellowstone National Park*. Lincoln: University of Nebraska Press, 2003.

Seawright, Jason, and John Gerring. "Case Selection Techniques in Case Study Research." *Political Research Quarterly* 61, no. 2 (June 2008): 294–308.

Sellars, Richard West. *Preserving Nature in the National Parks: A History*. New Haven, CT: Yale University Press, 1997.

———. *Preserving Nature in the National Parks: A History*. rev. ed. New Haven, CT: Yale University Press, 2009.

Servheen, Christopher, and Rebecca Shoemaker. "Delisting the Yellowstone Grizzly Bear: A Lesson in Cooperation, Conservation, and Monitoring." *Yellowstone Science* 16, no. 2 (2008): 25–9.

Shaw, Randy. *The Activist's Handbook: A Primer for the 1990s and Beyond*. Berkeley: University of California Press, 1996.

Singer, Francis J., and Paul Schullery. "Yellowstone Wildlife: Populations in Process." *Western Wildlands* 15 (Summer 1989): 18–22.

Skillen, James R. *The Nation's Largest Landlord: The Bureau of Land Management in the American West*. Lawrence: The University Press of Kansas, 2009.

Smith, Conrad. *Media and Apocalypse*. Westport, CT: Greenwood Press, 1992.

Smith, Douglas W. "Ten Years of Yellowstone Wolves, 1995–2005." *Yellowstone Science* 13, no. 1 (Winter 2005): 18, 20.

Smith, Douglas W., and Gary Ferguson. *Decade of the Wolf: Returning the Wild to Yellowstone*. Guilford, CT: The Lyons Press, 2005.

Smith, Rob Roy. "Unbearable? Bitterroot Grizzly Bear Reintroduction & the George W. Bush Administration." *Golden Gate University Law Review* 33, no. 3 (2003): 384–417.

Spence, Mark David. *Dispossessing the Wilderness: Indian Removal and the Making of the National Parks*. New York: Oxford University Press, 1999.

Turner, Tom. *Justice on Earth: Earthjustice and the People It Has Served*. Oakland, CA: Earthjustice, 2002.

Tweed, William C. *Uncertain Path: A Search for the Future of National Parks*. Berkeley: University of California Press, 2010.

Vale, Thomas R., ed. *Fire, Native Peoples, and the Natural Landscape*. Washington, D.C.: Island Press, 2002.

Varley, John, and Paul Schullery. "Reaching the Real Public in the Public Involvement Process: Practical Lessons in Ecosystem Management." *The George Wright Forum* 13, no. 4 (1996): 72, 74.

Wallace, Glenda, ed. *The Power of Politics, the Media and the Public to Affect Wildland/Urban Fire Protection Programs in the 1990s: Proceedings from the 1992 National Symposium and Workshop*. National Wildfire Foundation, 1993.

Wallace, Linda, ed. *After the Fires: The Ecology of Change in Yellowstone National Park*. New Haven, CT: Yale University Press, 2004.

White, P. J., Glenn E. Plumb, Michael B. Coughenour, and Rick L. Wallen. "Carrying Capacity and Movements of Yellowstone Bison." *Yellowstone Science* 19, no. 1 (March 2011): 8–14.

White, P. J., Douglas W. Smith, John W. Duffield, Michael Jimenez, Terry McEneaney, and Glenn Plumb. "Yellowstone after Wolves: Environmental Impact Statement Predictions and Ten-Year Appraisals." *Yellowstone Science* 13, no. 1 (Winter 2005): 34–41.

Whittlesey, Lee H. "Cows All Over the Place." *Wyoming Annals* 66 (Winter 1994–95): 42–57.

Wright, R. Gerald. *Wildlife Research and Management in the National Parks*. Urbana: University of Illinois Press, 1992.

Wuerthner, George, ed. *The Wildfire Reader: A Century of Failed Forest Policy*. Washington, D.C.: The Foundation for Deep Ecology by arrangement with Island Press, 2005.

Wuerthner, George. *Yellowstone and the Fires of Change*. Salt Lake City: Haggis House Publications, 1988.

Yochim, Michael J. "Aboriginal Overkill Overstated: Errors in Charles Kay's Hypothesis." *Human Nature* 12, no. 2 (2001): 141–67.

———. "Compromising Yellowstone: The Interest Group-National Park Service Relationship in Modern Policy-making." PhD diss., University of Wisconsin-Madison, 2004.

———. "The Development of Snowmobile Policy in Yellowstone National Park." *Yellowstone Science* 7 (Spring 1999): 2–10.

———. "The Recent Winter Use History of Yellowstone National Park: How Should the National Park Service Envision Its Dual Mission?" *Annals of Wyoming* 73 (2001): 33–46.

———. "Snow Machines in the Gardens: The History of Snowmobiles in Glacier and Yellowstone National Parks." *Montana: The Magazine of Western History* 53 (Autumn 2003): 2–15.

———. "Snowplanes, Snowcoaches and Snowmobiles: The Decision to Allow Snowmobiles into Yellowstone National Park." *Annals of Wyoming* 70 (Summer 1998): 6–23.

———. *Yellowstone and the Snowmobile: Locking Horns over National Park Use.* Lawrence: University Press of Kansas, 2009.

———. "Yellowstone City Park: The Dominating Influence of Politicians in National Park Service Policymaking." *Journal of Policy History* 23, no. 3 (2011): 381–98.

Government Documents

Burson, Shan. "Natural Soundscape Monitoring in Yellowstone National Park, December 2008–March 2009." Unpublished report to NPS, Yellowstone National Park, 2009.

———. "Natural Soundscape Monitoring in Yellowstone National Park." Unpublished report to NPS, Yellowstone National Park, 2008.

Congressional Record. 100th Congress, 2nd Session, daily ed., September 14, 1988.

Federal Register.

Foley, D. Mary. "Scientific Assessment of Yellowstone National Park Winter Use, March 2011." http://www.nps.gov/yell/parkmgmt/reports.htm, accessed May 9, 2011.

Franke, Mary Ann. *Yellowstone in the Afterglow.* Mammoth Hot Springs, WY: NPS, 2000.

McClure, Craig, and Troy Davis. "Wildlife Responses to Motorized Winter Recreation in Yellowstone." Unpublished report to NPS, Yellowstone National Park, 2008.

Meagher, Mary. *The Bison of Yellowstone National Park.* Washington, D.C.: U.S. Government Printing Office, 1973. NPS Scientific Monographs 1 Series.

Mills, Susan, ed. *The Greater Yellowstone Postfire Assessment.* Unpublished report for Greater Yellowstone Coordinating Committee, Yellowstone National Park, Wyoming, March 1989.

Murie, Adolph. *The Wolves of Mount McKinley.* Washington, D.C.: U.S. Government Printing Office, 1944.

Schullery, Paul. *Nature and Culture at Fishing Bridge: A History of the Fishing Bridge Development in Yellowstone National Park.* Yellowstone National Park, WY: NPS, 2010.

Schullery, Paul, et al. *Fishing Bridge and the Yellowstone Ecosystem, A Report to the Director*. Denver: U.S. Government Printing Office, November 1984.

Spear, Terry M., Julie Hart, and Dale J. Stephenson. "Yellowstone Winter Use Personal Exposure Monitoring." Unpublished report to NPS, Yellowstone National Park. 2006.

———. "Yellowstone Winter Use Personal Exposure Monitoring." Unpublished report to NPS, Yellowstone National Park. 2005.

USDA-USFS. *Gallatin National Forest/Forest Plan*. Bozeman, MT: U.S. Forest Service, 1988.

USDI-FWS. *The Reintroduction of Gray Wolves to Yellowstone National Park and Central Idaho*. Helena, MT: FWS, 1994.

USDI-NPS. *Brucellosis Remote Vaccination Program for Bison in Yellowstone National Park: Draft Environmental Impact Statement*. Yellowstone National Park, WY: NPS, 2010.

———. *Draft Environmental Assessment for Wildland Fire Management Plan*. Yellowstone National Park, WY: NPS, June 1991.

———. *Draft Environmental Impact Statement, Development Concept Plan*. Denver: NPS, 1987.

———. *Draft Winter Use Plan and Environmental Impact Statement*. Yellowstone National Park, WY: NPS, 2011.

———. *Final Environmental Impact Statement/Development Concept Plan, Fishing Bridge Developed Area, Yellowstone National Park*. Denver: NPS, 1988.

———. *Final Environmental Impact Statement, Grizzly Bear Management Program*. Denver: NPS, 1982.

———. *Lake Area Comprehensive Plan/Environmental Assessment*. Yellowstone National Park, WY: NPS, 2012.

———. *Master Plan, Yellowstone National Park*. Denver: NPS, 1974.

———. *Merced Wild and Scenic River Revised Comprehensive Management Plan and Supplemental Environmental Impact Statement*. Yosemite National Park, CA: NPS, 2005.

———. *Merced Wild and Scenic River Comprehensive Management Plan and Final Environmental Impact Statement*. Yosemite National Park, CA: NPS, 2000.

———. *Special Flight Rules Area in the Vicinity of Grand Canyon National Park: Actions to Substantially Restore Natural Quiet*. Grand Canyon National Park: NPS, 2011.

———. *Winter Use Plan Draft Environmental Impact Statement*. Yellowstone National Park, WY: NPS, July 1999.

———. *Winter Use Plans Environmental Assessment*. Yellowstone National Park, WY: NPS, 2008.

———. *Winter Use Plans Final Environmental Impact Statement*. Denver: NPS, October 2000.

———. *Winter Use Plans Final Environmental Impact Statement, Yellowstone and Grand Teton National Parks, John D. Rockefeller, Jr. Memorial Parkway*. Yellowstone National Park, WY: NPS, 2007.

———. *Winter Use Plans Final Supplemental Environmental Impact Statement.* Yellowstone National Park, WY: NPS, February 2003.

———. *Yellowstone National Park Wildland Fire Management Plan.* Yellowstone National Park, WY: NPS, March 1992.

———. *Yellowstone National Park Wildland Fire Management Plan.* Yellowstone National Park, WY: NPS, June 1991.

U.S. House Committee on Agriculture, Subcommittee on Forests, Family Farms, and Energy. *Recovery of Forest Resources from the Greater Yellowstone Wildfires, Exxon Valdez Oil Spill, and the Mount St. Helens Eruption.* Washington, D.C.: 102nd Congress, 1st Session, 1991.

U.S. House Committee on Government Operations, Subcommittee on Environment, Energy, and Natural Resources. *Federal Fire Management Policy: Evaluation of Changes Made after Yellowstone.* Washington, D.C.: 101st Congress, 2nd Session, 1990.

U.S. House Committee on Resources, Subcommittee on Energy and Mineral Resources. *New World Mine Proposed Buyout.* Washington, D.C.: 105th Congress, 1st session, 1997.

U.S. Senate Committee on Energy and Natural Resources and U.S. Senate Committee on Agriculture, Nutrition, and Forestry. *Current Fire Management Policies.* Washington, D.C.: 100th Congress, 2nd session, 1988.

Weaver, John. *The Wolves of Yellowstone.* Washington, D.C.: U.S. Government Printing Office, 1978.

Yellowstone Center for Resources. *Yellowstone Center for Resources Annual Report, 2001.* Mammoth Hot Springs, WY: NPS, 2002.

Yellowstone National Park, FWS, University of Wyoming, University of Idaho, Interagency Grizzly Bear Study Team, and University of Minnesota Cooperative Park Studies Unit. *Wolves for Yellowstone? A Report to the United States Congress.* Mammoth Hot Springs, WY: NPS, 1990.

Periodicals, Newspapers, and Newsletters

American Forests

American Rivers

The American Spectator

American Whitewater

Audubon

Backpacker

Billings Gazette

Bozeman (Montana) *Daily Chronicle*

The Buffalo Chip (Yellowstone's Resource Management quarterly newsletter)

Casper (Wyoming) *Star Tribune*

Chicago Tribune

Clementine newsletter (Mineral Policy Center, Washington, D.C.)

Cody (Wyoming) *Enterprise*

Defenders

Denver Post

Federal Parks & Recreation

Forum for Applied Research and Public Policy

Greater Yellowstone Report newsletter (Greater Yellowstone Coalition, Bozeman, MT)

High Country News
Hi-Way Herald newsletter
    (Good Sam Club)
Idaho Falls (Idaho) Post Register
Idaho Motorist
Insider's Report
Jackson Hole (Wyoming) News and Guide
Livingston (Montana) Enterprise
Los Angeles Times
Minneapolis Star-Tribune
The Missoulian (Missoula, MT)
National Geographic
National Parks
The New Republic
New York Times
New York Times Magazine
Newsweek
Outdoor Photographer
Powell (Wyoming) Tribune

The Pronghorn newsletter
    (Wyoming Wildlife Federation)
Renewable Resources Journal
Rocky Mountain News
San Francisco Chronicle
San Jose (California) Mercury News
Salt Lake Tribune
Sierra
Sunset: the Magazine of Western Living
Time
Toronto (Canada) Globe and Mail
Trailer Life
Trout
U.S. News & World Report
USA Today
Wall Street Journal
Washington Post
Washington Times
Wilderness

Index

access, motorized, 10, 121, 167, 169, 177;
importance of perceptions regarding,
32, 144; mentioned, 11, 46, 168, 178;
as not threatened by brucellosis
management policies, 160, 166;
as not threatened by wildfires,
74, 78, 79; as not threatened by
wolf reintroduction, 127–28, 134;
as threatened by elimination of
snowmobiles from Yellowstone, 142,
144, 149, 150, 170–71; as threatened
by Fishing Bridge Village closure, 27,
31–32, 36, 39, 170; as threatened by
New World Mine, 103, 109, 111, 113,
114, 117; in Yosemite National Park
Merced River controversy, 180
acid mine drainage, 89, 97, 103, 104, 106,
117
American Rivers, 92, 95, 100, 103, 110
Animal and Plant Health Inspection
Service, U.S. (APHIS), 151, 152, 154, 157,
158, 160, 171; relaxing brucellosis rules,
155, 160–61, 165, 167; desired solution
for brucellosis in bison, 158, 164
avalanches. *See* Sylvan Pass

Babbitt, Bruce: in New World Mine
controversy, 94–95, 96, 102, 116;
regarding wolf reintroduction, 124,
133, 166, 167, 173, 175. *See also* politics
and politicians

Babcock, Tim, 103
Balogh, Alex, 98–99
Bambi, 63–64
Bangs, Ed, 129
Barbee, Bob: and Earth First!, 33; and
Fishing Bridge, 20, 21, 28, 29, 30, 34,
42, 179, 195n37, 199n74; and fire policy
review, 57, 70, 74; and New World
Mine controversy, 85, 91, 94–95, 96,
102, 116; and wolf reintroduction, 125,
132, 133, 166
Barry, Don, 147, 150, 167. *See also* politics
and politicians
Baucus, Max, 98–99, 221n40. *See also*
politics and politicians
Bayer, Ian. *See* Noranda Minerals
Corporation
Bayh, Birch, 103, 111
bears, grizzly, 13; deaths at Fishing
Bridge, 19, 24, 26, 30, 33–35; dispute
between Craighead brothers and
NPS regarding management of, 18,
43; habitat, 15, 23–25, 26, 32, 33, 34–35,
40, 96–97, 191n4; habitat closures to
humans, 195n39; and human food, 18,
19, 24, 25, 40, 44; management plan,
19, 20; population recovery, 44, 131,
193n24; symbols of wildness, 38–39;
threatened species and recovery plan,
18–19, 21, 29; and whitebark pine, 89,
96. *See also under* science